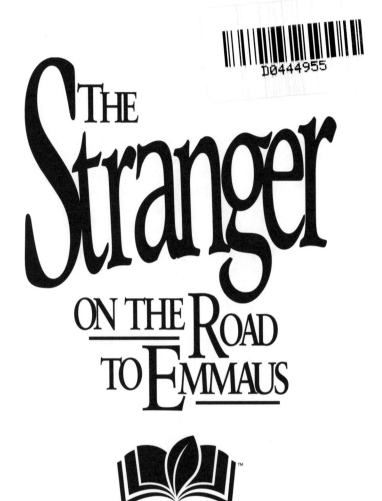

THE Stranger

ON THE ROAD TO EMMAUS

John R. Cross

Published by GoodSeed® International

THE STRANGER ON THE ROAD TO EMMAUS
Edition 3a

Copyright © 2007 by GOODSEED® International

First Printing: December 1996

All rights reserved. No portion of this book may be reproduced in any form without the written permission of the copyright holder. GOODSEED, www.goodseed.com, The Emmaus Road Message and silhouette logo design marks, are trademarks of GOODSEED INTERNATIONAL.

Published by GOODSEED® International
P.O. Box 3704, Olds, AB, T4H 1P5, Canada
Email: info@goodseed.com

Canadian Cataloguing in Publication Data

Cross, John R.

The stranger on the road to Emmaus

3rd ed.

Includes bibliographical references and index.

ISBN 978-1-890082-17-8 (bound)   ISBN 978-1-890082-14-7 (pbk.)

1. Bible – Criticism, interpretation, etc.   2. Christianity – Essence, genius, nature
3. Theology, Doctrinal – Popular works   I. Title

BS511.2.C76 2000   220.6   C00-930918-7

Printed in Canada 🍁

200710-075-15000

To my father and mother, both of whom taught me that the Bible has a message that cannot be ignored.

And to my wife and family, who have been constant in their support and encouragement.

ACKNOWLEDGMENTS

Centuries ago, a king known for his wisdom, wrote…

Is there anything of which one can say, "Look! This is something new"?

Certainly, as it relates to the Bible, one cannot take credit for original thoughts. I readily admit that I have included outlines and ideas that have been plundered from a thousand sources, both ancient and modern. Many of them are such common knowledge, no one would dare claim them as their own. Where sources were known, I have given credit in the end notes.

Of those I can identify, I especially want to thank Trevor McIlwain, who, in using a broad overview of Scripture, put the message in perspective. His approach to teaching has had a profound influence on my own, and for that I am deeply indebted to him. Trevor also provided many helpful critiques and suggestions on the original manuscript.

In the same vein, I wish to thank Nancy Everson for her input and encouragement; my brother David Cross and my wife Janice for help in hashing out subject details and flow; Dr. Carl Wieland for his input on science-related areas; Paul and Kathleen Humphreys, Barney and Mary Ann Iott, John Krajec, and Russ and Karyn Smyth, for their faithful support; and the artists: Don Dolton, Adah Biggs, Ian Mastin, and one who preferred anonymity. Many others deserve special recognition, but I have had to content myself with including their names below.

This third edition has reaped the benefit of three years of input, with scores of folk making helpful suggestions. Of those listed, and the list is far from complete, some zeroed in on content, simplicity, or grammar, while others helped with the art or administration. To all involved, my many and sincere thanks.

Stephanie Aldom, Robin Belanger, Tracy Bernard, Jenny Bowen, Mavis Brockman, Ron Carraway, John & Denise Cornish, Andrew Cross, Naomi Cross, Sally Cross, Thom Cunningham, Bryan Coupland, Audrey DeJager, Luke DeJager, Jim Delgatty, Carrianne Ducommun, Dave Ducommun, Deanne Dolton, Caleb Edwards, Jim Elliott, Nathaniel Enns, Theo Enns, Nathan Enns, Peter & Linda Enns, Jennifer Erickson, Eric Esau, Flip & Marguerite Felton, Andrew & AnneMarie Ferguson, Joseph Ferguson, Dr. Dun Gordy, Don Hogman, Paul Howells, David Humphreys, Mark Humphreys, Mieke Jacobs, Miriam Keung, Andy Kline, Andrew Krajec, Jason McClure, Alan McDougall, Jason McDougall, Dr. Andy McIntosh, Alexis McKay, Jeremy Meerstra, Art & Wim Meerstra, Joyce Meerstra, Mark Nelson, Don Pederson, Lily Pegg, Gaetan & Ivy Pilon, Chet & Anita Plimpton, Micah Plimpton, Nora Rainey, Jim & Jill Rowe, Don Roberts, Dennis Rokser, Benjamin Sanford, Marie Sanford, Tim & Sue Sanford, Miriam Schnee, Jonathan & Jessica Simmonds, Brad Sprague, Helen Sprague, Neil Stirling, Dr. Neil Stretch, Linda Swain, Alice Tucker, Klaas VanderHeide, Peter & Carol VanderHeide, Esther VanderHeide, Frank VanderMeulen, Aukie Vandevrie, Verdon & Barbara Watson, Beth Weaver, Tibby Westcott, Raewyn Wiebe, Nichole Zook

CONTENTS

To maintain ease in reading and remain consistent with the Bible text chosen, in most cases I have used small initial letters for pronouns and certain nouns that relate to God. In areas where there might be confusion about who is being referred to, I have used capital letters consistent with traditional grammar rules.

All Scripture portions are italicized and indented. Where Scripture text is boldfaced, an emphasis has been added. Square parenthesis in the Scripture text indicate additions for explanatory purposes.

PREFACE

It's not easy to write an objective book about the Bible. By its very nature, the Bible demands a response. Unfortunately, people's responses have been determined under less than ideal settings.

Many of us have experienced religious zealots, who cram shattered fragments of Bible down our throats with the predictable effect of stimulating the spiritual gag reflex. This has left people inoculated with just enough Bible information to create misunderstanding, but not enough to generate true comprehension. On such a basis, many have chosen to *reject* the book rather than *accept* it. Most try a neutral platform—they avoid it altogether.

With the above in mind, I've endeavored to stay away from that *preachy* tone that sets one's teeth on edge. I've worked to explain the Bible clearly, allowing it to speak for itself—to say what it says—letting you draw your own conclusions. Some may accuse me of losing objectivity because I've communicated the Bible as being true. I felt that was a risk I must run, as the Bible itself makes that claim. To do otherwise would not be true to the text. Indeed, I've tried to capture the spirit of the narrative to make it interesting as well as clear.

Secondly, I was determined to not *water down* the message. Where the Bible demands a choice, I've tried to illustrate that choice clearly. The Bible is quite direct about what it has to say and I've endeavored to reflect that reality by shunning any sort of vagueness. In keeping with this, I've avoided the confusion of being politically-correct at the expense of the message. Initially, I was perplexed at knowing how to express some words in our gender-neutral society. I eventually gave up on *humankind* and went with the traditional *mankind*.

As with any book, some may find it easy in the first few pages to decide that "it's not for me." I wish to challenge those who are inclined that way, to read the entire volume before deciding what to believe about the Bible. There was a time when I too would have thrown the Bible out with the proverbial bath water—but then I was challenged to pause and look again. I'm still looking, and continue to marvel over this *Book of all books*. There is a good chance you will too.

About the Bible:

…And let him who hears say, "Come!" Whoever is thirsty, let him come; and whoever wishes, let him take the free gift of the water of life.

I warn everyone who hears the words of the prophecy of this book: If anyone adds anything to them, God will add to him the plagues described in this book.

And if anyone takes words away from this book of prophecy, God will take away from him his share in the tree of life and in the holy city, which are described in this book.   Revelation 22:17–19

CHAPTER ONE

1 Prologue

The year—circa 33 A.D.

The sun burned midday hot. All was quiet. Even the birds refused to sing in the oppressive heat. Cleopas kicked a clod of dried mud from the dusty road, drew a large breath and blew out his cheeks in a weary sigh. Squinting into the haze, he could barely make out the next ridge. A few miles beyond lay Emmaus—home. Sunset would be on them before their arrival. Normally they would have left Jerusalem sooner—after all, seven miles is a decent walk—but the events of the morning had kept them hanging back, wishing for more concrete news. Emmaus wasn't much of a town, but today it seemed very attractive. Any place but Jerusalem, with its yelling rabble, its Roman cohorts, its governor—Pontius Pilate.

Cleopas' heavy thoughts were jerked back to the present as his irritated companion asked a question for the second time. The two of them had been discussing the day's events—the last few years' events—until it seemed no detail could be dissected more. Cleopas was tired, but more than that, he was confused by all that had transpired in Jerusalem. These days, it seemed, life held more questions than answers.

Trudging down the hill they rounded a bend. It was then they met the stranger.

Hours later, the same day, the same night, when the two of them stood hot and sweaty before their friends back in Jerusalem—for it was there they had rushed—they couldn't give a good answer as to how the stranger had joined their twosome. At first, Cleopas thought he had stepped out of the shadow of a big boulder, but that didn't jive with his friend's explanation. The bottom line was, they just weren't sure where he had come from. Lamely, Cleopas had said that the stranger had "kinda, well just sort of—appeared." That had been met with some derisive statements about the heat and too much sun.

But of one thing they were sure. The stranger had taken that ancient collection of books—the Bible—and starting at the very beginning, over the next several hours, had explained it in a way that made incredible sense. The stranger's message had driven all despondency and doubt from their minds. So thrilled were they by their new understanding that they had hurried all the way back to Jerusalem to tell their friends about The Stranger. Somehow, somewhere, they too needed to hear this message—the message they had heard on the Road to Emmaus.

So just what did The Stranger say about the Bible—a book that has puzzled so many—that made so much sense?

That is what this book is all about. And to understand it clearly, we will do what The Stranger did—start at the very beginning.

2 Getting Things Straight

When you stop and think about it, it's entirely reasonable— indeed, just plain logical—to take a few hours out of your entire life to gain an understanding of the Bible.

After all, the Bible has some very profound things to say about life ... and about death.

For centuries it has been a best seller. Anyone who claims to be the least bit informed should understand its basic content. Unfortunately, the Bible has fallen into disrepute, not because of what it says, but because some very prominent men and women, who claim to follow the Bible, have made some of the worst choices in life.

Even the message of the book has been attacked at times, often by well-meaning people who have never taken the time to really understand what it says.

But the Bible has not changed. And despite what the hypocrites or critics say, it does make good sense to know it for **yourself**—

> ... for **your own** peace of mind,

> ... for **your own** life and death's sake.

A PUZZLE

In many ways, the Bible is like a puzzle. By this, I do not mean that its message is hidden, but rather that to understand the Bible accurately, the biblical pieces must be put together in the right way. We can do this by applying four basic principles of learning.

FOUNDATIONS

The first principle is one we use all the time. To learn any new concept, it helps to build from the foundation up—to *move from the known to the unknown*. You don't start children in kindergarten by teaching them algebra. Rather, you begin with basic numbers, and *move from the simple to the complex*. If you skip the fundamentals, even rudimentary algebra will be beyond your grasp.

It's the same way with the Bible. If you neglect the foundations, your biblical understanding will incorporate some unusual ideas, resulting in the message being confused—the puzzle will present the wrong image. In this book we begin with the basics, and progress through each chapter, building on previously gained knowledge.

BUILDING A CLOTHESLINE

The second principle is especially important when learning history or reading a story. Simply put, it's this—*start at the beginning and move sequentially through to the end*. That may seem obvious, but many people tend to read the Bible in bits and pieces, never taking the time to tie them together. In this book we will cover key events, stringing them together in logical sequence—like hanging laundry on a clothesline. Since this overview is far from comprehensive, expect some gaps on the line. If you wish, the gaps can be filled in later, after you have the overall picture.

Although this clothesline cannot include every story, the events we do study will tie together in one continuous message. If you are a typical reader, by the time you have finished this book, the Bible will make remarkable sense. Whether you believe it or not is entirely up to you. I sincerely hope you will, but that is your choice. My job is to help you understand it clearly.

PICKLES AND PIE

The third principle is of critical importance. *Don't mix your subject matter—stick to one theme at a time.*

The Bible addresses many different issues. It might be compared to a cookbook with its many diverse recipes. Traditionally, the Bible has been broken down into topics, such as God, Angels, Man, and Prophecy. The intention was to create better understanding, but one needs to be careful. Some people, finding certain similarities between topics, attempt to combine the ideas, often resulting in a distortion of the original meaning.

It's like jumping from a pickle recipe to a pie recipe because they both share the initial letter "p." If you begin by making pickles and end with the pie recipe, you will bake the pickles until they are well-browned! Both may start with the letter "p," but combined they make bizarre food!

In the Bible, if you unintentionally leap from one topic to another, the end result will be confusion—your puzzle will be disjointed. To avoid this biblical chaos, we will stick to one *theme*.

MAJOR ON THE MAJORS

This last principle—*major on the majors*—should be applied to any learning situation where the content is unfamiliar to you. The idea is to learn the most important points first.

The Bible covers an incredible array of topics, but not all are of equal importance. In this book we will focus on one major theme—the most significant theme in the Bible. Once you understand it, the Bible will make profound but simple sense.

The mixing of various topics is one of the contributing causes as to why we find so many different church groups, religions and cults, that to varying degrees hold the Bible as their book. The pie has been mixed with the pickles. The puzzle has a jumbled picture. In some cases, the confusion is minor. In other situations, the mix-up has had catastrophic results.

3 A UNIQUE BOOK

There is no doubt about it; the Bible is a unique book. Actually, it's a collection of books, sixty-six in all. One author, in writing of the Bible's uniqueness, put it this way:

Here is a book:

1. *written over a 1500 year span;*
2. *written over 40 generations;*
3. *written by more than 40 authors, from every walk of life— including kings, peasants, philosophers, fishermen, poets, statesmen, scholars, etc.:*

    Moses, a political leader, trained in the universities of Egypt
    Peter, a fisherman
    Amos, a herdsman
    Joshua, a military general
    Nehemiah, a cupbearer
    Daniel, a prime minister
    Luke, a doctor
    Solomon, a king
    Matthew, a tax collector
    Paul, a rabbi

4. *written in different places:*

    Moses in the wilderness
    Jeremiah in a dungeon
    Daniel on a hillside and in a palace
    Paul inside a prison
    Luke while traveling
    John on the isle of Patmos
    others in the rigors of a military campaign

5. *written at different times:*

    David in times of war
    Solomon in times of peace

6. *written during different moods:*

    some writing from the heights of joy and others from the depths of sorrow and despair

7. *written on three continents:*

    Asia, Africa, and Europe

8. *written in three languages:*

    Hebrew ..., Aramaic ..., and Greek ...

> 9. Finally, its subject matter includes hundreds of controversial topics. Yet, the biblical authors spoke with harmony and continuity from Genesis to Revelation. There is one unfolding story ... [1]

This *one unfolding story* is what we want to look at—simply and without theological jargon. By far the most unique thing about the Bible is that it claims to be God's own words.

God-Breathed

Often referred to as Scripture, the Bible states that ...

> *All Scripture is God-breathed ...* [2]   2 Timothy 3:16

The whole concept of God *breathing out* Scripture is a study in itself. Just as when one exhales his breath, and that breath comes from his innermost being, so ultimately all Scripture is to be viewed as the very product of God himself. God and his words are inseparable, which is one reason the Bible is often referred to as *God's Word.*

Prophets

Highly simplified, it can be looked at this way. God told men what he wanted recorded and those men wrote it down. Most of these men were called *prophets.*

> *In the past God spoke to our forefathers through the prophets ...*   Hebrews 1:1

Today, we think of prophets as those who foretell the future, but in Bible times a prophet was a messenger who passed on God's words to the people. Sometimes the message had to do with future events, but more often than not, it was concerned with daily living.

God guided the prophets in such a way, that what was recorded was precisely what he wanted written. At the same time, God allowed the human writer to record *His Word—God's Word*—in the prophet's own unique style, but to do so without error. These men were not free to add their own private thoughts to the message; neither was it something they dreamed up on their own.

> *... you must understand that no prophecy of Scripture came about by the prophet's own interpretation. For prophecy*

never had its origin in the will of man, but men spoke from God as they were carried along… 2 Peter 1:20–21

God was not putting his stamp of approval on some literary effort of man. The phrase *carried along* is used elsewhere in the Bible in reference to the transporting of a paralyzed man.[3] Just as a disabled man could not walk by his own power, so the prophets did not write the Scripture at their own inclination. The Bible is clear on this point—it was *God's* message from beginning to end.

EXTREME ACCURACY

The prophets wrote God's words on a scroll, usually an animal skin or paper made from plant fiber. The originals were called *autographs.*

Since the autographs had a limited life span, copies were made of the scrolls. But such copies! And all by hand! The writers' awareness that what was being recorded was God's own *Word* resulted in one of the most remarkable *photocopy* jobs ever done. In writing the Hebrew text…

They used every imaginable safeguard, no matter how cumbersome or laborious, to ensure the accurate transmission of the text. The number of letters in a book was counted and its middle letter was given. Similarly with the words, and again the middle word was noted.[4]

This was done with both the copy and the original autograph to insure that they were exactly the same.

These scribes were so accurate in their transcription that, when the Dead Sea Scrolls were found (written in 100 BC), and compared with manuscripts resulting from centuries of copying and recopying to a period of time 1000 years later (900 AD), there were no significant differences in the text.[5]

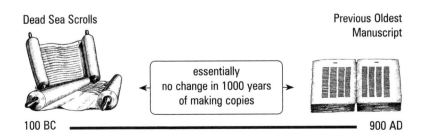

Dead Sea Scrolls

Previous Oldest Manuscript

essentially no change in 1000 years of making copies

100 BC ————————————————— 900 AD

Josephus, a Jewish historian from the first century A.D., summed it up for his people when he stated … *how firmly we have given credit to those books of our own nation, is evident by what we do; for during so many ages as have already passed, no one has been so bold as either to add anything to them, to take anything from them, or to make any change in them; but it becomes natural to all Jews … to esteem those books … divine.*[6]

These men were absolutely convinced that to meddle with the text was to tamper with God. We have ample reason to be assured that what we have today is essentially the same as what the prophets wrote.

Truly, the Bible is a unique book by any standard. No wonder the Bible is … *the most quoted, the most published, the most translated and the most influential book in the history of mankind.*[7]

Old and New Testament

As we begin to navigate through the Bible, it may be helpful to know that the Scriptures are divided into two major sections—the *Old* and *New Testament*. Historically, the *Old Testament* portion was further sub-divided into another two[8] categories:

1. the Law of Moses (sometimes referred to as *The Torah, The Books of Moses, or The Law*)
2. the Prophets (Later on, a third section called *the Writings,* was sub-divided out of *the Prophets.*)

In the Scriptures, the phrase, *the law and the prophets,* is a way of referring to the entire Old Testament—a part which comprises approximately two-thirds of the Bible. The remaining one-third is referred to as the *New Testament*.

God's Word

Remembering the biblical categories is not critical. The important thing to keep in mind is that the Bible claims to be God's Word—His message to mankind. We are told that through its pages we can become acquainted with God. Such a claim should cause even the most indifferent person to pause and consider what it has to say.

Your word, O LORD, is eternal; it stands firm …

Psalm 119:89

Dictionary Definition of *Bible* and *Scripture*[9]

Bi·ble (bī′bel) *noun*
1.   a. The sacred book of Christianity, a collection of ancient writings including the books of both the Old Testament and the New Testament.
  b. The Hebrew Scriptures, the sacred book of Judaism.
  c. A particular copy of a Bible: *the old family Bible.*
  d. A book or collection of writings constituting the sacred text of a religion.
2.   Often **bible**. A book considered authoritative in its field: *the bible of French cooking.*

Scrip·ture (skrîp′cher) *noun*
1.   a.   A sacred writing or book.
  b. A passage from such a writing or book.
2.   Often **Scriptures**. The sacred writings of the Bible. Also called *Holy Scriptures.*
3.   **scripture**. A statement regarded as authoritative.

CHAPTER TWO

1 IN THE BEGINNING GOD ...

The Bible starts with four very profound words:

In the beginning God ...   *Genesis 1:1*

There are no opening arguments for the existence of God—it is assumed he exists. God is just *there*.

ETERNAL

God has been *there* all along. God existed before plants, animals and people, before the earth and the universe. He had no beginning and he will have no end. God has always been and will always be. The Bible says that God has existed from everlasting past to everlasting future. God is eternal.

Before the mountains were born or you brought forth the earth ... from everlasting to everlasting you are God.
Psalm 90:2

The concept of an eternal God is difficult for us to grasp. It's so troublesome to our intellect that often we file it in our cranium under the label *impossible*. But there are illustrations to help our comprehension. For example, we can compare eternity with the cosmos.

Most of us can fathom our solar system—the sun surrounded by orbiting planets. We know it's vast, but space probes have made the farthest distances seem reachable. But go a step further and begin to measure the universe. If we were to climb into  a spaceship and travel at the speed of light, we would circle the earth *seven times in one second*! How did you enjoy your tour? A little brisk, perhaps? Heading out into space at the same speed, we would pass the moon in two seconds, the planet Mars in four minutes, and Pluto in five hours. From there you are off into our galaxy—the MILKY WAY.

At the speed
of light you
circle the
earth seven
times in one
second ...

... pass the
Moon in two
seconds ...

... and Plut
in five hour

Mars in
four minutes ...

At the speed of light, you will
reach the closest star in 4.3 years,
which means each second of those
years you travel 186,000 miles or
300,000 kilometers—a total distance
equivalent to 25,284,000,000,000 miles
or 40,682,300,000,000 kilometers.

Our star, the sun, is near the edge of the
Milky Way Galaxy. Our entire Solar System
with its orbiting planets could fit in this box.

The Milky Way Galaxy[1]

The band of stars you see in the night sky is part of a gigantic family of stars called the Milky Way Galaxy. Traveling at the speed of light, it would take 100,000 years to cross it from one side to the other. There are an estimated 100 billion galaxies in the Universe, many comprising billions of stars. Galaxies come in clusters and super-clusters. There are about twenty galaxies in our cluster, and thousands of galaxies in our super-cluster.

Want a star named after you?[2]

Based on the present population of the earth, you could have 16 *galaxies* named after you. That means *billions* of stars could carry your name!

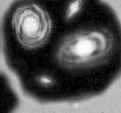

At the speed of light, you will reach the next closest galaxy in 2,000,000 years...

...and the next closest cluster of galaxies in 20,000,000 years.

At this point you have only begun to travel the Universe.

Yes, the thought of an eternal God is difficult to grasp, but so is the vastness of our universe. Both are mind-boggling, yet both are real. The Bible speaks emphatically on this point. God's eternal existence is such an inherent part of his nature that the Bible refers to it as his name…

> …the name of the LORD, the Eternal God.   *Genesis 21:33*

Many Names

God has many names or titles, each declaring something about his character. We will look at three:

1) I Am

> God said…, "I AM WHO I AM. This is what you are to say… 'I AM has sent me to you.'"   *Exodus 3:14*

The closest one can get to an explanation of this statement is this: *I Am the One who is* or *I Am the self-existent one*. God exists by his own power.

We need food, water, air, sleep, light—an endless supply of essential items to live—but not God. He requires nothing, nothing at all! He is the *self-existent one*, the *I Am*.

2) Lord

The title *I Am* is not commonly used in the Bible because its meaning is embedded in the word LORD.

> No one is like you, O LORD; you are great, and your name is mighty in power.   *Jeremiah 10:6*

The name LORD not only highlights God's eternal self-existent state, but also focuses our attention on his position—a position that is higher than all others. He is LORD of lords.

3) The Most High

This name ties in with the name LORD by emphasizing God's role as a sovereign ruler.

> Let them know that you, whose name is the LORD—that you alone are the Most High over all the earth.   *Psalm 83:18*

Just as ancient empires had absolute leaders or sovereigns who reigned over their domains, so God is King of the universe, the God Most High.

Even the word *God* itself emphasizes his position as supreme ruler. The word *God* means *strong one, mighty leader, supreme Deity.*

The idea of God as king may conjure up an image of an old man seated on a gold throne floating somewhere in the stratosphere. The Scripture nowhere illustrates God as an old man, but it does refer to God's throne—not ensconced in a cloud—but rather in a *holy temple* situated in Heaven.

> The LORD is in his holy temple; the LORD is on his heavenly throne. He observes the sons of men; his eyes examine them.
> Psalm 11:4

God rules from Heaven. We don't know much about this place called *Heaven*, but the little we do know is incredible. We will discuss this in greater detail later on, but for now it is enough to know that God is the supreme Ruler.

ONLY ONE GOD

The term *The Most High* speaks of God's unique place in the universe. There is no one else like him. He stands alone, the sovereign LORD of all.

> I am the LORD, and there is no other; apart from me there is no God.
> Isaiah 45:5

> Before me no god was formed, nor will there be one after me.
> Isaiah 43:10

There is no hierarchy of gods, with one big God ruling the roost as it were. No other gods exist *out there,* whether self-existent or created.

> This is what the LORD says... "I am the first and I am the last; apart from me there is no God."
> Isaiah 44:6

The Bible is emphatic—there is only one God.

A SPIRIT

Before we leave this subject, we need to understand one last thing. The Bible tells us that God is invisible because he is a spirit.

> God is spirit...
> John 4:24

You can't see a spirit because it doesn't have flesh and bones like we do. But just because you cannot see somebody doesn't make that person any less real.

Think of a funeral of a friend who has died. If the casket was open, you may have looked at the body. The body was there, but where was your friend? He was gone; your friend's spirit was no longer present. When we look at someone, we only see their house, the human body—we don't actually see the real person, the spirit.

We will see that the Bible indicates in many different ways that man's spirit starts at a point in time and then lives on forever. But God is different; he never had a beginning and he will never end. He is the only eternal spirit, living from everlasting past to everlasting future.

God:
He is a **spirit**
He is **eternal.**
He is the *I Am*—the self-existent one.
He is **the** *God Most High*, the Sovereign Ruler of all.
He is the **only God.**

And that's the way it was—*In the beginning…*

2 Angels, Hosts and Stars

God's first creative act is scattered across the pages of the Bible. You can pull together enough information to answer rudimentary questions, but that is where it stops. The Bible is not written to satisfy man's endless curiosity. It gives basic information on some events, but when it comes to further details, the pages fall silent. This is precisely the case with the subject of spirit beings.

Names

The Bible calls spirits by many different names—some singular, some plural. We often call them angels, but the Bible uses many terms to define them: cherubim, seraphim, angels, archangels, morning stars—the list goes on. Collectively they are referred to as multitudes, hosts, or *stars.

> *The host of heaven worships You.*
>
> Nehemiah 9:6 NKJV

*Not to be confused with stars in the night sky. Context reveals which meaning is in question.

They may all have personal names but only a few are mentioned, such as Gabriel and Michael.

INVISIBLE, INNUMERABLE

As with God, spirits are invisible, having no bodies of flesh and blood like you and me. Even though we can't see them, they must be everywhere. The Bible indicates that there are...

> *...thousands upon thousands of angels...*   Hebrews 12:22

The idiom used to number just those surrounding God's throne communicates an unfathomable sum.

> *Then I looked and heard the voice of many angels, numbering thousands upon thousands, and ten thousand times ten thousand. They encircled the throne...*
> Revelation 5:11

SERVANTS

The angelic beings were created to serve God and do his pleasure. They are called ministering spirits.

> *Praise the LORD, you his angels, you mighty ones who do his bidding, who obey his word. Praise the LORD, all his heavenly hosts, you his servants who do his will.*
> Psalm 103:20–21

> *Are not all angels ministering spirits sent to serve...?*
> Hebrews 1:14

The word *angel* is derived from the Greek term, meaning *messenger* or *servant*. Because God created them, they belonged to him and were to do whatever God asked them to do.

CREATOR–OWNER

The concept of the creator also being the owner has lost its strength in our industrialized, money-driven economy. I remember walking through a tribal village in Papua New Guinea. Every item I asked about—*"Whose paddle is this? Whose canoe is that?"*—elicited a response that designated an owner. Upon inquiring how they knew who the owner was, they looked at me incredulously. *"Well, the owner is the one who made it!"* The creator-owner connection was very strong. When I questioned them if it would be all right for me to break a paddle, they were just as emphatic that it would not be a good idea—unless I wanted to have trouble with the creator-owner. Taking it a step further, I asked if it was acceptable for the owner to break it. They gave a tribal shrug and a nod: *"It's okay for the owner to break it—he made it."*

God created the angels and so it was not out of place for them to be considered his possessions. And since they belonged to him, they were to do his bidding—as his servants and messengers. This was not some ancient form of servitude. There are no parallels here to forced bondage. The angels could have had no better Creator-Owner.

Extraordinary Intellect and Power

To carry out his directives, God created the angels with great intellect and power. Some of these angelic beings had more capability than others. The angels were created as perfect beings, without any evil. But they weren't robots either; they each had a will which gave them the ability to choose.[3]

Similar but Different

Angels share some similarities with man, though man is not nearly as powerful or intelligent. The Bible says that God made man…

> …a little lower than the angels…   Psalm 8:5 NKJV

Though similar, angels are distinct from man. They never die.[4] They neither marry nor reproduce.[5] Though normally unseen, on certain assignments they make themselves visible. When they talk to man, the language they use is understandable to the hearer.

The Anointed Cherub

The most powerful, the most intelligent and the most beautiful spirit ever created was a cherub. His name is translated as *Lucifer,*[6] which means *shining one* or *morning star.*

> …O Lucifer, son of the morning!   Isaiah 14:12 NKJV

Lucifer was referred to as an anointed cherub. The meaning of the word *anointed* has its origins in the ancient rite of pouring oil on someone or something to set it apart to God for a special task. This act was considered sacred and not to be taken lightly.

> You were anointed as a guardian cherub, for so I ordained you. You were on the holy mount of God…You were blameless in your ways from the day you were created…
>
> Ezekiel 28:14–15

It seems that Lucifer's job kept him in the presence of God at all times. Perhaps he somehow represented the rest of the angels and led them in worship and praise of their Creator-Owner. We will learn more about this anointed cherub later.

WORSHIP

The word *worship* comes from an old English word meaning *to declare a person's worth*. The Bible says that all the angels worshiped God.

> You give life to everything, and the multitudes of heaven worship you. *Nehemiah 9:6*

That is only fitting since God is the Sovereign King and, as such, rightly deserves to have his worth declared. By way of contrast, if I am boasting about a friend's deeds, someone else could call into question whether my friend deserves as much praise as I'm giving. But the Bible says God is worthy of all praise.

> You are worthy, our Lord and God, to receive glory and honor and power, for you created all things, and by your will they were created and have their being. *Revelation 4:11*

> …you are great and do marvelous deeds; you alone are God. *Psalm 86:10*

ALL THE ANGELS WATCH CREATION

God's creative act had begun. Now, as all the angelic host watched and rejoiced, God embarked on his next great work of art.

His canvas: the universe

His subject: the whole earth.

> "Where were you when I laid the earth's foundation? Tell me, if you understand. Who marked off its dimensions? Surely you know! Who stretched a measuring line across it? On what were its footings set, or who laid its cornerstone—while the morning stars [or spirit beings] sang together and all the angels shouted for joy?" *Job 38:4–7*

CHAPTER THREE

1 HEAVEN AND EARTH

The first book in the Bible is called Genesis.

Genesis means *beginnings.*

> *In the beginning God created the heavens and the earth.
> Now the earth was formless and empty, darkness was over
> the surface of the deep, and the Spirit of God was hovering
> over the waters. And God said, "Let there be light," and
> there was light. God saw that the light was good, and he
> separated the light from the darkness. God called the light
> "day," and the darkness he called "night." And there was
> evening, and there was morning—the first day.* Genesis 1:1–5

FROM NOTHING

"In the beginning God created..." To create is to exhibit
profound power. It is even more incredible to realize that
God created everything out of nothing. We as humans
create, but only with pre-existing material. We paint pictures
using oils and canvas. We build houses out of wood, mortar
and brick. But when God created, he used nothing.

ALL-POWERFUL

To create on such a grand scale with no materials, no
blueprints, no workshop and no tools, takes abilities totally
foreign to us. The Bible tells us that creation was possible
simply because God is able. God's power knows no limit.

> *Great is our Lord and mighty in power...* Psalm 147:5

He is truly *all-powerful.*

ALL-KNOWING

God not only has the power, but he also has the knowledge.
He is *all-knowing.*

> *Great is our Lord...his understanding has no limit.*
> Psalm 147:5

God knows everything. He doesn't need to check with
the architect or an engineer for further information. His
knowledge is unlimited. In creation, God was not confined
to someone else's blueprint.

EVERYWHERE PRESENT AT ONE TIME

When man is in the process of building or shaping an object, he needs a workplace, such as a shop or studio. But God needed no workshop in which to fashion his creation, for the Bible tells us that the Lord is *everywhere present at one time.*

> *"Am I only a God nearby,"* declares the LORD, *"and not a God far away? Can anyone hide in secret places so that I cannot see him?"* declares the LORD. *"Do not I fill heaven and earth?"* declares the LORD.   Jeremiah 23:23–24

Only God possesses this triad of attributes—**all-knowing, all-powerful**, and **present everywhere at one time**—and only a faultless combination of these three attributes would be able to create the complex realm in which we live.

> *He made the earth by his power; he founded the world by his wisdom and stretched out the heavens by his understanding.*   Jeremiah 51:15

The *angels* possess none of these characteristics, even as powerful and intelligent as they are. And us? We don't even come close to this sort of ability.

For us to construct even the most simple object takes combined human effort. For example, let's say we decide to make a simple metal chair—the folding kind you find in a school auditorium.

For starters we need metal.

> *But where do you find the right kind of metal?*

In rocks.

> *But who knows which stones contain the required metal?*

We need a geologist and a prospector who know a great deal about finding the rocks which carry iron ore.

> *Assuming we have found the right rocks, what's the next step? The rocks are in the ground!*

We need someone with the know-how to manufacture dynamite and assorted mining equipment. We need miners who have the expertise to extract the ore safely from the ground.

> *But you still can't build a chair with a mound of iron ore.*

It needs to be melted down.

Can you build a fire hot enough to melt rocks?

We need those who know the smelting and alloy process.

So we found those fellows, but guess what?

They just poured for us a glob of steel. At this point we might be willing to sit on the ingot—after it has cooled down, that is! But if we are going to make a chair, it will necessitate having someone who understands how to roll that block into a flat piece of metal, just the right thickness. Then we'll need to bend the steel and weld it.

Welding?

Sounds like we need someone with knowledge in electricity and how to generate it.

As you can see, making a chair is a complicated process. And we haven't even touched on how to make paint, specifically the kind that will adhere to metal and in the color we want.

And what about the feet of the chair?

They are plastic.

Plastic?

Hmmm. Doesn't that get into petroleum products? Now let me see. Drilling a well to find oil takes … !???

And all we wanted to do was make a metal chair. To create even the simplest object takes hundreds of people with combined knowledge and allied skills. **No one person knows it all.**

None of us, human or angelic, can be compared in even the smallest way to God who **knows** all things, who has all the **power** to create from nothing, and is **everywhere**—so that he can place the object he has made wherever he chooses. God stands alone.

> *Ah, Sovereign LORD, you have made the heavens and the earth by your great power and outstretched arm. Nothing is too hard for you.*   Jeremiah 32:17

GOD SPOKE

The account of this monumental creative act is recorded simply and concisely. The most staggering information is stated in just a few words. For example, the biblical text makes only passing reference to the *means* by which God accomplished his creation. He didn't use hands or tools. The Lord just spoke the cosmos and all it contained into existence.

> *And God said, "Let there be light,"* ... *Genesis 1:3*

> *...the universe was formed at God's command...*
> *Hebrews 11:3*

Once again, such ability confounds our imagination. We can't comprehend speaking a metal chair into existence, let alone the universe! But then, what would you expect from an almighty God? When you think about it, you would expect him to be just that powerful. The Bible states it as fact.

> *By the **word** of the LORD were the heavens made, their starry host by the breath of his **mouth**... Let all the earth fear the LORD; let all the people of the world revere him. For **he spoke**, and it came to be; **he commanded**, and it stood firm.* *Psalm 33:6,8–9*

So, that's the way it all started. God spoke light into existence. He named the light *day*, and the darkness he called *night*. According to the Bible, the first day of creation was complete.

Ancient but Accurate

Centuries ago it was commonly believed that the earth was flat. This thinking never had its origins in the Bible. The Scripture uses a word that alludes to the spherical shape of the globe when it states...

> *He sits enthroned above the circle of the earth...* *Isaiah 40:22*

Some ancients speculated that the earth sat on a strong foundation or was supported by a mythological god. The Bible says God...

> *...suspends the earth over nothing.* *Job 26:7*

Ptolemy in the 2nd century catalogued 1,022 stars, which was considered authoritative until Galileo's invention of the telescope in the 17th century. Though only about 5000 stars are visible to the unaided eye, the Bible from its earliest pages relates the number of stars to...

> *...the sand which is on the seashore...* *Genesis 22:17*

EVERYWHERE PRESENT AT ONE TIME

Not all the attributes of God are equally comprehensible. Somehow it's easier for us to envision God being *all-powerful* and *all-knowing* than to see him being present in all places at the same time. But over and over again, the Scripture teaches us that God is *everywhere-present.*

When you stop and ponder the idea, it really is comforting. If I am traveling away from my family, I want to know that God is with them. But at the same time, I want the Lord to be with me. If I am in trouble, I don't want to have to *find God* to get help. I may need assistance—NOW! And, of course, I want that to be true for my family as well.

On the other hand, it can be frightening to know that God is everywhere present. If I do wrong, there's no place to hide.

In the 10th century BC, a king of Israel wrote these words as he was directed by God:

> *Where can I go from Your Spirit? Where can I flee from Your presence?*

> *If I go up to the heavens, You are there; If I make my bed in the depths, You are there. If I rise on the wings of the dawn, if I settle on the far side of the sea, even there Your hand will guide me, Your right hand will hold me fast. If I say, "Surely the darkness will hide me and the light become night around me," even the darkness will not be dark to You; the night will shine like the day, for darkness is as light to You.* Psalm 139:7–12

The fact that God is *everywhere at one time* needs to be differentiated from the concept of *pantheism.* Simply put, pantheism teaches that God is *in* everything, and everything *is* God. In contrast, we will see that the Bible teaches that the Lord is distinct from his creation—he is not part of it. The Scripture defines God as a *being*, not some sort of abstract *force* or *transcendent reality.*

> *Do you not know? Have you not heard? The LORD is the everlasting God, the Creator of the ends of the earth. He will not grow tired or weary, and his understanding no one can fathom.* Isaiah 40:28

2 IT WAS GOOD

God had begun his creative work. The curtains had been pulled back. As all the angelic host watched, heaven and earth were placed on the stage. With a word, the sovereign God turned on the floodlights. Act One was completed: Day One was finished. Now five more acts of God's great drama were to follow in the next five days of creation.

> Do you not know? Have you not heard? Has it not been told you from the beginning? Have you not understood since the earth was founded? He sits enthroned above the circle of the earth, and its people are like grasshoppers. He stretches out the heavens like a canopy, and spreads them out like a tent to live in.   Isaiah 40:21–22

The Bible compares the earth to a tent. It's a place in which to dwell, the most unique homestead in the universe. But for planet earth to be a suitable dwelling, major construction needed to be done. We see the angels hush. The curtain goes up on Day Two with the creation of the *expanse*. The expanse? What is that? Let me explain.

DAY TWO

> And God said, "Let there be an expanse between the waters to separate water from water." So God made the expanse and separated the water under the expanse from the water above it. And it was so. God called the expanse "sky." And there was evening, and there was morning—the second day.   Genesis 1:6–8

When God created the world, the earth was covered with water. On Day Two, we see the first indication that the world as originally created was different from what we now know. The Bible says God took some of the water and placed it high in the heavens. Though some commentators have suggested that this refers simply to the clouds, others have theorized the existence of a transparent canopy of water vapor surrounding the globe. Whether the *waters above* suggest a canopy or not, there is evidence that the climate was substantially different from what we now know.

It seems to have been uniformly tropical. It is known that an atmosphere containing more water vapor would have achieved some sort of *greenhouse effect*. Later on we will see what may have changed everything to what we now know. Whatever the case, according to the Bible, God created an *expanse, probably synonymous with what we presently call the atmosphere.

*The word *expanse* is synonymous with *space*, and can apply to either earth's atmosphere or deep space.

DAY THREE

At the beginning of Day Three, the water under the expanse still constituted one vast ocean with no visible dry land. Once again, God spoke.

> And God said, "Let the water under the sky be gathered to one place, and let dry ground appear." And it was so. God called the dry ground "land," and the gathered waters he called "seas." And God saw that it was good. Then God said, "Let the land produce vegetation: seed-bearing plants and trees on the land that bear fruit with seed in it, according to their various kinds." And it was so. The land produced vegetation: plants bearing seed according to their kinds and trees bearing fruit with seed in it according to their kinds. And God saw that it was good. And there was evening, and there was morning—the third day.　Genesis 1:9–13

Day Three can be divided into two parts. First, we see the dry land appear. Apparently, as the ocean bottom sank, forming huge basins for the water, dry land appeared, rising out of the watery depths. Second, we see the creation of plants and trees.

> For this is what the LORD says—he who created the heavens, he is God; he who fashioned and made the earth, he founded it; he did not create it to be empty, but formed it to be inhabited—he says: "I am the LORD, and there is no other."　Isaiah 45:18

From the very beginning, God had been preparing the world to be inhabited, and now plant life was created to provide for our physical needs: food to eat, oxygen to breathe and wood for building.

Day Four

On the first day of creation, God had drawn back the curtain of darkness when He spoke light into existence. On the fourth day, God created the light-givers.[1]

> And God said, "Let there be lights in the expanse of the sky to separate the day from the night, and let them serve as signs to mark seasons and days and years, and let them be lights in the expanse of the sky to give light on the earth." And it was so.
>
> God made two great lights—the greater light to govern the day and the lesser light to govern the night. He also made the stars. God set them in the expanse of the sky to give light on the earth, to govern the day and the night, and to separate light from darkness.
>
> And God saw that it was good. And there was evening, and there was morning—the fourth day.   Genesis 1:14–19

If it seems strange to us that God would create light before He created the sun, we must remember that it is just as easy for God to create the light as it is for him to create the light-givers.

> I am the LORD, who has made all things, who alone stretched out the heavens...   Isaiah 44:24
>
> The moon marks off the seasons, and the sun knows when to go down.   Psalm 104:19

Order

The sun, moon and stars reveal that the Master Designer is a God of order. Order is the rule of the universe. It ticks with the precision of an atomic clock and, indeed, it is a kind of timekeeper. We write tidal charts years in advance with the confidence that they will be accurate. We launch satellites, certain that they will rendezvous with distant planets at a precise moment, just as *programmed. The whole planet relies on the regularity of the sunrise and sunset. Without that set pattern, nothing would survive.

* NASA's Galileo probe traveled six years before reaching Jupiter precisely as scheduled.

The order observed in the universe is the result of physical laws that govern all things. We can study those laws through various sciences such as astronomy, biology, physics and chemistry. God established these physical laws to hold the universe together with astonishing precision.

> *He is before all things, and in Him all things hold together.*
> Colossians 1:17 NASB

We take these laws so much for granted that we never consider what the world would be like without them. But just imagine the result if—for a few seconds, at random, every few days—the law of gravity was suspended. Chaos and death would reign. It would be like someone instantly removing all the traffic lights, stop signs and speed limits from our city streets. Those laws are there for a purpose. Laws define uncompromising boundaries as to how something will function.

> *The day is yours, and yours also the night; you established the sun and moon. It was you who set all the boundaries of the earth…*
> Psalm 74:16–17

Almost instinctively we treat these natural laws with great respect. For example, we walk very carefully along the edge of a cliff because we know that to defy the law of gravity will have serious repercussions. *Whenever you have a law, you also have a consequence.* Unless one's a daredevil, we avoid flirting with those consequences like we avoid the plague.

These laws—this structure and order—are a reflection of God's nature. It's the way he is.

DAY FIVE

On the fifth day, God created the whole kaleidoscope of sea life and birds.

> *And God said, "Let the water teem with living creatures, and let birds fly above the earth across the expanse of the sky." So God created the great creatures of the sea and every living and moving thing with which the water teems, according to their kinds, and every winged bird according to its kind. And God saw that it was good.*
>
> *God blessed them and said, "Be fruitful and increase in number and fill the water in the seas, and let the birds increase on the earth." And there was evening, and there was morning—the fifth day.*
> Genesis 1:20–23

Day Six

The sixth day was the pinnacle of God's creative act. God began the day by creating the land animals.

> And God said, "Let the land produce living creatures according to their kinds: livestock, creatures that move along the ground, and wild animals, each according to its kind." And it was so.
>
> God made the wild animals according to their kinds, the livestock according to their kinds, and all the creatures that move along the ground according to their kinds. And God saw that it was good.   *Genesis 1:24–25*

Kinds

On days three, five and six, it is respectively stated that plants, sea life, birds and animals were to reproduce according to their kind. What does it mean when it says, *according to their kind?* Simply put, it means that cats give birth to cats, dogs to dogs and elephants to elephants. We don't need to worry that, when we plant tulip bulbs, cedar trees will sprout.

Creatures can give rise to different varieties,[2] but still be the same kind. For instance, you can breed various types of dogs and end up with a whole array of canines—poodles to Great Danes—but they are all still dogs. Nothing new has been added, in fact, each of them contains less genetic information than the mongrel stock from which they were bred. On the other hand, because kinds are fixed, a farmer need not be concerned about the neighbor's pig breaking into his pasture and interbreeding with his son's pony. Once again, we can see that God embedded in the system physical laws to maintain order.

Perfect, Flawless, Holy

As the universe was created, the Bible says repeatedly that…

> God saw that it was good.   *Genesis 1:25*

It's another of those concise statements which is loaded with meaning. When God created, he made things truly good.

> As for God, his way is perfect; the word of the LORD is flawless.   *Psalm 18:30*

We humans can never make something flawless. What we produce may be quite acceptable, but it will still have defects. But when God created, he made all things without fault.

The Bible says that God himself is perfect—without blemish. We use words like *holy* and *righteous* to describe aspects of that perfection.

> Holy, holy, holy is the LORD Almighty... Isaiah 6:3

> Splendid and majestic is His work, and His righteousness endures forever. Psalm 111:3 NASB

> ...the holy God will show Himself holy in righteousness. Isaiah 5:16 NASB

We will take a deeper look at these words as we progress through the Bible. For now, all we need to know is that the words, *holy* and *righteous*, are used to describe aspects of the Lord's perfect nature.

The absolute holiness of God cannot be over-emphasized. It's a point that must not be missed in the overall story. It's a piece that cannot be left out of the puzzle. Keep this in mind as you continue to read.

Perfection is fundamental to God's character. Because he is perfect, he could only make a perfect creation. Creation has changed, as we will see, but in the beginning it was just right! God said, *it was good.* It was perfect.

God Cares

God could have created all plants and animals black and white, but instead he made everything with an endless variety of pigmentation and hues. Not only did he invent color, but also created eyes able to see the color.

God ensured a vast variety of foods that would taste good. He could have created all food to taste like liver! Some may not mind liver, but we all know people who would have been very disappointed. The Lord not only created endless flavors, but he also provided us with taste buds able to enjoy the fine nuances of a seemingly endless variety of cooking styles.

Along with many other things, he gave fragrance to flowers and he created the nose with its ability to appreciate a multitude of scents. Everything could have smelled like rotten eggs, but that is not the way God designed it.

God could have limited His creation of plant life to a few kinds. Indeed, just a few would have provided our needs quite adequately. But no, we see an overwhelming variety. It is evident that the Lord is a God who truly cares. The Bible says that he...

> *... richly provides us with everything for our enjoyment.*
> *1 Timothy 6:17*

Not only did God have all the ability and power to create the boundless variety, but that power was combined with loving concern. He is a God who revealed himself with acts of kindness in the world about us.

God is still impressing mankind with his creation. For centuries, much has been hidden from man's view because of our inability to see and understand it. But then, as we developed electron microscopes, atom-smashers, orbiting telescopes and other technology, we were able to peer into some of those hidden areas. And we have not become bored in our discoveries. Rather, the more we discover, the more fascinated we are, the more impressed we become, and the more we are aware of what we do not know. And yet it has been there all along, created by an awe-inspiring God.

> *Great is the LORD, and highly to be praised, and His greatness is unsearchable.* *Psalm 145:3*

There was yet one more step before the sun set on Day Six—before God's universe was complete; that step was the creation of man and woman.

3 MAN AND WOMAN

> *For this is what the LORD says—he who created the heavens, he is God; he who fashioned and made the earth, he founded it; he did not create it to be empty, but formed it to be inhabited—he says: "I am the LORD, and there is no other."* *Isaiah 45:18*

DAY SIX (CONTINUED)

The sixth day began with the creation of animals. Now the focus of the whole story changes. Up to this time, God had been preparing the earth *to be inhabited*. The watching angels must have wondered what God had in mind for the grand finale. Would the earth be for them? Whether such angelic conjecture went on or not we don't know, but certainly the way God went about the creation of man held its share of surprises.

> Then God said, "Let *us make man in *our image, in *our likeness, and let them rule over the fish of the sea and the birds of the air, over the livestock, over all the earth, and over all the creatures that move along the ground." So God created man in his own image, in the image of God he created him; male and female he created them.
>
> Genesis 1:26–27

* Perhaps you are wondering who God was talking to when he said "Let **us** make man in **our** image…" We will cover that later on in the book.

THE IMAGE OF GOD

The Bible says the Lord created man in the *image of God*. Now obviously this doesn't mean we are exact duplicates. None of us are all-knowing, all-powerful, or everywhere present at one time. Nor does the Bible teach that we are *little gods*. Rather, man is like a mirror which reflects the image of the object but is not the object itself. In a sense, when you look at man, you see many things that he holds in common with God.

First of all, God created man with a **mind**. In a sense, God gave us a dab of his intellect. Because we have a mind, we are able to investigate, understand and create, abilities which God possesses. But, although we have an intellect, we are not all-knowing. Indeed, we are born into this world with very little knowledge. All our *knowing* must be learned.

God also created man with **emotions**. The word *emotion* can have negative overtones, but there is a positive side. The ability to *feel* is a very important aspect of being human. Without *feelings*, your response to others would be like that of a robot—cold and calculated. In contrast to an emotionless robot, the Scripture tells us that the Lord is compassionate; he is tender; he feels anger when he sees injustice. A heartless, unaffected god without the capacity to feel love or show compassion would be truly frightening. God created us with *feelings*, because *he* has feelings.

God also created man with a **will**. Man's ability to make decisions for himself is often taken for granted. But the capacity to choose and have preferences is what gives mankind endless variety. Some like rice, others prefer potatoes. For breakfast you can have grape, apple or orange juice. The choices are unlimited.

The ability to choose separates us from robots which cannot make independent decisions—they only feed back what is programmed in. Man was given a *will* so he could freely follow God, not as a robot, but as one who has intelligently grasped that God cares for him, and therefore knows that God is looking out for his best interests.

Having an *intellect*, *emotions* and a *will* are all aspects of being created in God's image. There are other areas we could look at as well, but let's move on in the story. The Bible says...

> ... the LORD God formed the man from the dust of the ground and breathed into his nostrils the breath of life, and the man became a living being.　　*Genesis 2:7*

The words *breath of life* are often associated with the *spirit* or non-material side of man. This is an additional reflection of God's image, for God is Spirit. As we stated before, spirits cannot be seen since they have no bodies. However, in man's case, God chose to provide a physical house of flesh and bones for man's spirit to dwell in—a *house* formed from *the dust of the ground*. Once formed, the body would have laid there, complete in every way, but entirely lifeless. It was when God breathed the spirit into man, that the body became alive. Only God can impart life; no person or angel has that ability. Once again, we see that the Lord is completely distinct from all his created beings—He is greater than them all.

A COMPANION

The first and only man God created was named *Adam,* which means *man.* God then created the woman.

> The LORD God said, "It is not good for the man to be alone. I will make a helper suitable for him." Genesis 2:18

> So the LORD God caused the man to fall into a deep sleep; and while he was sleeping, he took one of the man's ribs and closed up the place with flesh. Then the LORD God made a woman from the rib he had taken out of the man, and he brought her to the man.

> The man and his wife were both naked, and they felt no shame. Genesis 2:21–23,25

These few verses have generated heated arguments. Some have understood that when God made woman, he made her a second-class citizen. This is not so. God took woman out of man's side—to be a companion, not from man's heel—to be his slave. Adam gave his wife the name *Eve,* meaning *lifegiver.*

THE PERFECT GARDEN

God took Adam and Eve and placed them in a special garden which he had created for them. The garden was called *Eden.*

> Now the LORD God had planted a garden in the east, in Eden; and there he put the man he had formed. And the LORD God made all kinds of trees grow out of the ground—trees that were pleasing to the eye and good for food. Genesis 2:8–9

All the gardens and zoos of the world could not compare with God's garden. It was a perfect paradise—with luxuriant foliage, sparkling clear water teeming with a myriad of fish, an incredible variety of animals—with beauty beyond description! The weather was different too. The Bible says…

> … the LORD God had not sent rain on the earth … but streams came up from the earth and watered the whole surface of the ground. Genesis 2:5–6

We have very little idea of what Eden was like—but, obviously, God did not create a garden where Adam and Eve were struggling to survive. The garden had an abundance, and everything they could possibly need was adequately provided by God. It was a perfect world in which to live.

Creator–Owner

God didn't ask Adam and Eve if they would like to live in Eden—he knew what was best for them. God could act without consulting anyone simply because, as Creator, he was also Owner. (Remember the tribal illustration: He who makes the canoe paddle also owns the paddle.)

> Yours, O LORD, is the greatness and the power and the glory and the majesty and the splendor, for everything in heaven and earth is yours.　　　1 Chronicles 29:11

> The earth is the LORD's, and everything in it, the world, and all who live in it ...　　　Psalm 24:1

> Know that the LORD is God. It is he who made us, and we are his; we are his people ...　　　Psalm 100:3

Just as the angels belonged to God because he created them, so man belonged to God because the Lord was his Creator. And just as the angels were given the position of being God's servants, so God gave man the responsibility of taking care of the earth.

> The LORD God took the man and put him in the Garden of Eden to work it and take care of it.　　　Genesis 2:15

Trial Period

Just because God did not consult with Adam and Eve about placing them in the garden did not mean that they were without a choice. God had created man with a will—the ability to choose. However, when it comes to some areas of life, such as love, having the capacity to choose is meaningless unless there are alternatives. So God placed before man a very simple option involving two trees.

> ... In the middle of the garden were the tree of life and the tree of the knowledge of good and evil.　　　Genesis 2:9

The first tree mentioned is the *tree of life*. If man ate of this tree, he would live forever. No problem.

The second tree, however, came with a warning. It was *the tree of the knowledge of good and evil*. Adam and Eve knew about *good*, but *evil* was another matter. They had both been created as perfect beings and were innocent of all wrong. Their experience was limited to God's goodness. The Bible says that if Adam and Eve ate the fruit of this one tree, then not only would they know what was good but also what was evil.

> And the LORD God commanded the man, "You are free to eat from any tree in the garden; but **you must not eat from the tree of the knowledge of good and evil,** for when you eat of it you will surely die." *Genesis 2:16–17*

Earlier on we saw that to defy one of God's physical laws, such as gravity, has repercussions. That principle—*a broken law has consequences*—applies to any of God's laws or commands. In this case, God gave man one simple rule. "Don't eat the fruit from that one tree." The consequence of breaking that command was made just as plain—man would die. We will discuss death in detail later.

This single tree was what distinguished man as a human and not a robot. Man had a choice—to eat or not to eat, to obey or disobey. Given that choice, Adam and Eve were removed from the realm of androids, programmed to do only what they were told. There is a big difference between a person who is programmed to say *"I will obey you"* and someone who does so of his or her own free will. Having the ability to *choose* is what gives the word *obey* meaning and depth. Choice makes a relationship genuine.

This one restriction on the first humans was scarcely a hardship. The situation was not as some paintings depict, with Adam and Eve sitting under two lonely trees having very little fruit from which to choose. They had an abundance.

> …the LORD God made **all kinds of trees** grow out of the ground—trees that were pleasing to the eye and good for food. *Genesis 2:9*

CREATED FOR HIS GLORY

In giving Adam and Eve a choice, God was not intending them to run off and establish their own agenda. Rather, man was created to reflect God's grandeur—to honor Him.

> "You are worthy, our Lord and God, to receive glory and honor and power, for you created all things, and by your will they were created and have their being." *Revelation 4:11*

When a son is obedient to his dad, he honors his dad. So it is between man and God. Man was created with a will so that, by the obedient choices he made, he would honor the Lord. Indeed, as Creator of the universe, God deserves all the honor man could give him. Showing such respect would result in tremendous benefits. The Bible says that when man fits into God's plan for him, he finds the greatest happiness, fulfillment and reality. So it was for Adam and Eve.

> God blessed them and said to them, "Be fruitful and increase in number; fill the earth and subdue it. Rule over the fish of the sea and the birds of the air and over every living creature that moves on the ground." Genesis 1:28

MAN—THE FRIEND OF GOD

God was committed to the well-being of Adam and Eve. He was there to fill every need they had.

> Then God said, "I give you every seed-bearing plant on the face of the whole earth and every tree that has fruit with seed in it. They will be yours for food. And to all the beasts of the earth and all the birds of the air and all the creatures that move on the ground—everything that has the breath of life in it—I give every green plant for food." And it was so. Genesis 1:29–30

The Bible speaks of God coming in the cool of the evening to walk with man. Adam and Eve were able to do this, as they were innocent of any sort of evil or wrong—they had a perfection that allowed them to be in God's company. *Only perfect[3] people can live in the presence of a perfect God.*

What an experience that must have been for this new couple—to stroll in the garden with the Creator of the universe! It's quite conceivable that God spent time explaining in detail how he made things, imparting profound knowledge on intricate flowers, calling down birds concealed high in the treetops, introducing secluded forest animals—pointing out things that had escaped their notice. No doubt he explained the laws that kept everything running so precisely. What an education and what an Educator! No one could have better informed them as to how to care for the garden. The world was a perfect place in which to live.

But God wasn't some sort of crusty, distant super-professor. The Creator was Adam's and Eve's *best* friend. In life, the ideal family relationship is one in which the parents give loving care, and a child in turn gives honor to his parents by loving obedience. This was the relationship Adam and Eve had with God. God lovingly provided for them, and they lovingly obeyed the Lord—honoring him. It was the way God created things to be.

CREATION COMPLETED

> *God saw all that he had made, **and it was very good.** And there was evening, and there was morning—the sixth day.*
>
> Genesis 1:31

We often start projects with great gusto, dabble sporadically, and finally peter out, placing the half-finished product on a shelf high in the closet. But God always finishes what he sets out to do. We may change our minds about our plans, but his character doesn't change.

> *…the plans of the LORD stand firm forever, the purposes of his heart through all generations.*
>
> Psalm 33:11

Creation was done. The Bible tells us that God rested on the seventh day, not because he was tired, but because his creation was complete. It was time to lean back and enjoy!

What about Evolution?

The Bible does not mention evolution. The Creation-Evolution debate has generated much controversy, couched as a debate between religion and science. This book is not written to address this topic, but here is a little food for thought.

First of all, it is not entirely safe to designate Evolution as science, and Creation as religion. Since Charles Darwin first published the theory in 1859, classic Darwinism has been largely replaced by Neo-Darwinism and Punctuated Equilibrium—theories that differ greatly from each other. No agreed-upon body of facts exists that explains origins. Many well-studied people argue that Evolution is not pure science, but embraces key aspects of religion. This religion presupposes that there is no God, choosing to put its faith in massive amounts of time and chance. They point out that evolution violates basic laws of physics.

On the other hand, to put Creation wholly in the religion category may not be correct either. A significant community of scientists has concluded that this complex universe could only exist if there was a designer (such as God), or a team of designers. Solely using science, they point out that the world has an irreducible complexity[4] at even the smallest level. They demonstrate that such universal complexity and order could only exist if it was planned from the ground up—it could not evolve by random chance. Though some of these scientists do not categorize themselves as Bible believers, many do take the Bible at face value. The latter group is referred to as Creation Scientists.

Since the mid-sixties, there has been an explosion of written material on the subject (see Appendix). Much of it is readable for the lay person. I would encourage you to keep reading and studying before you make up your mind.

Some wonder about the feasibility of the Creation account as it relates to the dinosaurs. From a biblical viewpoint, there is no reason not to believe that God created them along with the rest of the animals. Evidence exists that the dinosaurs lived at the same time as man.

Others wonder about the earth's age—it appears very old, but the Bible does not allow for eons of time. It is true that scientists have developed numerous astronomical, solar, terrestrial, and biological clock models[5] in an effort to determine the age of the universe, but while these models employ reasoned calculations, the computed ages have left scientists scratching their heads. Depending on the clock used, ages range from a few thousand years to billions of years. Darwin theorized 400 million years for biological evolution. Today, a common estimate starts at 4.6 billion years. Whose clock is right?

Is there a reasonable answer that fits the biblical account? Going strictly by the Bible, we know that God created a mature earth. On the day of his creation, Adam could have walked among towering trees, marveled at immense animals, and gazed at stars in the night sky. Perhaps he thought, *"Wow! This place has been around for a long time."* However, God would have told him that it was, at most, six days old—he had created the whole universe in a fully functioning state. Scientists, in looking back, try to determine the past by what they observe—just like Adam. The Bible, however, records the origins of the earth from the perspective of an eyewitness—God himself.

So, did God mean it when he said he created the universe? Who are we to believe? Whose word is to be trusted?

Centuries ago, a king pondered his place in the world:

> *When I consider your heavens, the work of your fingers, the moon and the stars, which you have set in place, what is man that you are mindful of him, the son of man that you care for him?*
>
> *You made him a little lower than the heavenly beings and crowned him with glory and honor.*
>
> *You made him ruler over the works of your hands; you put everything under his feet: all flocks and herds, and the beasts of the field, the birds of the air, and the fish of the sea, all that swim the paths of the seas. O LORD, our Lord, how majestic is your name in all the earth!*   Psalm 8:3–9

CHAPTER FOUR

1 I Will

Creation ended with God's stamp of approval. He pronounced it *very good*. All was in order. There was no pain, no disease, no struggle for the survival of the fittest, no discord, and above all, no death. Between God and man there was a unique relationship, a fellowship, a friendship. Eden was the perfect place to live. Everything was very good.

But today we have pain and disease and only the fittest survive. At times we wish that verbal discord was our only problem. Instead, at any given time, the tyranny of war dominates in many parts of the world. Everything runs down, breaks down or wears out. From every corner of the animal kingdom to all mankind, life involves perpetual struggle. The world is *not* a *very good* place. What happened?

Lucifer

It all goes back to the garden of Eden. The Bible says of Lucifer...

> *You were in Eden, the garden of God; every precious stone adorned you...*
> Ezekiel 28:13

Lucifer, you will remember, was the most powerful spirit God created. His name means *morning star*. He belonged to the angelic order called *cherubim* and was selected by God for special responsibilities that took him into God's presence.

> *You were anointed as a guardian... You were on the holy mount of God...*
> Ezekiel 28:14

Lucifer was perfect. He is described as having incredible beauty and wisdom.

> *You were blameless in your ways from the day you were created...*
> Ezekiel 28:15

> *You were the model of perfection, full of wisdom and perfect in beauty.*
> Ezekiel 28:12

Although Lucifer was the most powerful angel, there is no direct indication that he ruled the other spirit beings.

PRIDE

The time when the next event in history occurred is open to debate. It probably took place sometime soon after creation was completed. There may be a difference of opinion over *when*, but *what* happened is very clear. The Bible says Lucifer became proud. His beauty and power *went to his head*, so to speak. With pride came ambition. Five times Lucifer said, *"I will."* A whole study could be done on these *I will's*, but, in brief, it's enough to say that Lucifer wanted to stage a celestial revolt.

> *O morning star, son of the dawn… You said in your heart,*
>   *"**I will** ascend to heaven;*
>   ***I will** raise my throne above the stars [or angels] of God;*
>   ***I will** sit enthroned on the mount of assembly, on*
>   *the utmost heights of the sacred mountain.*
>   ***I will** ascend above the tops of the clouds;*
>   ***I will make myself like the *Most High."***   Isaiah 14:12–14

Not only did Lucifer want to take over Heaven, but he was resolved to be like the Most High. Lucifer was determined to lead a coup d'état to replace God with HIMSELF. Then HE would be the leader of all the angels and the universe would be HIS to rule. Lucifer's heart was bursting with prideful ambition.

*The Most High is one of God's names.

The only loophole in Lucifer's plan was that God knew all about it. God is *all-knowing* and Lucifer's thoughts did not escape him. The Bible says that God hates pride. It's the first on the list of things he detests.

> *These six things the LORD hates, yes, seven are an abomination to Him: **a proud look** …*   Proverbs 6:16–17 NKJV

Lucifer was deliberately going contrary to God's plan for him. We must remember that God did not create angels as robots. They were created with a will. Their choice to serve was an expression of willing submission to the sovereign God. But Lucifer became dissatisfied with being an angel. He had something bigger and better in mind. He became proud and chose to rebel. Lucifer despised both his design and his Designer. The dictionary says that to despise means: *to regard with contempt; to look down upon; to dislike intensely; loathe.*

God called Lucifer's attitude *sin*.

JUDGMENT

Because God is perfect, he could not tolerate Lucifer's sin as if it did not matter. *Perfection, by its very nature, demands the absence of imperfection.* We will see this truth repeatedly as we progress through the Bible.

God who is right (*righteous*), can have no part with wrong.

God's *holiness* leaves no room for sin.

God who is sinless, cannot tolerate sin in his presence.

This is a reality as certain as any physical law that governs the universe.

God's response to Lucifer's sin was immediate. He expelled him from his position in Heaven.

> …you sinned. So I drove you in disgrace from the mount of God, and I expelled you, O guardian cherub…Your heart became proud on account of your beauty, and you corrupted your wisdom because of your splendor. So I threw you to the earth…   *Ezekiel 28:16–17*

Lucifer did not go without a battle. He still was a very strong being and, on top of that, many other angels followed him. The Bible gives some precise details of what happened. To help you understand the account, I have tied the context together. As you read, you will see that any confusion about *whom* this may be speaking of, is removed in the latter parts of the text.

> Then another sign appeared in heaven: an enormous red dragon… His tail swept a third of the stars out of the sky and flung them to the earth…
>
> And there was war in heaven. Michael and his angels fought against the dragon, and the dragon and his angels fought back. But he was not strong enough, and they lost their place in heaven.
>
> The great dragon was hurled down—that ancient serpent called the devil, or Satan, who leads the whole world astray. He was hurled to the earth, and his angels with him.[1]
>
> *Revelation 12:3–4, 7–9*

DEVIL, SATAN, DEMONS

The text indicates that one-third of the angels followed Lucifer in his rebellion. Lucifer became known as the *Devil* or

Satan. Just as God's names describe his attributes, so Lucifer's names reveal his character. Satan means *adversary* or *enemy*; Devil means *false accuser* or *slanderer*. The rebellious angels that followed Satan were now called *demons* or *evil spirits.*

LAKE OF FIRE

When God cast the Devil and his demons from Heaven, it was only the first phase in judging these rebellious spirits. The Bible says that God has a place of final punishment, an...

> ...*eternal fire prepared for the devil and his angels.*
> Matthew 25:41

This location is commonly referred to as *the Lake of Fire.* Often cartoons are drawn depicting Satan and his demons standing waist-deep in flames, conniving and plotting mischief. However, the Bible tells us that Satan is not yet there. He was cast out of Heaven, but not into the Lake of Fire. Later, after many events occur involving him and his demons, Satan will be forever confined to this place of punishment. Referring to this future time, the Bible says...

> *The devil, who deceived them, was cast into the lake of fire...And they will be tormented day and night forever and ever.* Revelation 20:10 NKJV

WAR

Although God had expelled Satan and his demon followers from his presence, they retained their immense power and intellect. Now they were enemies of the Most High God. It would be all-out war. Satan would be against everything good, everything that God planned to do, and everything that God stood for. Satan would fight dirty.

As to the exact events that occurred right after Satan's rebellion, we can only speculate. You can almost see the Devil, consumed with jealousy and hatred, casting his shifty eyes around the universe looking for a weak link in God's armor.

There was absolutely none!

There must be some way to get even with God.

Satan's eyes settled on the earth...and he saw man.

Slowly—he smirked.

2 HAS GOD SAID...?

When God created man, he didn't just place him on earth and walk away. The Bible says that God visited Adam and Eve in the garden and, in the offhand way it's mentioned, one can assume that this was a regular event. On a number of occasions, the Scripture speaks of God taking on the form of a human to show himself to man. This was obviously one of those times. Adam and Eve were on intimate terms with their Creator-Owner, and God took care of their every need.

THE DECEIVER

But then Satan slinked into the garden. He did not arrive with a blast of trumpets, announcing who he was and what he was about. Satan is much too subtle for that. The Bible tells us that Satan is the great deceiver—the devil. He is incapable of telling uncorrupted truth.

> ...the devil...was a murderer from the beginning, not holding to the truth, for there is no truth in him. When he lies, he speaks his native language, for he is a liar and the father of lies. *John 8:44*

The word *lie* in the original Greek text is *pseudos*—a conscious and intentional falsehood. We use the word ourselves. It implies *imitation*.

Several years ago, I was reading an article on Satan in a popular news magazine. He was illustrated as having a red body with horns on his head, a pointed tail and carrying a pitchfork. The overall rendering was hideous. According to the Bible, that picture is deceptive to the extreme. The Bible says that...

> ...Satan himself masquerades as an angel of light. *2 Corinthians 11:14*

He comes in all his eye-catching splendor, mimicking God as closely as he can. A better picture of the Devil might have been a good-looking young man in a black suit with a clerical collar. Satan loves religion. He closely imitates the truth, but he cannot be trusted, because by his very nature he is an impostor—a counterfeit, a teller of deliberate falsehoods.

I am sure Satan was quite happy with the red suit, pitchfork-in-hand drawing. It's easier to deceive people if they're looking in the wrong direction for the wrong thing. He would also have been pleased with other statements in the magazine—"*theologians have all but scratched *Old Scratch.*" The implication was that *no one believes in that guy anymore!* What better way to deceive than for the Devil to have theologians telling people that he is a myth!

> *This is an idiom used for the Devil with no biblical connections.

DECEPTION

So Satan arrived in the garden of Eden with all the subtlety he could muster. No trumpets, no fanfare. He came in the embodiment of a snake, a reptile that is often identified with the Devil. The Bible records several incidents of evil spirits living inside both humans and animals, speaking through them or causing them to act abnormally. On this occasion Satan spoke through the reptile. He addressed Eve.

> *Now the serpent was more crafty than any of the wild animals the LORD God had made. He said to the woman, "Did God really say, 'You must not eat from any tree in the garden'?"*   Genesis 3:1

The fact that a snake could speak did not seem to disturb Eve. No doubt every day she discovered a new and fascinating part of God's creation. Perhaps she thought this was just another one of those new creatures. We don't really know.

DOUBT

Whatever the case, it is interesting that Satan approached Eve with a question about God. He planted something in her mind that she had never considered—*the creature can question the Creator.* The question came in a slightly condescending tone, "Did God really say ... ?"

"I mean, *really*—did God *really* say that?"

With his *you've got to be kidding* approach, Satan implied that man was rather simple-minded or naive to accept the Lord's word at face value.

"Perhaps God is holding back something good from you. I mean, how do you know? Maybe the Lord isn't as good and loving as he makes himself out to be."

There was a hint that God wasn't being completely honest, not entirely forthright. Satan passed himself off as being concerned for man, looking out for man's best interests. The Devil counterfeited God's goodness. His twisted logic questioned God's Word and in questioning, he planted doubt.

In addition, Satan grossly overstated God's prohibition. God had NOT forbidden eating from *every* tree. He had only mentioned *one* tree: the tree of the knowledge of good and evil. But the overstatement produced the desired reaction.

> *The woman said to the serpent, "We may eat fruit from the trees in the garden, but God did say, 'You must not eat fruit from the tree that is in the middle of the garden, and you must not touch it, or you will die.'"* Genesis 3:2–3

Eve tried to defend God, even though the Lord does not need to be defended. In her zeal she added to God's command. God had told man that he should not *eat* of the tree, but he had never said they could not *touch* it. When you *add* to God's Word you always *take away* something from it. Eve made God out to be more demanding than he really was, and in the process marred God's character. Getting people to add or subtract from the Bible is the sort of math Satan specializes in. The Devil loves the resulting confusion. The addition was *oh so little*, but it was all that Satan needed. A crack had appeared in the dike.

DENIAL

> *"You will not surely die," the serpent said to the woman. "For God knows that when you eat of it your eyes will be opened, and **you will be like God**, knowing good and evil."* Genesis 3:4–5

Not content with questioning God's word, Satan outright denied it. He blatantly called God a liar. He suggested that the reason the tree was forbidden was because God feared Adam and Eve would learn too much. Cleverly, Satan mixed truth with error. It was true that their eyes would be opened and they would know good and evil, but it was false to imply that they would be like God with all his attributes. It was also erroneous to state that they would not die. Satan was deliberately and knowingly lying. Although he knew by experience the consequence of going against God's word, he cruelly enticed man to partake of his own destruction.

Disobedience

> *When the woman saw that the fruit of the tree was good for food and pleasing to the eye, and also desirable for gaining wisdom, she took some and ate it. She also gave some to her husband, who was with her, and he ate it.*
> Genesis 3:6

Satan had succeeded. You can almost hear his howl of laughter echoing through the garden. As usual, Satan did not hang around to help pick up the pieces. He never does. The Bible says…

> *…the devil prowls around like a roaring lion looking for someone to devour.*
> 1 Peter 5:8

The Devil leaves the bones—picked clean. He may come across as a great provider—providing pleasure, fun, a good time—but it's only temporary and often very empty. In reality, Satan never gives. If he imparts anything, it's only gut-wrenching heartache. He's a malicious playmate, a cruel companion.

Over the years some have blamed the woman for this outright disobedience against God's command. However throughout Eve's entire conversation with Satan, it seems that her husband was with her. Adam could have prevented his wife from eating the fruit, and certainly did not have to eat the fruit himself. But they *both* ate.

What Adam and Eve did is similar to children playing in the street against their mother's instructions. The disobedient youngsters think they know *better than mom* what is safe and fun. They are showing that they don't entirely trust their mother's knowledge of safety. They are disregarding her authority. In the same way, Adam and Eve sinned when they felt they knew *better than God* what was good for them. Their choice made a statement. They didn't quite trust their Creator—they weren't sure God was telling the truth.

Adam and Eve had all the reasons in the world to tell the Devil that HE was the liar, but they chose to believe Satan instead of God. They disobeyed God's clear instructions, and joined the Devil's rebellious ranks. The Bible says:

ENEMY

> *Anyone who chooses to be a friend of the *world becomes an enemy of God.*
> James 4:4

*The *world* as influenced and controlled by Satan.

That's the natural outcome of choosing sides. Adam and Eve had abandoned their friendship with God and joined Satan. They had rejected a pure, perfect world to experiment with a forbidden one.

A Broken Friendship

But such a choice has ramifications. As we saw before, *a broken law has consequences.* The Scripture teaches us that sin's effects are very costly. Adam and Eve's defiant choice to follow Satan's lies opened a vast gulf in the relationship between God and man. A perfect God could not allow mixed loyalties, half friendships or partial betrayals. Unless there was trust, no relationship could exist. The friendship was over.

> Therefore God gave them … the sinful desires of their hearts … They exchanged the truth of God for a lie, and worshiped and served created things [Satan] rather than the Creator—who is forever praised.[2]   Romans 1:24–25

Fig Leaves

> Then the eyes of both of them were opened, and they realized they were naked …   Genesis 3:7

Adam and Eve immediately sensed that something was wrong. They had feelings they had never experienced before—very uncomfortable ones—called guilt and shame. They were devastated. The Bible says they were afraid and for the first time they realized they were naked. Casting their eyes around for a solution …

> … they sewed fig leaves together and made coverings for themselves.   Genesis 3:7

Perhaps they thought that if they fixed up their *outward appearance*, God would never notice that things had changed on the *inside*. They would just gloss things over and pretend that everything was okay. It was man's first attempt to make things right in a world gone wrong.

There was only one problem with the *fig leaf* solution: it didn't work. The condemnation remained. Having a good outward appearance did not remedy the inner reality. Perfection was gone. Feelings of guilt churned within. The gulf was still there.

> Then the man and his wife heard the sound of the LORD God as he was walking in the garden in the cool of the day, and they hid from the LORD God among the trees of the garden.
>
> *Genesis 3:8*

Only guilty people run and hide—one doesn't hide from a friend. A barrier, a chasm now existed between God and man. The friendship was over.

Is God Picky?

Some may say: But the sin was over such a little thing—just a bite of fruit! True. God had not put a big stumbling block in man's path. Indeed, it was no stumbling block at all. There were dozens of trees from which Adam and Eve could have freely eaten. This was the smallest of possible tests, but it defined man as being human—as having a free will.

Suppose a young lady met a fellow who seemed to be the nicest person on earth. He showed real love for her—going out of his way to do special things for her, comforting her when she hurt, sharing in her humor, telling her he loved her. Then she found out he had no choice—that he was programmed to be *loving* … well, it would be a terrible disappointment. It would all seem so artificial, so meaningless, so empty. And it would be.

3 WHERE ARE YOU?

Satan had deceived Adam and Eve into thinking that they could be equal with God. That was exactly what the Devil had craved for himself. But God hadn't created man to be governed by his own instincts or ideas. The important thing was to do what God said, and HE had said...

> "...you must not eat from the tree...for when you eat of it you will surely die." Genesis 2:17

They had eaten, and in an instant everything had changed. It happened just as God said. His word had not altered. It never does.

> Then the man and his wife heard the sound of the LORD God as he was walking in the garden in the cool of the day, and they hid from the LORD God among the trees of the garden. Genesis 3:8

Man was given a choice, a simple one, which was very easy to keep. But this one choice made a huge difference. Having this choice: to eat or not to eat
   to obey or disobey
   to love or not to love
                              ...defined man as human.

Man was not a robot. Man was able to love by his own free choice. Adam and Eve's love for each other was real, not artificial. And their initial obedience and love for God was genuine as well.

Although the test itself may have seemed a small concern, it is a serious thing to disobey the Lord in even the smallest of matters. The Bible says that God is perfect—he is holy and righteous—he cannot tolerate even the least of sins. It states explicitly that to disobey is wrong. It is sin. 1 Samuel 15:23

It's not recorded what Adam and Eve were thinking as they crouched out of sight in the shrubbery of the garden, listening to the Lord God approaching—but if you have had the experience of having thrown a baseball through your neighbors' window when they are gone, and then seeing them drive up...well, you get the idea. But it wasn't the next door neighbor Adam and Eve had offended. Rather, they had disobeyed the word of the Lord of the universe, the Holy Sovereign God. What would their Creator-Owner say? What would an almighty, all-powerful God do?

> Then the LORD God called to Adam and said to him, "Where are you?" Genesis 3:9 NKJV

What an immense relief! Apparently God didn't know anything had happened. He didn't even know where they were! Like two children who had just raided the cookie jar, they poked their heads out. Their faces were masked with innocence. Ahh, are you looking for us? Adam spoke:

> ... "I heard you in the garden, and I was afraid because I was naked; so I hid." Genesis 3:10

He spoke, but he erred. Like a boy playing hooky from school and then writing his own absentee note signed, "my mom," Adam overlooked the fact that he had never felt fear before, and that his nakedness had never bothered him. Adam had cookie crumbs on his face. God said...

> "Who told you that you were naked? Have you eaten from the tree that I commanded you not to eat from?" Genesis 3:11

Questions, Questions!

Why was God asking all these questions? Did not an all-knowing God know *where* Adam and Eve were hiding? And would not God know *why* they were feeling naked? Was the Lord really so limited that he had to ask the culprits whether they had eaten of the forbidden fruit? The truth of the matter was that God knew *exactly* what had occurred—but he was asking questions to help Adam and Eve sort out in *their* minds precisely what had happened. They had disobeyed the Lord! *They had trusted Satan instead of God.*

As we continue through the Bible we will see that God often questions man to help him see things clearly.

GOD'S FAULT

The Lord's questions also gave Adam and Eve an opportunity to *come clean* on their own.

> *The man said, "The woman you put here with me—she gave me some fruit from the tree, and I ate it."* Genesis 3:12

Uh-oh! Adam admitted to eating the fruit—sort of—but only because *that woman* God created gave him the fruit. Adam was a victim!

> "It was all God's fault."

> "If God hadn't created the woman ... then the woman wouldn't have given me the fruit, and then I wouldn't have eaten." Well, you can see it very clearly. It was God's fault after all!

> *Then the LORD God said to the woman, "What is this you have done?" The woman said, "The serpent deceived me, and I ate."* Genesis 3:13

Aha! So now the truth was out. Neither of them were to blame. It was the snake's fault. Eve was a victim too. And, of course, if God hadn't created snakes ... then she wouldn't have sinned either. God had messed up!

God never quizzed the snake. Some comic has said the snake had *no leg to stand on* anyway. The truth of the matter was that both Adam and Eve had chosen to sin of their own accord. God had given them an opportunity to own up, and they had blown it—they had refused to admit their guilt.

What they said.	What they should have said.
Adam: *The man said, "The woman you put here with me—she gave me some fruit from the tree, and I ate it."*	*"God I have failed you miserably. I have disobeyed your clear directions to not eat of the fruit. I have sinned. Please forgive me."*
Eve: *The woman said, "The serpent deceived me, and I ate."*	*"Lord God, I too have sinned by disobeying your command. I want to see our relationship restored to what it was. Please tell me how."*
Victim mentality Blames others	Responsible for own actions Seeks ways to restoration

Adam and Eve had said the wrong thing. Perhaps if they had been truly apologetic, God would have restored the friendship somehow—His way—right then and there. We don't know.

God did not annihilate Adam and Eve. If we had been the judge, jury and executioner, we would have given the thumbs down, and squashed them both. But God shows love far beyond anything we can imagine.

A Promise

This initial sin of man had severe consequences on the rest of mankind. As we will see, Adam and Eve were acting on behalf of the whole human race. Their sin brought a curse, but God in his love also gave a promise.

> So the LORD God said to the serpent, "Because you have done this…I will put enmity between you and the woman, and between your offspring and hers; he will crush your head, and you will strike his heel." *Genesis 3:14–15*

These sentences deserve a closer examination. God was not talking about women and snakes having an aversion for each other. The promise had two facets:

The Devil and his followers	The Woman and her male offspring
So the LORD God said to the **serpent**, "Because **you** have done this… I will put enmity between **you**	and the woman, and…
…between **your offspring**	and hers [**offspring**];
	…**he** will <u>crush</u>…
…**your head**, and **you** will <u>strike</u>	**his heel**."

The Lord God was saying that he would some day deliver man from Satan. There would be a male child, born of the woman, who would *crush* Satan's head—a fatal wound. True, Satan would also hurt the child, but only with a *strike* at the heel—a temporary injury that would heal.

This was the first of many promises to come about the future offspring of Eve. This male child would be known as THE ANOINTED ONE, because of the special task given to him by God. The task God had in mind for this *chosen one* was to *deliver* or *save* mankind from the consequences of sin and the power of Satan. For this reason, he would also be known as THE PROMISED DELIVERER. This must have been very good news to Adam and Eve.

This promise of a DELIVERER added another name to the list of terms that reveal God's character. He would be known as the *one who saves* or THE SAVIOR.

An offspring of **EVE**

↓

THE PROMISED DELIVERER

> ... there is no other God besides Me, A righteous God and a **Savior**; There is none except Me. "Turn to Me and be saved, all the ends of the earth; For I am God, and there is no other."
> Isaiah 45:21–22 NASB

A CURSE

As we saw before, sin has its consequences. It always does. Just as defying the law of gravity brings broken bones, so violating God's word has ramifications. God could not condone the sin of Adam and Eve. He could not say, *"Oh, forget it,"* or, *"You couldn't help it. We'll pretend it never happened,"* or, *"It was just ONE little sin."* No. The damage was done. Adam and Eve were guilty. One sin brought judgment. One sin brought fear and shame. One sin brought more sin. The earth and everything in it suffered from the curse. The animals, the sea, the bird life, even the very ground was affected. No longer was creation perfect. As a result of the curse, the Bible says...

> ... the whole creation groans and labors... Romans 8:22 NKJV

Man would enter the world through the pain of childbirth and leave it by the agonies of death. While on this planet, life would be full of injustice, sweat and misery. God told Adam...

> By the sweat of your brow you will eat your food until you return to the ground, since from it you were taken; for dust you are and to dust you will return. Genesis 3:19

The thorns and thistles of life, whether real or symbolic, would make man's existence one of pain and struggling to survive. Man had set off a chain reaction of sorrow. But the most bitter consequence of man's sin was the very thing that God had warned them about. It was death.

4 Death

> And the LORD God commanded the man, "You are free to eat from any tree in the garden; but you must not eat from the tree of the knowledge of good and evil, for when you eat of it **you will surely die**." *Genesis 2:16–17*

In a very real sense, when Adam and Eve chose to defy God's warning, they tested God to see if he would keep his word. *Did God really mean what he said? Would man die? Or was God just talking, uttering empty threats—bombast without teeth?* The Scripture's reply is quite emphatic:

> …it is easier for heaven and earth to pass away than for one stroke of a letter of the Law [or God's Word] to fail. *Luke 16:17 NASB*

We don't like talking about death. It's a taboo subject. I have traveled all over the world visiting some of the most remote people groups on the planet and I have never found a society that enjoyed death. I have stood at many open graves, some in churchyards, some in jungles, but they all shared one common denominator—grief. It is burnt into the human psyche with the branding iron of reality that death means one thing—separation. The loved one has slipped out of our presence to never return. The sense of loss and separation we feel at that time actually brings us very close to the meaning Scripture gives the word. In the Bible, death implies some sort of *separation*. It does *not* mean annihilation or non-existence.

It is also helpful to understand that death cannot be disassociated from its origin—it came about because of sin. The Bible speaks of it as a reward or payment for wrongdoing. Just as a person is paid wages for working, so…

> …the wages of sin is death… *Romans 6:23*

The Scripture speaks about *death* in a number of different ways. We will look at three.

DEAD

1. Death of the Body (Separation of man's spirit from his body)
Physical death is not hard for us to grasp. We are only too well acquainted with it. But we need to understand something more as it relates to Adam and Eve.

When you cut a leafy branch off a tree, the leaves don't instantly wither and look dead. In the same way, when God told Adam *"for when you eat of it you will surely die,"* God did not mean that Adam would drop dead as soon as he ate the fruit. Rather, God meant that Adam would be cut off from his source of life, and then, just like a branch, his body would eventually wear out and stop functioning. The body would…

> … *die and return to the dust.*　　　　Psalm 104:29

Though the body dies, the Bible says the spirit goes on living— it will continue to exist forever.

2. Death to a Relationship (Separation of man's spirit from God)
We have already seen that Adam and Eve's disobedience ended their close friendship with the Lord. But the consequences went even further. The children of Adam and Eve, and their children's children—indeed all mankind to this day—have been born into this world separated from God.

The relationship between God and man is so thoroughly finished, so profound, so complete, that even though we live physically, God views all mankind as being…

> … *dead in your transgressions and sins.*　　　　Ephesians 2:1

There's a dynamic here that we must not miss. Let me illustrate.

I have spent a significant portion of my life either traveling or living in tropical countries. For a time, my wife and I lived in a house set on low stilts. On one occasion, a very large rat chose to crawl into the narrow space under our house and die. Unfortunately, the vermin expired right under our little bedroom. Initially, we thought we had no option but to let the body decay into oblivion. The carcass rotting in the hot, humid climate sent a stupefying odor into our bedroom, giving new meaning to the word *foul*. The rat smelled so rank that my wife and I found it impossible to sleep. We were forced to retreat to another part of the house. Sleeping in close proximity to that evil-smelling carcass was not normal or natural to us. We fled.

The next morning, my son, Andrew, volunteered to remedy the situation. He located a long stick, and reaching deep into the crawl space under the house, slowly worked the dead rat towards the opening. As it got close, Andrew pulled back in revulsion, grimaced and said, "Dad! The beast is full of maggots." Oh gag! Andrew took a plastic bag and sticking it over his hand reached far under the house. Grabbing the miserable creature by its tail, he pulled the worm-infested cadaver out into the open. Holding the offending remains far from his body, he ran towards the jungle that bordered our property and, with a mighty swing, flung the rat far from his presence.

If that rat had been alive and able to sense Andrew's emotions, he would have been aware that Andrew was highly displeased with him—angry. And if that rat could have read Andrew's thoughts as he was flung far into the woods, he would have heard him say, "Get out of here!" And if the rat could have spoken and said, "For how long?," Andrew would have answered, "Forever!"

The dead rat actually illustrates three different ways God feels about sin. First, he is angry. This is not a wrath full of malice or meanness. God is not a hothead who has lost his temper. Rather, it is a reflection of God's pure, perfect character. It might best be understood as a type of *righteous indignation*. Just as we were perturbed with the rotten rat, so the Lord is angry about sin. *It grieves him.* God created the world to be a delightful place to live, but sin has changed much of it into hard work. Every time we do an unpleasant job, it's a reminder that sin has ravaged God's creation. Pain and suffering, sorrow and grief, filth and stench, bullies and drunkenness, earthquakes and war—all were not part of God's original creation. Sin has been like a drop of cyanide on a lavish, scrumptious meal—it didn't take much but it ruined it all. Sin has been like a bee sting to the face—it's a small thing, but it affects your whole being. *Sin went beyond breaking the law; it was an affront to God's entire character.* It's for this reason that the Bible says...

> ... *God's wrath comes on those who are disobedient.*
> *Ephesians 5:6*

Adam and Eve had disobeyed God when they ignored the Lord's clear instructions. Disobedience against God is a hallmark of sin. The Bible says...

> *The wrath of God is being revealed from heaven against all the godlessness and wickedness of men ...* *Romans 1:18*

We label sin as fun or evil, harmless or sadistic, big or small. The Bible does recognize certain differences when it comes to consequences, but with God, all sin is a stench in his holy nostrils. It's cyanide in his feast.

Secondly, just as the rat drove my wife and me to sleep in another room, and just as Andrew flung that revolting carcass out of his presence, so God has removed himself from sinful man. The Scripture says...

> ...*your iniquities have separated you from your God; your sins have hidden his face from you*...   Isaiah 59:2

Sometimes I've heard folks say that God seems distant, far away. Well, the Bible does say that man IS *estranged* from his Creator.

ESTRANGED

> ...*you were alienated from God*...   Colossians 1:21

Holiness demands the absence of sin. If sinful man were to enter into the radiant purity of God's presence, it would be like a host of resurrected, rotten rats traipsing into my mother-in-law's living room, begriming its freshly cleaned, ivory-colored carpet. Nothing they stepped on would be considered pure again. The whole place would be corrupted. In the same way, a perfect God cannot allow sin in his presence, for...

> *[His] eyes are too pure to look on evil; [he] cannot tolerate wrong.*   Habakkuk 1:13

This brings us to the third point that the dead rat illustrates. Just how long does God feel we should be separated from him? The answer is pretty clear. *Forever!* Sin has infinite and eternal ramifications. Just like we would not want to live with the rotten rat next week, or at any time, God will never allow sin to dwell in his presence.

This is difficult news but keep reading. Good news is coming. For now, though, it is important to understand that when the Bible speaks of man's relationship with God as being finished, it speaks with intensity. It is truly cut off—it's dead.

3. Death to a Future Joy—The Second Death
(Separation of man's spirit from God forever)

When a young couple is engaged, they look forward with delight and anticipation to all the future joys of marriage. They browse house designs, discuss where to live and what they will do together. But if the engagement goes sour and the relationship ends, all their prospective plans die too.

The Bible tells us that God is preparing a wonderful home for man after death. It's called Heaven. Heaven is an incredible place, designed by God for man's future joy. Eternal life is part of the plan. Just being free of sin, suffering and *death* will be wonderful.

ETERNAL
JUDGMENT

But just as there is eternal life, so there is **eternal death**. When the Bible uses the word *death*, by implication it sometimes refers to the *death of God's original plan* for mankind. This death is also called the *second death*, probably because it occurs after physical death. This *second death* is reserved for those people who will not be in Heaven. Instead, the Bible says they will go to the *Lake of Fire*, an appalling place that God created specifically for punishing Satan and his demons.

> *Then I saw a great white throne and him who was seated on it…And I saw the dead, great and small, standing before the throne, and books were opened. Another book was opened, which is the book of life.*
>
> *The dead were judged…*
>
> *The lake of fire is the second death. If anyone's name was not found written in the book of life, he was thrown into the lake of fire.*   Revelation 20:11–12, 14–15

The Bible speaks of being *[a]thrown alive into the fiery lake of burning sulfur,* and of being *[b]tormented day and night forever and ever.* It will be a place of *[c]sorrow, devoid of happiness.* The Scriptures talk of *[d]worms* (literally maggots), of an intense *[e]darkness,* of people weeping and gnashing their teeth in extreme anguish, of being parched with *[f]thirst,* and of remembering this life and of wishing for no one to join them. It's a place of lonely suffering, not some buddy-buddy celebration of debauchery.

[a] Rev. 19:20
Though the physical body dies the spirit continues to live.

[b] Rev. 20:10

[c] Psalms 116:3

[d] Mark 9:48

[e] Matthew 8:12; 22:13; 25:30

[f] Luke 16:24

> *But the cowardly, the unbelieving, the vile, the murderers, the sexually immoral, those who practice magic arts [or witchcraft], the idolaters and all liars—their place will be in the fiery lake of burning sulfur. This is the second death.*
>
>   Revelation 21:8

Later in the book, we will learn more about man's destiny.

A SIN NATURE

Sin and death now reigned in Adam's bloodline, seemingly passed on through the generations by the father. Like begets like. Apples reproduce apples, cats reproduce cats, sinful man reproduces sinful man.

Adam by nature had become a sinner—Adam would die.

> *Therefore, just as sin entered the world through one man, and death through sin, and in this way death came to all men, because all sinned.* Romans 5:12

Because of Adam's sin, all his offspring would inherit his sin nature. And because he died, all his offspring would die.[3]

All of Adam's descendants would have the sin nature. All would die.

We often connect a list of crimes with the word *sinner*, but the Bible says it is more than that. Man has a *sin nature*, often called *Adam's nature*. This nature is a *condition* or *state of being*. For example, the doctor has told a friend of mine that he has a heart condition. That *condition* reveals itself with *symptoms*. When he climbs the stairs, he huffs and puffs and his face changes color. On occasion, he pops a nitroglycerin tablet under his tongue. In the same sense, we can say that every human has a *condition*, called the sin nature. The *symptoms* of that *condition* are acts of sin.

AN HONEST GOD

If all this talk of sin and death seems morbid, it should be a reminder to us that God doesn't make unpleasant subjects pretty. He tells it like it is. Sin and death are two things all humans have in common, and we need to know what the Bible says about them. To be told the truth is what one would expect from a perfect God.

A REVIEW

In the beginning, God and man were close friends, living in harmony in a perfect world. Only perfect people can live with a perfect God.

The relational bridge was broken when Adam and Eve believed Satan's word instead of the Lord's, and disobeyed God's clear instructions. The whole world changed. It became a place of guilt, sorrow and death.

After Adam and Eve sinned, they adjusted their outward appearance in an effort to look better than they really were. They tried to cover their sin. It didn't work. The gulf remained.

As we continue our story, we will see that it is in the nature of man to deny his true sinfulness; to devise ways to reach God; to seek a way back to a perfect world.

What have Geneticists Found?

"It makes us realize that all human beings, despite differences in external appearances, are really members of a single entity that's had a very recent origin in one place. There is a kind of biological brotherhood that's much more profound than we ever realized." So said Stephen Jay Gould, the Harvard paleontologist and essayist in a NEWSWEEK 1988 cover article entitled, *"The Search for Adam and Eve."*[4]

According to the article, scientists *"... trained in molecular biology ... looked at an international assortment of genes and picked up a trail of DNA that led them to a single woman from whom we all descended."* ... *"There weren't even telltale distinctions between races."*

> The Bible says: *Adam named his wife Eve, because she would become the mother of all the living.*
> *Genesis 3:20*

Then in 1995, TIME[5] had a brief article saying there was scientific evidence that *"... there was an ancestral 'Adam,' whose genetic material on the chromosome is common to every man now on earth."*

> The Bible says: *From one man he made every nation of men that they should inhabit the whole earth...*
> *Acts 17:26*

These studies of human DNA conclude that we all have *one man* and *one woman* in our ancestry. Some scientists agree; others disagree. Even those who agree are quick to point out that this may not be the biblical Adam and Eve. Whatever the case, it's interesting to note that the findings are consistent with the Bible. This and other discoveries of modern molecular biology confirm what the Scripture has indicated for millennia, that we are all very closely related.

CHAPTER FIVE

1 A PARADOX

In these first few chapters we have learned a little of what God is like. As we progress, we will learn more, but we need to stop and compare a couple of God's characteristics with man's new predicament.

It is helpful to understand that just as God established physical laws to govern the universe, so he established spiritual laws that govern the relationship between God and man. And just as a knowledge of physics and chemistry helps us make sense of the world around us, so a knowledge of these spiritual laws helps us make sense of life and death. These spiritual laws are not difficult to understand. First, let's look at man's situation.

MAN'S PROBLEM

Centuries ago in the Middle East, when one incurred a debt, an official certificate was drafted so that the parties involved would not forget the amount payable. Those who were unable to pay their debts were considered criminals under the full penalty of the law. In the same way, the Bible teaches that on the moral ledger, our sin incurs a debt. There's a price to be paid. We are faced with...

DEBTOR

> ... *the law of sin and death.*   Romans 8:2

That law says:

> *The soul who sins shall die.*   Ezekiel 18:20 NKJV

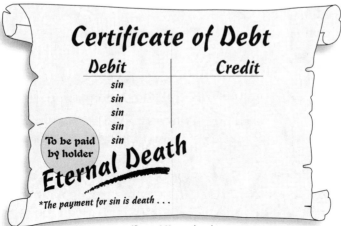

Certificate of Debt

Debit | Credit

sin
sin
sin
sin
sin

To be paid by holder

Eternal Death

*The payment for sin is death . . .

*Romans 6:23 - paraphrased

The question then remains: Are we able to pay that debt? The answer is a qualified yes. However, since death exists for eternity, it's hard to call it paid—for the transaction is never completed. To pay it, we must bear the full consequences of death in all its three-part meaning. Frankly, most thinking people find themselves very reluctant to pay. The problem is this—we must pay. It's our debt. Mankind is in a dilemma.

Two Facets

This dilemma has two facets, like opposite sides of the same coin.

❖ **We have something we don't want**—a sin problem. Because of our sin, we experience guilt, shame, pain, separation from God, and eventually the Second Death.

❖ **We need something we don't have**—perfection. We need a level of goodness that makes us acceptable in God's presence.

So the question is twofold: **How can we get rid of our sin? And, how can we gain** *a righteousness that is* <u>*equal*</u> *to God's righteousness,* **so that we can be accepted in his presence?**

Here is another way of putting it. Mankind, by creation, was designed to live in God's presence. But when man disobeyed God, his whole being changed. He lost that sinless nature which made him acceptable to God. So, *how can man gain back that perfection which allows him to live with God?*

We will be keeping these questions in mind as we progress through the Bible.

God's Situation

To understand God's situation, we need to look at two different attributes that are part of his character.

1. Perfectly Just

We have seen that the Lord is a perfect God, entirely without sin. To be sinless also means that God is honest and fair—just.

> He is the Rock, his works are perfect, and all his ways are just.
> A faithful God who does no wrong, upright and just is he.
> Deuteronomy 32:4

We would say that God is a good judge because he does not treat one person one way, and another person another way. God enforces his rules equally and fairly. Here on earth a person may hide a crime, lie about it, bribe the judge, or just simply not get caught. But with God, no perpetrator will get away with his sin. No one will escape God's justice.

> For God will bring every deed into judgment, including every hidden thing, whether it is good or evil. *Ecclesiastes 12:14*

Honesty and fairness are fundamental to God's perfect nature.

> Righteousness and justice are the foundation of Your throne.
> *Psalm 89:14 NASB*

Because God is perfect, we can count on him being absolutely fair. We like that. But here's the bad news. Perfect justice demands that sin be punished with a penalty equal to the offense. It's indicative of just how seriously God views sin by the penalty assigned to it. As we have seen, the Bible says that our sin-debt can only be paid with our death—in all its three-part meaning.

This is not good news. Fortunately, the other aspect of God's character comes into the picture.

2. Perfectly Loving

God is not only perfectly just, but he is also completely loving. By his very nature, God loves.

- ❖ God revealed a type of love when he created the world—a care and concern.

- ❖ But then God unveiled a deeper love—an undeserved love. This love is often referred to by using the words *grace, mercy, kindness* and *compassion*. As sinners, we don't deserve God's kindness, yet God loves us with a perfect love in spite of our sin. Because God is perfect, no one could be better than he at demonstrating grace and mercy.

PARADOX

Now we find a paradox. To be completely *just,* God must enforce our payment of the sin-debt—we must die. But because God is *loving,* he has no desire to destroy us. Both qualities of his character are equal. God is not more *loving* than he is *just.* So how can God maintain *justice* and still be *loving*?

To begin with, God judges all sin, either here on the earth or after physical death. He is 100% consistent on that score. We all must die.

> *Like water spilled on the ground, which cannot be recovered, so we must die.*   2 Samuel 14:14a

But then the other attribute of God's nature comes into play. Because God is by nature loving…

> *…he devises ways so that a banished person may not remain estranged from him.*   2 Samuel 14:14b

Although God allows our physical bodies to die, he lovingly provides a way whereby we can escape the eternal aspects of the death penalty. At the same time, God makes it possible for us to live in his presence again. So how does God judge sin and rescue us at the same time? How does God punish sin without punishing us? We will study that in the following chapters.

PRIDE

One last thing before we move on. The Bible says that pride is what caused Satan to rebel. We often look at pride as being a good thing, but the Bible says pride is what keeps us from coming to God for help. We are often too proud to humble ourselves and say that we need the Lord.

> *God opposes the proud but gives grace to the humble.*
> 1 Peter 5:5

2 ATONEMENT

After eating the fruit, the first thing that Adam and Eve did was to clothe themselves in fig leaves. In spite of having these clothes, Adam told God that he felt naked—exposed. There is a reason for this. The Bible tells us that…

> *… The LORD does not look at the things man looks at. Man looks at the outward appearance, but the LORD looks at the heart.*   1 Samuel 16:7

God was looking right through their feeble attempts to clothe themselves. He could see their hearts.

The Bible tells us that God rejected Adam and Eve's attempts at self-improvement. The fig leaves covered their nakedness, but their hearts were full of sin. He wanted to teach them that man could do nothing, outwardly or inwardly, to remove the sin problem. So, he refused to accept their *fig leaf* clothes.

A COVERING

Only God could supply them with clothing that was acceptable to him. God took animals, killed them and ...

> The LORD God made garments of skin for Adam and his
> wife and clothed them. *Genesis 3:21*

This was a graphic illustration of the fact that *sin brings death.* Adam and Eve had never seen death before. If they watched, it must have been a jarring experience—seeing the blood spilled on the ground, the gasping for life, the shine pass from the animal's eye, comprehending the finality. Whatever the case, God made the awful reality of death understandable to them immediately. Animals died in order that they might be clothed.

BANISHED

Although man had sinned, he still lived in the garden and had access to the tree of life. Eating of this tree would mean that man would live forever. So God removed man from the garden.

> And the LORD God said, "The man has now become like one of *us, knowing good and evil. He must not be allowed to reach out his hand and take also from the tree of life and eat, and live forever."
>
> So the LORD God banished him from the Garden of Eden to work the ground from which he had been taken.
>
> After he drove the man out, he placed on the east side of the Garden of Eden cherubim and a flaming sword flashing back and forth to guard the way to the tree of life. *Genesis 3:22–24*

*Notice the word *us.* Since the Bible clearly states that there is only one God, it is logical to ask ourselves—who is God talking to when he says, "... man has become like one of **us**?" That question will be answered as we progress through the Scriptures.

This was an act of mercy. God did not want men to live forever entrapped as sinners. Can you imagine what the world would be like if all the evil men and women down through the ages were still alive today? By putting man outside of the garden, God allowed the consequences of sin to take its eventual toll, namely physical death. But God was thinking beyond the grave. He was thinking of his plan to deliver man from the Second Death, a way to escape the Lake of Fire.

CAIN AND ABEL (see time line, pages 162–163)

> *Adam lay with his wife Eve, and she became pregnant and gave birth to Cain. She said, "With the help of the LORD I have brought forth a man." Later she gave birth to his brother Abel.* Genesis 4:1–2

Both Cain and Abel were born outside of the garden. Because they had been conceived as a result of Adam's union with Eve, they had Adam's sin condition, and were separated from God. For God to be *just*, he must enforce his law. Cain and Abel also had to die for their sin.

But God loved them, so in his mercy he provided a way for them to escape judgment. That way had two dimensions:

Inward—A Faith in God

Cain and Abel were to simply trust God—believe that what the Lord said was true. For example, God had promised Adam and Eve that THE DELIVERER would crush Satan's head and save them from sin's consequences. *Was that possible? Was it true? Did God really mean it?* Cain and Abel individually had to decide for themselves whether or not to believe God.

Outward—A Visual Aid

God also wanted to show them *what it would take* to remove sin. It involved a rather vivid visual aid. It is a little startling, so hang on to your chair.

A thorough study[1] of Scripture leads us to the understanding that God apparently and specifically told Cain and Abel to take an animal, kill it and let its blood run out on an *altar. Why was this? The very thought of animal sacrifices strikes most of us as horrible—repulsive. What conceivable reason would God have for such an explicit instruction? The Bible says…

*Altars were stone or earthen platforms upon which sacrifices were made.

> *…without the shedding of blood there is no forgiveness.* Hebrews 9:22

God was saying that man's sin-debt could only be paid, or forgiven, if there was death. But why the blood?

> *For the life of a creature is in the blood, and I have given it to you to make atonement for yourselves on the altar; it is the blood that makes atonement for one's life.* Leviticus 17:11

This concept of a blood sacrifice has two aspects:

❖ **Substitution**: Normally, man would die for his own sin. But now, based on certain future events, God was saying that he would accept an innocent animal's death in man's place—as a substitute. It was a life for a life, the innocent dying in place of the guilty. The sacrifice pictured *the law of sin and death* being obeyed and justice being fulfilled. But could not a sacrifice be killed without the shedding of blood, perhaps by drowning?

❖ **Atonement**: God said that the blood would make *atonement* for sin. The word *atonement* means *covering*. The shed blood would *cover* man's sin, therefore when God looked at man, he would no longer see the sin. Man would be viewed as *righteous* and therefore acceptable by God. The relationship would be restored. Man would still die physically, but the eternal consequences would no longer apply (i.e. separation from God forever in the Lake of Fire).

Through faith in God, as illustrated by the substitutionary death and the atoning blood on the altar, man would find forgiveness for sin and a new relationship with God.

ATONEMENT—A COVERING FOR SIN

The word *atonement* carries with it the idea of the *just, holy, righteous* side of God's nature being satisfied. God's law required death as the penalty for sin. When God saw the death of the innocent sacrifice, he was satisfied that the demands of his law had been carried out.

Sacrificing an animal on an altar did not take away the sin. Man was still sinful. The sacrifice only pictured what was necessary for sin to be forgiven—death and shedding of blood. The blood provided an *atonement* or *covering* for sin. In effect, the same way that God covered the nakedness of Adam and Eve with acceptable clothing, so man's sin was covered by the blood and man found acceptance with God. It would be right to say that the Lord temporarily overlooked man's sin as if it had been obliterated.

With God's instructions clear in our minds, we'll now return to the story of Cain and Abel and see what happens.

TWO SACRIFICES

> *Now Abel kept flocks, and Cain worked the soil. In the course of time Cain brought some of the fruits of the soil as an offering to the LORD. But Abel brought fat portions from some of the firstborn of his flock.* Genesis 4:2–4

Cain and Abel both brought sacrifices to the Lord. This is what God had told them to do. God wanted them to show by their actions that they were putting confidence in His Word as being true. But there was a problem. Although they were both bringing sacrifices, there was a disparity.

Abel brought an animal which could be killed and its blood shed. That was good—it was what God had said to do. But Cain brought garden produce. Vegetables do not shed blood. Cain was offering a sacrifice, but it was the wrong one.[1] He had come up with his own version of the *fig leaves*.

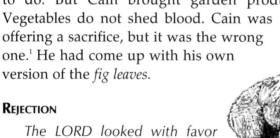

REJECTION

> *The LORD looked with favor on Abel and his offering, but on Cain and his offering he did not look with favor.* Genesis 4:4–5

God rejected Cain's sacrifice. Cain erred in two ways.

First, his actions revealed that he really didn't trust God. Secondly, Cain failed by doing things his own way. But God doesn't accept personal ideas on how to get right with him. Man may have the best intentions in the world, but sincerity is not enough—it does not bridge the gap.

We often look at independentthinking as a good thing, and there is some merit to that thought. However, we need to be careful. An independent spirit can also be very self-centered. When the *I'll do my own thing* mentality spills over into relationships—as to who's right and who's wrong, who gets and who doesn't, or even how we run entire countries—it can become very ugly.

Cain was *doing his own thing*. He felt he knew better than God what was right.

ACCEPTANCE

On the other hand, Abel offered the kind of sacrifice that God had commanded—an innocent animal that would die and shed blood. Abel deserved to die for his own sin, but God in his mercy allowed the animal to die in his place as a substitute. As Abel placed his sacrifice before the Lord, he was trusting God to keep his word—to send a DELIVERER—to somehow save him from sin's awful penalty. It is doubtful if Abel knew how THE DELIVERER would accomplish his role, but it is clear that Abel was trusting God with the solution to sin.

> ... by faith Abel offered God a better sacrifice than Cain did. By faith he was commended as a righteous man, when God spoke well of his offerings ...   Hebrews 11:4

As Abel approached God in faith, his sacrifice provided an atonement-covering for sin. When God looked at Abel, he did not see his sin. In a sense, God overlooked it. In God's eyes, Abel was righteous or perfect, and could now be accepted in His presence.

GOD'S GENTLENESS

As for Cain, he wasn't happy with God.

> *… Cain was very angry, and his face was downcast.*
>
> *Then the LORD said to Cain, "Why are you angry? Why is your face downcast? If you do what is right, will you not be accepted? But if you do not do what is right, sin is crouching at your door; it desires to have you, but you must master it."*
>
> Genesis 4:5–7

God gently tried to show Cain that he was headed for trouble, that his sin nature would destroy him. He pointed out to Cain that he too would be accepted if he came the same way Abel had come. There is no record of Cain replying. He was sulking.

QUESTIONS, QUESTIONS

> *Now Cain said to his brother Abel, "Let's go out to the field." And while they were in the field, Cain attacked his brother Abel and killed him.*
>
> *Then the LORD said to Cain, "Where is your brother Abel?"*
>
> Genesis 4:8–9

Just like God quizzed Adam and Eve, now we see the Lord asking Cain questions. God didn't need to ask Cain what had happened. God knows everything; he knew exactly what had taken place. He was giving Cain a chance to come clean. But just like Adam and Eve, Cain's words revealed his heart:

> **Cain:** *"I don't know," he replied. "Am I my brother's keeper?"*
> **God:** *"What have you done? Listen! Your brother's blood cries out to me from the ground."*
>
> Genesis 4:9–10

Sin cannot be hidden. Cain had murdered his brother and then had tried to wrangle his way out of a confession. God put his finger on Cain—You did it! There is no record of Cain ever expressing remorse for his actions. God could have destroyed him, but in his mercy, He moved him to another region. The human race had gotten off to a scandalous start.

SETH (see time line, pages 162–163)

> *Adam lay with his wife again, and she gave birth to a son and named him Seth, saying, "God has granted me another child in place of Abel, since Cain killed him."*

Seth also had a son, and he named him Enosh. At that time men began to call on the name of the LORD. Genesis 4:25–26

Although Seth was born with a *sin nature,* he trusted God just like Abel. It was through Seth and his descendants that God would send THE SAVIOR. God was keeping his promise.

DEATH

Well, it's time to leave Adam. The Bible says he had a large family and lived to be extremely old. Some scholars have proposed that a greenhouse effect in the original creation could have shielded man from harmful cosmic rays allowing for the incredible life spans recorded in early history. Others have noted that the accumulation of degenerative mutations would have been in its infancy, allowing for longer life spans. Though there may be merit in these theories, scientists increasingly believe that the length of one's life is the result of a genetically determined limit. Originally, that genetic limit could have been set much higher. We will see later what may have caused the change. Whatever the reason, the Bible says that God's word finally came true for Adam.

After Seth was born, Adam lived 800 years and had other sons and daughters. Altogether, Adam lived 930 years, and then he died. Genesis 5:4–5

DEAD

WHO DID SETH AND CAIN MARRY?

The Bible says Adam and Eve had other sons and daughters. It is implied that at this point in history brothers and sisters would have married each other. Because there had not been enough time for a significant number of mutant genes to arise in the genetic pool shared by the children, no harmful effects would have resulted from this kind of intermarriage. Later in the history of the Bible, we see this type of marriage forbidden.

What Happened to Abel when he Died?

Although the Bible does not explicitly mention where Abel's spirit went when he was murdered, we know from other Scriptures that those who died went to a place called *Paradise*, a place God prepared for believing men and women. Some Bible scholars would differentiate between Paradise and Heaven during this time in history, but all agree that they are now merged.

The Bible does not tell us a lot about Heaven, possibly because it's difficult to get our fog-bound mortal brains to comprehend it. One biblical writer who was given a peek at the place was left wanting for concrete words—he resorted to word pictures to get his point across. When you look at the world God created in six days, it's rather staggering to think about what he could do with eons of tinkering. The Bible does say that Heaven is a real place, with real people living there. It will be like Eden, only incomparably better.

Man's sin nature will be gone.

> Nothing impure will ever enter it, nor will anyone who does what is shameful or deceitful, but only those whose names are written in the … book of life.　　　　*Revelation 21:27*

Man will a have a righteousness that is completely acceptable to God. In thinking of seeing the Lord, one biblical writer wrote …

> … in righteousness I will see your face … I will be satisfied with seeing your likeness.　　　　*Psalm 17:15*

Man's unique relationship with God will be restored.

> Now the dwelling of God is with men, and he will live with them. They will be his people, and God himself will be with them and be their God.　　　　*Revelation 21:3*

Everything about life will be perfect.

> [God] will wipe every tear from their eyes. There will be no more death or mourning or crying or pain, for the old order of things has passed away. He who was seated on the throne said, "I am making everything new!"　　　　*Revelation 21:4–5*

There will be no funerals or fractured relationships, no graves or broken-hearted good-byes, no hospitals or homelessness, no crippled bodies or ailing health, no crutches or canes.

Instead, Heaven will be a place of endless joy and pleasure.

> ...you will fill me with joy in your presence, with eternal
> pleasures at your right hand.   Psalm 16:11

Our bodies will not be limited by time or space. It seems we will
be able to move about instantly. Evidently we will also be able to
recognize people we have known or heard about here on earth.

At least part of Heaven will be occupied by a large city. It has
been calculated that if only 25% of the city was used, 20 billion
people could be accommodated with plenty of room to spare.
This city is called the New Jerusalem.

> And he...showed me the holy city, Jerusalem,...having the
> glory of God. Her brilliance was like a very costly stone, as a
> stone of crystal-clear jasper. It had a great and high wall, with
> twelve gates, and at the gates twelve angels...
>   Revelation 21:10-12 NASB

> And in the daytime (for there shall be no night there) its gates
> shall never be closed...   Revelation 21:25 NASB

> And the street of the city was pure gold, like transparent glass.
>   Revelation 21:21 NASB

> Then the angel showed me the river of the water of life, as
> clear as crystal flowing from the throne of God...   Revelation 22:1

This will be a city like none we have ever known—no
pollution, no rust, no decay, no thieves, no crime,
no fear—perfect in every detail. All residents of Heaven
will live there for eternity.

ETERNAL
LIFE

> They will not need the light of a lamp or the light of the sun,
> for the Lord God will give them light. And they will reign for
> ever and ever.   Revelation 22:5

> ...I will dwell in the house of the LORD forever.   Psalm 23:6

Perhaps we can end this section with the following verse which,
though not limited to heavenly realms, certainly carries the idea
of what God has in store.

> "No eye has seen, no ear has heard, no mind has conceived
> what God has prepared for those who love him."   1 Corinthians 2:9

3 TWO BY TWO

Many people view the Bible as a constant sequence of stunning miracles. Actually, miracles were very much the exception. Centuries would pass before anything earthshaking would happen. At this point in our story, the Bible records that no less than ten generations passed before the next big event unfolded in world history. Each one of those generations represents a long life span during which time the population of the world increased dramatically.

Hundreds and hundreds of years passed, but God did not forget His commitment to send THE PROMISED DELIVERER. Each generation had those who believed God. Though the population of the world was increasing by leaps and bounds, the number who trusted God did not increase at the same rate. The Bible records that all but a few turned their backs on him.

VIOLENCE

Mankind had not only rejected God but was intent on following Satan with all the gusto man could muster. The Bible says:

> The LORD saw how great man's wickedness on the earth had become, and that every inclination of the thoughts of his heart was only evil all the time.
>
> Now the earth was corrupt in God's sight and was full of violence. God saw how corrupt the earth had become, for all the people on earth had corrupted their ways.
>
> Genesis 6:5,11–12

If you consider some of the nations of the world whose daily news fills our TV screens with accounts of anarchy, war, violence and rape, then you have an idea of what it must have been like. The Scripture says that man's thoughts were consumed with evil continually. Perversion and chaos reigned. The world had become a deadly place in which to live.

LIVING FOR SELF

In addition, the Bible declares that the society of that day was focused on living for self.[2] What God said wasn't important anymore. Man had scorned God's plan and had developed a philosophy of life that excluded any desire to seek after him. Man wasn't even attempting to bridge the gap.

Though righteousness was far from man's mind, sin was a different matter.

GOD

Cain OWN IDEAS

Adam OUTWARD APPEARANCES

MAN

People of Noah's Day

> For although they knew God, they neither glorified him as God nor gave thanks to him, but their thinking became futile and their foolish hearts were darkened. Although they claimed to be wise, they became fools and exchanged the glory of the immortal God for images made to look like mortal man and birds and animals and reptiles.

> Therefore God gave them over in the sinful desires of their hearts to sexual impurity for the degrading of their bodies with one another. They exchanged the truth of God for a lie, and worshiped and served created things rather than the Creator—who is forever praised. Amen.

> Because of this, God gave them over to shameful lusts. Even their women exchanged natural relations for unnatural ones. In the same way the men also abandoned natural relations with women and were inflamed with lust for one another. Men committed indecent acts with other men, and received in themselves the due penalty for their perversion.

> Furthermore, since they did not think it worthwhile to retain the knowledge of God, he gave them over to a depraved mind, to do what ought not to be done.

> They have become filled with every kind of wickedness, evil, greed and depravity. They are full of envy, murder, strife, deceit and malice. They are gossips, slanderers, God-haters, insolent, arrogant and boastful; they invent

ways of doing evil; they disobey their parents; they are senseless, faithless, heartless, ruthless. Although they know God's righteous decree that those who do such things deserve death, they not only continue to do these very things but also approve of those who practice them.[3]

Romans 1:21–32

The Bible says that at this time in history, man had sold his soul to sin. But as we have seen before, sin has its consequences. It always does. Just as defying the law of gravity results in bruises and broken bones, so ignoring God's word has ramifications. God could not condone the sin. The Bible says God was grieved by it all.

So the LORD said, "I will wipe mankind, whom I have created, from the face of the earth ... "

Genesis 6:7

Man may have had a philosophy of life that excluded God, but God still held man accountable for his behavior.

NOAH (see time line, pages 162–163)

However, one man and his family were different. The Scripture says that ...

Noah found favor in the eyes of the LORD ... Noah was a righteous man, blameless among the people of his time, and he walked with God.

Genesis 6:8–9

Though Noah was a good-living man, the Bible makes it plain that he still was a sinner. According to the law of sin and death, Noah had to die for that sin. But the Bible also indicates that Noah brought an animal sacrifice to God, evidence that he recognized the need to have an innocent substitute pay that death penalty for him. Noah believed that the Lord would somehow save him from sin's consequences. The Scripture says that because Noah trusted God, the Lord looked upon him as being righteous. Noah had a right relationship with the Lord, indicated by the words, "... *he walked with God.*"

So God said to Noah, "I am going to put an end to all people, for the earth is filled with violence because of them. I am surely going to destroy both them and the earth. So make yourself an ark of cypress wood; make rooms in it and coat it with pitch inside and out."

Genesis 6:13–14

THE WAY OF ESCAPE

God told Noah to build an ark—a boat. This was no rowboat. It was a large ship, similar to modern ocean-going freighters. It had several decks, a built-in ventilation system and a door—only one door. The vessel was built of wood covered with a coat of tree pitch, a common means in past centuries of sealing a ship.[4] The Ark remained the largest vessel ever built until its size and ratio were almost duplicated in 1844 by the ship Great Britain. The dimensions of the Ark are still considered ideal for a large stable boat. It was not built for speed, only to preserve life. God told Noah:

> *"I am going to bring floodwaters on the earth to destroy all life under the heavens, every creature that has the breath of life in it. Everything on earth will perish.*
>
> *But I will establish my *covenant with you, and you will enter the ark—you and your sons and your wife and your sons' wives with you.*

*Covenant: an agreement, promise or contract.

> *You are to bring into the ark two of all living creatures, male and female, to keep them alive with you. Two of every kind of bird, of every kind of animal and of every kind of creature that moves along the ground will come to you to be kept alive. You are to take every kind of food that is to be eaten and store it away as food for you and for them."*
>
> *Noah did everything just as God commanded him.*
>
> Genesis 6:17–22

OBEDIENCE

Because Noah believed God, he obeyed him. That still didn't make God's directions any easier to follow. Noah had never built a boat before, certainly not one this size. And how would he explain the notion of a worldwide deluge to his neighbors?

God had said it would be 120 years before the Flood would take place.[5] During this time Noah not only oversaw the construction of the boat, but he also warned all who would listen that judgment was coming.[6]

The Bible tells us that before the Flood people lived to be hundreds of years old. Various theories have been suggested as to why this was so, but no reason is given in the Bible.

It is simply stated as fact. Considering the long time people lived, 120 years for building the ark was well within the usual life span. After the Flood, life spans were shortened considerably so that a man of 90 was regarded as old.

Many excellent books have been written on the Flood regarding the impact it had on the world climate and geography. These books are reasoned theories based on the biblical account and scientific observations. With such detailed sources available, I have not attempted to duplicate them. However, in the next few pages, I will briefly refer to some of these theories, with the hope that they will help your understanding without getting bogged down.

> The LORD then said to Noah, "Go into the ark, you and your whole family, because I have found you righteous in this generation." Genesis 7:1

> And Noah did all that the LORD commanded him. Genesis 7:5

> On that very day Noah and his sons, Shem, Ham and Japheth, together with his wife and the wives of his three sons, entered the ark.

> They had with them every wild animal according to its kind, all livestock according to their kinds, every creature that moves along the ground according to its kind and every bird according to its kind, everything with wings. Pairs of all creatures that have the breath of life in them came to Noah and entered the ark. The animals going in were male and female of every living thing, as God had commanded Noah.

> Then the LORD shut him in. Genesis 7:13–16

ONE DOOR

The ark took seven days to load. With a few exceptions, Noah only took one pair of each kind on board. Even allowing for extinct kinds, the ship had adequate room to house them all, with the animals occupying only an estimated 60% of the vessel.[7] The remaining space probably carried feed. Taking the young of large beasts may have been another space saver. To save on food, some may have hibernated. Of course, God was quite able to sustain them in any way he chose.

After the loading was completed, God shut them in. When judgment came and the waters began to rise, no amount of banging on the ark could move Noah to open the hatch. Nor did Noah and his family need fear that the door might be torn open in the pounding deluge. They were perfectly safe because God had shut the door—the one and only door to safety. He had shut in those who believed and shut out the rebellious.

God is gracious. He had given mankind 120 years to turn from their sinful ways and take advantage of his mercy. Now their time was up. Judgment came, just as God had said it would. Man sometimes threatens and never delivers, but God always keeps His Word.

> *In the six hundredth year of Noah's life, on the seventeenth day of the second month—on that day all the springs of the great deep burst forth, and the floodgates of the heavens were opened. And rain fell on the earth forty days and forty nights.*　　　　　Genesis 7:11–12

THE SPRINGS AND FLOODGATES

Cartoons have been drawn of an old man on a little houseboat, surrounded by animals, all getting soaked to the skin by a rain squall. Those efforts to illustrate the story are in error. You would have been crazy—and dead—to have remained outside in the storm that burst upon the earth.

First of all, the earth ruptured, releasing massive amounts of underground water. The Bible talks about *the springs of the great deep bursting forth*. It has been theorized that water under extreme pressure was spewed high into the sky. Then it, along with other water in the atmosphere, came down as the *floodgates of heaven were opened*. Such a rupturing of the planet's crust had to have included enormous volcanic activity. It is possible that at this time the whole process known as *continental drift* occurred. Using super-computers, one of the world's leading researchers in plate tectonics has modeled in 3D the whole process of continental drift occurring in a few months.[8] As fissures tore open the crust of the earth, huge slabs of the surface were thrust deep into the earth's interior, recycling the ocean basins and continental land.

The Hebrew word to describe this event means *a catastrophic deluge*. In the Bible, that word is solely used to describe this Flood. No other inundation has ever come close to equaling it. Though many of the things that happened in the cataclysm can be explained by natural science, we must remember that an all-powerful God could create the Flood circumstances and the attending catastrophic results without any limitation.

The *rain* lasted for 40 days, but it seems from the text that water continued to flow out of the underground *fountains* for 150 days.

> *For forty days the flood kept coming on the earth, and as the waters increased they lifted the ark high above the earth. The waters rose and increased greatly on the earth, and the ark floated on the surface of the water. They rose greatly on the earth, and all the high mountains under the entire heavens were covered.* Genesis 7:17–19

> *Everything on dry land that had the breath of life in its nostrils died. Every living thing on the face of the earth was wiped out; men and animals and the creatures that move along the ground and the birds of the air were wiped from the earth. Only Noah was left, and those with him in the ark.* Genesis 7:22–23

> *But God remembered Noah and all the wild animals and the livestock that were with him in the ark, and he sent a wind over the earth, and the waters receded. Now the springs of the deep and the floodgates of the heavens had been closed, and the rain had stopped falling from the sky. The water receded steadily from the earth.* Genesis 8:1–3

It is believed that prior to the Flood, the mountains were not as high as they are now. Today, if you were able to take the surface of the globe and smooth it out, the water would cover the earth to a depth of approximately two miles (3 km). The Bible says that after the Flood, the mountains we see today *rose up* and the *valleys sank down,* presumably forming the ocean basins.

> *The waters were standing above the mountains. At Your rebuke they fled…The mountains rose; the valleys sank down to the place which You established for them. You set a boundary that they may not pass over, so that they will not return to cover the earth.* Psalm 104:6–9 NASB

A DIFFERENT PLANET

Noah and his family were in the boat for 371 days before God opened the door and let them out. Long before that day, the waters had receded, and the ark had lodged in a mountainous region. When they left the ark, the ground was not only dry but producing again. It was a very different planet from before. It was the earth on which we now live.

> *Then God said to Noah, "Come out of the ark, you and your wife and your sons and their wives. Bring out every kind of living creature that is with you—the birds, the animals, and all the creatures that move along the ground—so they can multiply on the earth and be fruitful and increase in number upon it."*
>
> *So Noah came out, together with his sons and his wife and his sons' wives.*
>
> *Then Noah built an altar to the LORD and, taking some of all the clean animals and clean birds, he sacrificed burnt offerings on it. The LORD smelled the pleasing aroma…* Genesis 8:15–18,20–21

A Promise

The first thing Noah did after leaving the ark was to build an altar and offer an innocent animal as a blood sacrifice to God. The sacrifice did not remove the sin, but it did picture what was necessary to pay the penalty—blood shed in death. It was evidence that Noah had confidence in God, believing that the Lord would keep his word, and somehow save him and his family from the consequences of sin. God was pleased.

> *Then God blessed Noah and his sons, saying to them, "Be fruitful and increase in number and fill the earth.* Genesis 9:1
>
> *I now establish my covenant with you and with your descendants after you…Never again will all life be cut off by the waters of a flood; never again will there be a flood to destroy the earth."*

What about Dinosaurs, Fossils, Coal, and Oil?

We do not find the word *dinosaur* in the Bible—the word is recent, invented in 1841 by an English anatomist. However, the early books of the Bible do record references to animals that have no present parallels. Two of the larger animals mentioned have an intriguing resemblance to the fossil record.[9]

From what the Bible says, one can assume that the dinosaurs were created by God and lived with man from the beginning. Dinosaurs appear to have been reptiles, most of which continue to grow throughout their lifetime. If they had the long *life spans humans had before the Flood, it could account for the huge size some attained.

*Many people lived over 900 years.

The Bible indicates that two of every kind of land animal were ordered onto the Ark. It makes sense that only the young were taken, not only to conserve space, but also to maximize breeding time in the post-flood years. Since the average size of a dinosaur was that of a small pony, and even the largest dinosaurs at birth were no bigger than a football, calculations show that there was ample room for them on the Ark.

As to what caused their demise, we can only conjecture. In the last few decades, many creatures have become extinct, but even

> *And God said, "This is the sign of the covenant I am mak-*
> *ing between me and you...I have set my rainbow*
> *in the clouds, and it will be the sign of the covenant*
> *between me and the earth."*   Genesis 9:9,11–13

God promised to never destroy the earth with a flood again. Whenever it rained, the rainbow would be a reminder of that promise. Although thousands of years have passed since the Flood, God has kept his Word.

> *The sons of Noah who came out of the ark were Shem,*
> *Ham and Japheth. These were the three sons of Noah,*
> *and from them came the people who were scattered*
> *over the earth.*   Genesis 9:18–19

Man now had a fresh start.

> *Altogether, Noah lived 950 years, and then he died.*   Genesis 9:29

---

in these recent cases, it's hard to nail down the exact cause. Going back millennia makes it even harder. Since the climate seems to have changed radically after the Flood, it has been theorized that it would have been difficult for such animals to survive.

The conditions created by the deluge answer many questions we see in the natural world. For example, the massive amount of sediment created by the Flood, the extreme weight of the water, the tremendous amount of erosion—all could account for the deposits of coal, oil and fossils we now find. Many of the fossils show overwhelming evidence that they were swiftly and catastrophically buried, frequently in vast fossil *graveyards*. The very existence of any well-preserved fossil, such as a fish, means it was buried rapidly, with the encasing sediment hardening quickly before scavengers, bacteria and decay destroyed its features.

Many thought-provoking books have been written to discuss the Creation-Flood perspective. They present reasoned and logical explanations for much of what we see. If you have nagging questions, consult the Appendix for a list of resources that give you an analysis of these issues.

4 BABEL

The tenth chapter of the book of Genesis is often called *"The Table of Nations."* It tells us where the major ethnic groups came from, beginning with Noah's three sons. The chapter ends with this verse:

> *These are the clans of Noah's sons, according to their lines of descent, within their nations. From these the nations spread out over the earth after the flood.* Genesis 10:32

Once again, centuries of time passed and the population of the earth increased. Our story now moves on to what historians call the cradle of civilization: ancient Mesopotamia, now modern-day Iraq.

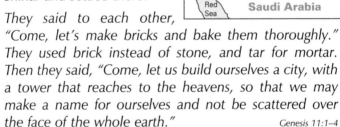

> *Now the whole world had one language and a common speech. As men moved eastward, they found a plain in Shinar and settled there.*
>
> *They said to each other, "Come, let's make bricks and bake them thoroughly."* They used brick instead of stone, and tar for mortar. Then they said, "Come, let us build ourselves a city, with a tower that reaches to the heavens, so that we may make a name for ourselves and not be scattered over the face of the whole earth."* Genesis 11:1–4

MAN'S AGENDA

After the Flood, God had told man to…

> *Be fruitful and increase in number and fill the earth.* Genesis 9:1

But now man was not only trying to change the agenda, but to add something of his own.

First: Man felt that everyone should stay in one place and build a big city. This was in direct disobedience to God's instruction. Once again, man felt that he knew *better than God* what was right.

As you can see, man has a problem with obedience. Have you ever wondered why you don't need to teach little children to disobey Mom and Dad? It comes very naturally because defiance is natural to the human heart. Basically, as humans we don't want to be told what to do. We prefer to do our own thing. This was the problem with the people of Babel.

Second: Along with the city, man wanted to build a tower to bring honor to himself. The people were saying, "We want to...

> *...make a name for ourselves..."*   Genesis 11:4

You can't help but hear the evil whisperings of Satan. That had been his ambition too.

It is noticeable that God didn't fit into any of the plans. When man is busy trying to be a *somebody*, to make a *name* for himself, then you can be sure pride is involved. God will have to be left out of the picture. It's preposterous to attempt to exalt yourself when you're standing next to a God who is so resplendent, so supreme, so majestic, and so powerful. HE's going to cause any other name-maker to look ridiculous. As we have seen before, the Bible says that *God* is the only one worthy to have His name exalted.

So man's plans did not square with the Lord's instructions at all. Once again, man was functioning independently of the Most High God.

Babel is the first incident of an organized religion recorded in the Bible. Babel, or what became known as Babylon, is often used in the Scripture as an example of man's religious efforts. The people, in trying to build a tower to the heavens, were devising their own way of reaching God. You can imagine them slaving away in the tropical heat, as they collected mud, baked the bricks and glued them together with tar. It must have been dreadful toil, all so they could reach the heavens. But it didn't work. There is only one way to God—God's way.

A good definition for the word religion is this: **man's efforts to reach God**. Man, by nature, tends to be very religious. He is constantly searching for or creating new ways to find God. It's a hopeless pursuit. We will see that the Bible says that mankind is in a spiritual wilderness—he is LOST—and cannot find his way back to God on his own.

LOST

Man can neither get rid of his sin nor find adequate righteousness to make himself acceptable to the Lord.

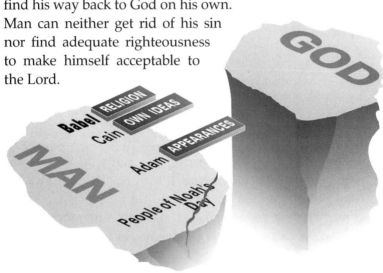

In contrast to religion, the Bible teaches that the only true way to God was provided by the Lord himself when, in his mercy, he reached down to man and provided man with a way to escape the punishment for sin. It is God who rescues us. He's the Savior. The Bible makes it clear that it is the Lord who...

> ...devises ways so that a banished person may not remain estranged from him.   2 Samuel 14:14

The people of Babel ignored that fact. Of course, none of their impressive construction efforts escaped God's notice. God was fully aware of what was going on.

> But the LORD came down[10] to see the city and the tower that the men were building. The LORD said, "If as one people speaking the same language they have begun to do this, then nothing they plan to do will be impossible for them."   Genesis 11:5–6

God knew what history has proven to be true, that with a common language, man's progress in technology is much faster. It seems to be a pattern. The more advanced and comfortable things are, the less man feels he needs God. Though God had given man a free will, he did not want man to live independently of him.

SCATTERED

The story speaks for itself. God took action to confront man's defiance. God said ...

> "Come, let *us go down and confuse their language so they will not understand each other."
>
> So the LORD scattered them from there over all the earth, and they stopped building the city. Genesis 11:7–8

*Once again, notice the word us. The Bible clearly states that there is only one God. So, just who is the Lord talking to when he says "us"? We will study that later.

The suggested migration of native North and South American tribal people across the Aleutian land bridge has never been well-founded. Though some language associations have been made, linguistically it has been impossible to prove. Why tiny, linguistically-isolated pockets of humanity should end up in such remote locations, from northern Greenland to the depths of the Amazon jungle, is beyond reasonable explanation. The Bible says God scattered them—and it seems that's just the way it happened. No doubt, he also equipped them with the knowledge of how to live in their new environments.

Whatever the case—whether via a land bridge or literally— when God scattered them, he gave them new languages. He did a thorough job. Anyone who has ever embarked on the formidable task of learning another tongue knows you don't just create a new language on a whim. Some of the languages God created are so complex that it can take trained linguists years to grasp, and even then, they do not completely understand them.

The city the people were building didn't disappear, but it did take on a name. It means *confusion*.

> That is why it was called Babel—because there the LORD confused the language of the whole world.
>
> From there the LORD scattered them over the face of the whole earth. Genesis 11:9

WHERE DID ALL THE RACES ORIGINATE?[11]

In one sense there is only one race—the human race. The Bible distinguishes people by national or tribal groupings, not by skin color or by physical appearance. But those differences do exist. How could it have happened?

For the sake of explanation, we will choose skin color, but the same would apply to eye and nose shape, hair texture, stature, etc.

We usually think of skin as having many colors, but actually skin essentially has only one color: melanin. If we have only a little melanin, we are light-skinned; if we produce a large quantity, we are dark-skinned. There are a few other minor factors which contribute to skin color, but they are not unique to any particular race, and the explanation below applies to them as well.

It has long been known that if a black person marries a white, the end result is a brown skin color. If two of that offspring marry, their children can either be black, white, or any shade of color in between. Why? Because the parents each possess the range of genes required to give the entire spectrum of color.

Now if you take children that were born with pure black skin (from the above marriage) and they marry other offspring of the same color, and migrate to an area where their children could not marry those of another color, then their offspring would be consistently black. They would no longer have the genes required to produce white skin. Under similar circumstances, this would apply to those with white skin, who would no longer have the genes required to produce black skin. Such diversification in two different color groups, which does not involve any new gene being added to those already created, can happen after only a few generations. Although the above explanation has been much abbreviated, one can see that it is not the problem as it may first appear.

The Bible says that all the nations of the earth came from Noah, his three sons and their wives, who were presumably brown, as they would have had genes enabling both white and black skin to appear in their descendants.

CHAPTER SIX

1 ABRAHAM

After the confusion of languages at Babel, many generations passed before the Bible records the next intervention by God in history. All through these passing years the Lord did not forget his promise to send a DELIVERER. Though the majority of people lived with little thought of God, each generation had those who believed his promises. One such couple was Abram and Sarai.

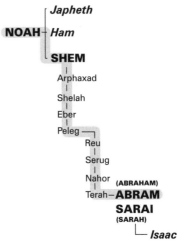

> *Now Sarai was barren; she had no children.* Genesis 11:30

Abram's home town was the city of Ur, just south of Babel. However, following the Lord's instructions, he left home and moved to Haran. It was here that God spoke to him a second time.

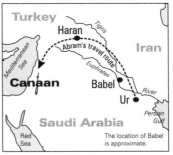

The location of Babel is approximate.

> *The LORD had said to Abram, "Leave your country, ... and go to the land I will show you." So Abram left, as the LORD had told him ... Abram was seventy-five years old[1] when he set out from Haran.* Genesis 12:1,4

For Abram this was a big step. He couldn't consult an atlas, research the country on the Web, or discuss plans with a travel agent. He didn't even know where he was going! God had not told him. As he traveled, he would have to trust God to lead him one day at a time. His unknown destination was Canaan, which is modern-day Israel.

> *So they came to the land of Canaan. And there he built an altar to the LORD, who had appeared to him.* Genesis 12:5,7 NKJV

Because Abram believed God to be his Savior from sin's consequences, he offered a blood sacrifice on an altar as an *atonement-covering* for his sin. Although the animal offerings were only a picture of what was needed for sin to be removed,

Abram's sacrifice was clear evidence that he recognized the need to have a substitute pay the death penalty for him. He was trusting God just as Abel, Noah and all the other righteous people had done in the ages past.

Abram lived a semi-nomadic life, so much so that the locals called him a *hebrew*, a name which carried the connotation of *a wanderer, the one from beyond*. From this time on, Abram and his descendants were referred to as *Hebrews*.

FOUR PROMISES

God also gave Abram four specific promises:

1. *I will make you into a great nation...*[2]

2. *I will make your name great...*[3]

3. *I will bless those who bless you, and whoever curses you I will curse...*[4]

4. *...all peoples on earth will be blessed through you.* Genesis 12:2–3

When God **blesses**, he bestows favor and well-being.

When God **curses,** he brings misfortune.

God's first promise was good news to Abram. In order to become a great nation, he would have to father children. However, since he had no offspring and Sarai was past childbearing age, he was perplexed as to how this would happen. But God had promised, so it must be true.

The last promise hinged on the first, and was a direct reference to THE DELIVERER. God was telling Abram that one of his descendants would be THE ANOINTED ONE, and that HE would be a blessing to everyone. The Bible says Abram believed God and rejoiced at *"the thought of seeing"* the day of THE DELIVERER'S arrival.[5]

> After this, the word of the LORD came to Abram in a vision: "Do not be afraid, Abram. I am your shield, your very great reward."
>
> But Abram said, "O Sovereign LORD, what can you give me since I remain childless...?"
>
> God...took him outside and said, "Look up at the heavens and count the stars—if indeed you can count them." Then he said to him, "So shall your offspring be."

*Abram believed the LORD, and he credited it to him as
righteousness.*
Genesis 15:1–2,5–6

This last sentence is loaded with meaning. We will look at
three words that have far-reaching implications. They are
the words *righteousness*, *credited* and *belief*. The last one is so
important I will commit an entire section to it.

RIGHTEOUSNESS

We saw earlier that the word righteousness is used in reference to God's perfection; that he is flawless, holy, pure, clean,
totally without blemish or sin.

CREDITED

The word *credited* carries the thought of settling a monetary
account through a payment. The term has common usage
today in our financial world. We like seeing money *credited*
to our bank account, as it shows we've been on the receiving
end! But what does the Bible mean when it says,

> "*Abram believed the LORD, and he credited it to him
> as righteousness.*"?
Genesis 15:6

Remember that *Certificate of Debt* that every human has as a
result of sin? Well, Abram had one too. But because Abram
believed God's promises, God placed a credit on his account.
He gave Abram *righteousness*.

DEBTOR

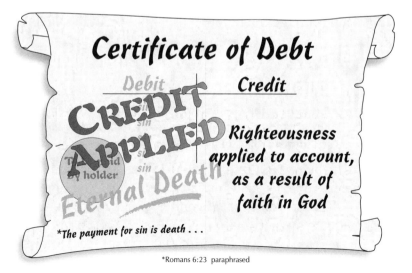

Certificate of Debt

Debit | Credit

CREDIT APPLIED

*Righteousness
applied to account,
as a result of
faith in God*

*The payment for sin is death . . .

*Romans 6:23 paraphrased

It was like God was saying, "Abram, because you are trusting me, I'm going to make an advance payment on your sin account. I'm going to place *my* perfection on your ledger. Now you need to understand, *my* righteousness far exceeds your sinfulness. What I am giving you will more than offset all your sin. You can consider your sin-debt as paid. And because what I am giving you is *my* righteousness, it will not only take care of your sin-debt, but it will fully provide you with all the perfection needed to live with me in Heaven."

The Bible says Abram had such confidence in God keeping his word, that he…

> …was looking forward to the city with foundations, whose architect and builder is God.   Hebrews 11:10

Although Abram's body would eventually die, Abram would not experience the horrific penalty associated with the second death. He knew he would live forever with God in Heaven.

Earlier on we asked that two-sides-of-the-same-coin question, "How can we get rid of our sin and gain *a righteousness equal to God's righteousness* so we can be accepted in his presence?" For Abram, the answer was simple: trust the Lord, believe his promises, and God will provide.

2 Belief

This third word can be easily misunderstood. We need to understand some things about it as it appears in the Bible:

❖ The words or concepts of *belief, faith, trust* and *confidence* are often used interchangeably.

Abram **believed** the LORD.	He **believed** what God said.
Abram put **faith** in the LORD.	He had **faith** in His Word.
Abram **trusted** the LORD.	He knew God to be **trustworthy**.
Abram had **confidence** in the LORD.	His **confidence** was in God alone.

❖ True belief is built on fact, not feelings. When you sit in a chair, you trust that it will hold you up. You don't sit in it because you have a wonderful feeling or an overwhelming passion about chairs. Rather, you observe that the chair is substantial, and based on that fact, you rest yourself upon it. Abram's faith rested on fact—God's promise. It was a matter of simple arithmetic.

God said, "You will have a son"
+ The Creator God is all-powerful and tells the truth
= Abram will have a son

❖ It's not the *amount* of faith[6] you have, but *in whom* you are placing your trust. Abram's faith may have wavered at times, but his confidence was firmly placed in God.

❖ True biblical belief does not stop with mental assent to the facts. If it did, it would not be genuine faith.

Faith can be illustrated the following way: Two friends are at a county fair. One asks the other, "Do you believe that the roller coaster will stay on those tracks?" The other replies, "Of course I do!" Then the first friend says, "Okay, let's go for a ride!" If the second friend is reluctant and begins making excuses for not joining in the fun, it's doubtful that he really believes. Although he may say so with his mouth, more importantly, he doubts it in his heart.

Roller coasters may deserve misgivings and there may be other good reasons for not taking a ride, but the point is this: belief or faith affects our actions.

Abram's belief went beyond agreement. He staked his life, his reputation, and his actions on it. Because he believed, he was obedient to God and traveled to a foreign land. Because he believed, he offered sacrifices, trusting God to save him from sin's consequences.

It's important to understand that Abram's obedience wasn't an attempt to prove to God or to others the genuineness of his faith. Rather, because he trusted God, the natural result was that he did the things God wanted him to do. So when we read the words, *"Abram believed the LORD..."* we need to be thinking of all that is implied.

Because of Abram's faith, God changed his name to Abraham, which means *father of many,* and Sarai became Sarah, meaning *princess.* It was God's way of saying he would keep his promise, although they were both past childbearing age.

3 ISAAC

Now the LORD was gracious to Sarah as he had said, and the LORD did for Sarah what he had promised. Sarah became pregnant and bore a son to Abraham in his old age, at the very time God had promised him. Abraham gave the name Isaac to the son Sarah bore him. Genesis 21:1–3

God had kept his promise to Abraham and Sarah, even in their old age. He always keeps his word and he delights in doing the impossible.

Some time later God tested Abraham. He said to him, "Abraham!"

"Here I am," he replied.

Then God said, "Take your son, your only son, Isaac, whom you love, and go to the region of Moriah. Sacrifice him there as a burnt offering on one of the mountains I will tell you about."

Early the next morning Abraham got up and saddled his donkey. He took with him two of his servants and his son Isaac. When he had cut enough wood for the burnt offering, he set out for the place God had told him about. On the third day Abraham looked up and saw the place in the distance. He said to his servants, "Stay here with the donkey while I and the boy go over there. We will worship and then we will come back to you."

Abraham took the wood for the burnt offering and placed it on his son Isaac, and he himself carried the fire and the knife. As the two of them went on together, Isaac spoke up and said to his father Abraham, "Father?"

"Yes, my son?" Abraham replied.

"The fire and wood are here," Isaac said, "but where is the lamb for the burnt offering?"

Abraham answered, "God himself will provide the lamb for the burnt offering, my son." And the two of them went on together.

When they reached the place God had told him about, Abraham built an altar there and arranged the wood on it. He bound his son Isaac and laid him on the altar, on top of the wood. Then he reached out his hand and took *the knife to slay his son. But the *angel of the LORD called out to him from heaven, "Abraham! Abraham!"*

"Here I am," he replied.

"Do not lay a hand on the boy," he said. "Do not do anything to him. Now I know that you fear God, because you have not withheld from me your son, your only son."

Abraham looked up and there in a thicket he saw a ram caught by its horns. He went over and took the ram and sacrificed it as a burnt offering instead of his son. So Abraham called that place The LORD Will Provide. And to this day it is said, "On the mountain of the LORD it will be provided."

The angel of the LORD called to Abraham from heaven a second time and said, "I swear by myself, declares the LORD, that because you have done this and have not withheld your son, your only son, I will surely bless you and make your descendants as numerous as the stars in the sky and as the sand on the seashore. Your descendants will take possession of the cities of their enemies, and through your offspring all nations on earth will be blessed, because you have obeyed me." Genesis 22:1–18

> *The Angel of the Lord—in this case a synonym for God. Compare Genesis 22:15,16

This is a most profound story. At first glance it appears that God is endorsing child sacrifice!! But look deeper.

YOUR ONLY SON

The setting is simple. God asked Abraham to take his son and sacrifice him on an altar—to put him to death. This is no idle request. The Lord reminded Abraham that this was his only son. His memory hardly needed the assistance. For years he had waited for this child, and Isaac was the very son that God had promised would be the father of countless descendants. The Lord had been very specific about that and it was obvious that a dead son could have no offspring!

God's request must have bewildered Abraham. In all probability he had witnessed the human sacrifices practiced by other nations of his day and knew it was a common form of appeasing their gods. Yet God's command to sacrifice Isaac went against everything Abraham knew about the Creator.

God, in his love, had promised Isaac as a descendant that would bear many children. There was no earthly way to harmonize God's previous promise with His present command. How could God be so inconsistent? And yet Abraham had learned that the Lord was utterly trustworthy, so he did just as God requested. Calling his son, he saddled the family donkey and, taking the trappings for sacrifice-making, he set off to do the Lord's bidding. His heart must have been torn with anguish! Being obedient was an immense step for Abraham, but that step showed his absolute faith in God's goodness.

The Bible does not leave us guessing Abraham's thoughts. It tells us that Abraham clung to God's promise, convinced that even if he sacrificed Isaac, the Lord would raise him from the dead.

> By faith Abraham, when God tested him, offered Isaac as a sacrifice...Abraham reasoned that God could raise the dead, and...receive Isaac back from death. Hebrews 11:17,19

The Bible says that God was testing Abraham's faith. We'll understand the reason why in a few more pages. This ultimate test of offering his own son revealed to Abraham, and to us, his genuine confidence in the Lord.

Abraham and Isaac, along with two other young men, headed off to the mountains of Moriah. When they got nearer, Abraham and Isaac went on alone with Isaac carrying the wood. Somewhere along the way Isaac queried his father. No doubt, Isaac had witnessed many sacrifices and it didn't take a college degree for him to realize that one of the essentials was missing—the sacrifice itself. Where was the lamb?

> "The fire and wood are here," Isaac said, "but where is the lamb for the burnt offering?" Genesis 22:7

One can't help but wonder if Isaac was thinking about the prevalence of child sacrifice in neighboring religions. He, too, was trusting in the Lord and in no small way! When his father replied that God Himself would provide the lamb, Isaac went on willingly. It says they went together.

God showed them the exact place to erect the altar on one of the mountains of Moriah. Many years later, the Jewish temple would be built on Mount Moriah, perhaps on the same site Isaac was offered.

BOUND

When they reached the place God had told him about, Abraham built an altar there and arranged the wood on it. He bound his son Isaac and laid him on the altar, on top of the wood.
Genesis 22:9

Isaac was no infant. The Hebrew word translated *boy* was used of young males all the way up to military age. He was certainly old enough to put up a fight and, in spite of the fact that Abraham was not a young man, there is no record of a struggle. It is obvious that Isaac willingly submitted to his father, an act which showed implicit confidence in his dad, whom he knew to be a follower of God's Word.

Once bound on the altar, Isaac was helpless. He was under direct and specific orders from God to be slain. There was no way he could save himself. The Bible says Abraham stretched out his arm and took the knife. You can see the old man's hand shake. His jaw sags. His heart is about to break.

This is his only son! The strain of the moment is incredible. Slowly the trembling arm is raised and in the somber light of the day, the cold metal of the knife glints. Deliberately, the mind commits itself to the plunge, and then ... and then God intervened. The Angel of the Lord called to Abraham from heaven and said ...

> *"Do not lay your hand on the lad, or do anything to him; for now I know that you fear God, since you have not withheld your son, your only son, from Me."* Genesis 22:12 NKJV

There must have been tears. You can see Dad and son weeping in overwhelming relief. God had intervened. The sentence of death was gone!—at least for Isaac it was gone. But still there was a death.

A Substitute

The Bible says that God provided an animal.

> *Abraham looked up and there in a thicket he saw a ram caught by its horns.* Genesis 22:13

Entangled in this way, the sheep could not injure itself in an effort to be freed.

> *He went over and took the ram and sacrificed it as a burnt offering instead of his son.* Genesis 22:13

There was death all right, but it was the ram's death instead of Isaac's. Isaac went free because a ram died. God had provided a substitute. This event so imprinted itself on Abraham's mind that he named the mountain as a reminder of what God is like.

> *So Abraham called that place The LORD Will Provide. And to this day it is said, "On the mountain of the LORD it will be provided."* Genesis 22:14

Abraham found that God is truly a...

> *... Savior in time of distress...* Jeremiah 14:8 NASB

The story ends with God reaffirming his promise to Abraham. His offspring would be many—the whole nation of Israel. Included in God's promise was the fact that THE ANOINTED ONE would be one of the descendants of Abraham and Isaac. It was said that HE would be a blessing to all people.

> *"I swear by myself," declares the LORD... "through your offspring all nations on earth will be blessed, because you have obeyed me."* Genesis 22:16,18

God's request of Abraham to sacrifice Isaac was a *once in a lifetime—once in the history of man* sort of request. God wanted to communicate certain truths not only to Abraham, but also to us—truths having to do with judgment, faith, and deliverance through a substitute.

Just as Isaac was under God's direct order to die, so all mankind is under the sentence of death.[7] Isaac could not save himself. But Abraham trusted the Lord, believing that somehow his loving God would make the difference. And God did intervene. He provided a way of escape through a substitute. It was a life for a life—the innocent dying for the guilty.

Just as Abel had offered a sacrifice to die in his place, so the ram had died in Isaac's place. And just as God had viewed Abel's sacrifice as acceptable, so God saw fit to provide a ram as an acceptable sacrifice in Isaac's place. It was God's idea. It was man coming to God in God's way, believing that His Word was true.

CHAPTER SEVEN

1 ISRAEL AND JUDAH

2 MOSES

3 PHARAOH AND THE PASSOVER

1 ISRAEL AND JUDAH

God had promised both Abraham and Isaac that THE DELIVERER would be one of their descendants. Both these men lived long lives and died.

JACOB (ISRAEL)

Isaac had two sons: Esau and Jacob. Esau was like Cain, patterning his life around his own ideas, doing his own thing. On the other hand, Jacob trusted God and, because of that, the Lord considered him righteous. Jacob often came to God offering blood sacrifices on an altar.

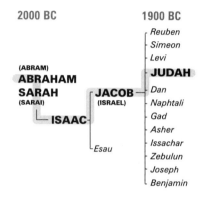

2000 BC   1900 BC

> So Jacob…built an altar there…because there God appeared to him.   *Genesis 35:6–7 NKJV*

Jacob believed the principles found in God's Word, that…

> …without the shedding of blood there is no forgiveness.   *Hebrews 9:22*

> For the life of a creature is in the blood, and I have given it to you to make atonement for yourselves on the altar; it is the blood that makes atonement for one's life.   *Leviticus 17:11*

Although Jacob often failed in life, God was the ultimate focus of his trust. Later his name was changed to *Israel*, which means *God prevails*. Today the nation of Israel, which descends directly from Jacob, has named itself after this man.

God also renewed his promise with Jacob, the same promise he had made to Abraham and Isaac. The Lord told Jacob…

> "I am the LORD, the God of your father Abraham and the God of Isaac…All peoples on earth will be blessed through you and your offspring."   *Genesis 28:13–14*

God was saying that one of Jacob's descendants would be a blessing to every nation—a reference to THE PROMISED DELIVERER.

Jacob (or Israel) had twelve sons from whom descended twelve tribes.[1] Before Jacob died, he told his son *Judah* that it would be through his tribe that THE DELIVERER would come.

Egypt

Abraham, Isaac and Jacob lived semi-nomadic lives in Canaan (what we know today as Israel). In the final years of Jacob's life, famine hit the country and he, along with his sons and their families, moved into Egypt. At the time, this ragtag band numbered only seventy souls. Egypt received and treated them well.

Three hundred and fifty years later they were still in Egypt, but by then it is estimated that there were two and a half million Israelites. The descendants of Abraham, Isaac, and Jacob had indeed become a great nation but there was a problem—they were in the wrong country. They had been promised the land of Canaan, not Egypt. However, the Lord had told Jacob long before the seventy had fled the famine in Canaan…

> *"I am with you and will watch over you wherever you go, and I will bring you back to this land. I will not leave you until I have done what I have promised you."* Genesis 28:15

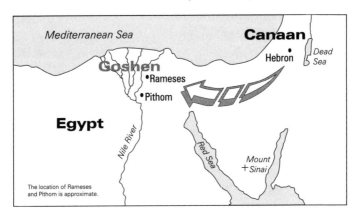

The location of Rameses and Pithom is approximate.

2 Moses

Two and a half million Israelites in Egypt could hardly be ignored. The Egyptian king (or Pharaoh) came up with an idea.

> *"Look," he said to his people, "the Israelites have become much too numerous for us. Come, we must deal shrewdly with them or they will become even more numerous and, if war breaks out, will join our enemies, fight against us and leave the country."*

*So they put slave masters over them to oppress them
with forced labor, and they built Pithom and Rameses as
store cities for Pharaoh.*   Exodus 1:9–11

Not only were the Israelites enslaved, they were slaves
condemned to hard labor.

*But the more they were oppressed, the more they
multiplied and spread; so the Egyptians came to dread
the Israelites and worked them ruthlessly. They made
their lives bitter with hard labor in brick and mortar and
with all kinds of work in the fields…*   Exodus 1:12–14

But God had not forgotten his promises. The Bible says…

*God heard their groaning and he remembered his covenant
with Abraham, with Isaac and with Jacob. So God looked
on the Israelites and was concerned about them.* Exodus 2:24–25

The time had come for the them to leave. The Lord had his
man in place, an Israelite named Moses.

Moses had been born in Egypt to Israelite parents. At birth,
he was condemned to die. Providentially, he was rescued
and raised as a member of Pharaoh's household with access
to the best education in the land. As an adult, he murdered
an Egyptian in defense of an Israelite, and then fled for his
life into the desert. It was here that he became a shepherd,
and for the next forty years learned to lead sheep. It was an
education designed by God.

*Now Moses…led the flock to the far side of the desert
and came to Horeb, the mountain of God. There the
angel of the LORD appeared to him in flames of fire from
within a bush. Moses saw that though the bush was on
fire it did not burn up.*   Exodus 3:1–2

One can't help but think that Moses stood staring at the
bush for some time. He must have been perplexed. What's
going on here?! Wouldn't his wife be glad to hear about
this—a wood that burned yet wasn't consumed would make
great fuel for her kitchen stove!

*So Moses thought, "I will go over and see this strange
sight—why the bush does not burn up."*

*When the LORD saw that he had gone over to look, God
called to him from within the bush, "Moses! Moses!"*
                                                 Exodus 3:3–4

A talking tree no less! One can imagine Moses looking around, all in a sweat, hoping no one was listening. What would he look like, carrying on a conversation with a shrub?!

> *And Moses said, "Here I am."*
>
> *"Do not come any closer," God said. "Take off your sandals, for the place where you are standing is holy ground." Then he said, "I am the God of your father, the God of Abraham, the God of Isaac and the God of Jacob."*   Exodus 3:4–6

Moses' blood must have chilled. He knew all about the eternal Most High God. He knew that God was the Creator-Owner of all living. He knew that the Lord was a holy God who separated himself from mankind because of their sin. Moses himself was a sinner—a murderer.

> *Moses hid his face, because he was afraid to look at God.*
>
> *The LORD said, "I have indeed seen the misery of my people in Egypt. I have heard them crying out because of their slave drivers, and I am concerned about their suffering.*
>
> *So now, go. I am sending you to Pharaoh to bring my people the Israelites out of Egypt."*   Exodus 3:6–7,10

Moses must have sighed with relief. God was not coming to judge his sin, but to give him a job. But there was a problem. Moses was a shepherd and the task looked formidable. Who was he anyway? People wouldn't put reams of confidence in a fellow who said he spoke to a bramble bush. Moses said to God,

> *"Suppose I go to the Israelites and say to them, 'The God of your fathers has sent me to you,' and they ask me, 'What is his name?' Then what shall I tell them?"*
>
> *God said to Moses, "I AM WHO I AM. This is what you are to say to the Israelites: 'I AM has sent me to you.'"*
>   Exodus 3:13–14

I AM means *the self-existent one*, the God who exists by his own power.

> *This is my name forever, the name by which I am to be remembered from generation to generation.*
>
> *Go, assemble the elders of Israel and say to them, 'The LORD, the God of your fathers—the God of Abraham, Isaac and Jacob—appeared to me and said: "I have watched over you and have seen what has been done to you in Egypt.*

> *And I have promised to bring you up out of your misery in Egypt into…a land flowing with milk and honey."'*
>
> *The elders of Israel will listen to you."*   Exodus 3:15–18

Though Moses struggled with misgivings, he also knew that when God made a promise, he always kept His Word. So Moses packed his bags and headed back to Egypt, back to Pharaoh and the Israelite slaves. On the way, he met his brother Aaron whom God had sent to be his spokesman.

> *Moses and Aaron brought together all the elders of the Israelites, and Aaron told them everything the LORD had said to Moses.*
>
> *…and they believed. And when they heard that the LORD was concerned about them and had seen their misery, they bowed down and worshiped.*   Exodus 4:29–31

It happened just the way that God said it would. The people believed and worshiped the Lord. God was keeping his promise.

3 Pharaoh and the Passover

It was one thing for Moses and Aaron to convince the leaders of Israel that God had spoken, but the whole effort of selling Pharaoh on the idea conjured up a quagmire of nightmarish problems.

> *Afterward Moses and Aaron went to Pharaoh and said, "This is what the LORD, the God of Israel, says: 'Let my people go…'"*
>
> *Pharaoh said, "Who is the LORD, that I should obey him and let Israel go? I do not know the LORD and I will not let Israel go."*   Exodus 5:1–2

Well, Pharaoh was right on one account—he did not know the LORD. Egypt venerated a plethora of gods—the sun-god, the god of storms, the Nile River—even Pharaoh was a god. Each god was represented by a different symbol: the vulture, the frog, the scorpion, and so on. The Egyptians worshiped the creation rather than the Creator. Not only was Pharaoh ignorant of the true God, he was closed to the whole idea of becoming acquainted. For him to worship the Creator would mean a considerable loss of power and status, and letting the

Israelites go would be hard on the economy—a major loss of free labor. Pharaoh was adamantly opposed to such an idea.

> Then the LORD said to Moses, "Now you will see what I will do to Pharaoh... I will bring you out from under the yoke of the Egyptians. I will free you from being slaves to them... with mighty acts of judgment." Exodus 6:1,6

God told Moses that He would bring judgments on Egypt in the form of plagues. Only under these conditions would Pharaoh let the Israelites go. Such news was rather disconcerting. If God brought plagues on Egypt, what would Pharaoh do in retaliation? The Lord encouraged the Israelites by reminding them of his promise to their forefathers.

> "I will take you as my own people, and I will be your God... And I will bring you to the land I swore [or pledged] with uplifted hand to give to Abraham, to Isaac and to Jacob. I will give it to you as a possession. I am the LORD." Exodus 6:7–8

GOD'S PEOPLE

God said the Israelites would be *his* people. This did not mean that *only* the people of Israel could follow the true God, but it did mean that the Lord was making it easier for the different nations of the earth to know just what God was like and how he related to man. All that the world would need to do is look at Israel and they would see a full-color, surround-sound, living lesson of how God dealt with mankind!

God had said he would bring plagues on Egypt in order to deliver Israel. In the process, he would teach both nations something about himself.

Israelites: The lesson to be learned...

> "Then **you will know that I am the LORD your God**, who brought you out from under the yoke of the Egyptians." Exodus 6:7

Egyptians: The lesson to be learned...

> "And **the Egyptians will know that I am the LORD** when I stretch out my hand against Egypt and bring the Israelites out of it." Exodus 7:5

God was going to teach both nations the same thing: that He alone is God. However, Pharaoh would have nothing to do with Moses and Aaron. So God told them:

> "Go to Pharaoh in the morning as he goes out to the water. Wait on the bank of the Nile to meet him … Then say to him, 'The LORD, the God of the Hebrews, has sent me to say to you: Let my people go … But until now you have not listened.'
>
> "This is what the LORD says: 'By this you will know that I am the LORD: … I will strike the water of the Nile, and it will be changed into blood. The fish in the Nile will die, and the river will stink; the Egyptians will not be able to drink its water.'" Exodus 7:15–18

And that's exactly what happened. God struck right at the heart of the Egyptian religion by making one of their gods, the Nile, turn to blood. God made their god stink. He made the river abhorrent to them! But…

> …Pharaoh's heart became hard; he would not listen to Moses and Aaron…and did not take even this to heart. Exodus 7:22–23

GOD VERSUS GODS

And so a cycle began. God would warn Pharaoh to let the Israelites go; Pharaoh would say NO; and God would bring a plague, each one targeting another of the Egyptian gods.

First the Nile was turned to *blood*.

Then God sent a scourge of *frogs*—in every nook and cranny. In food, in beds—everywhere.

This was followed by swarms of aggressive *gnats*.[2]

Flies supplanted the gnats.

Then an epidemic struck the *cattle*—they all died.

After that, the people were tormented with festering *boils*.

Then a massive *hail* storm ravaged their crops.

What the hail left behind was devoured by a horde of *locusts*.

Finally, the true God struck at the false god, the sun, with a curse of *darkness* so thick it could be felt.

In all, God sent ten plagues—the last and most devastating one was yet to come. God spoke to Moses and Aaron:

Now the LORD had said to Moses, "I will bring one more plague on Pharaoh and on Egypt. After that, he will let you go from here, and when he does, he will drive you out completely."

*"This is what the LORD says: 'About midnight I will go throughout Egypt. **Every firstborn son in Egypt will die,** from the firstborn son of Pharaoh, who sits on the throne, to the firstborn son of the slave girl, who is at her hand mill...'"* Exodus 11:1,4–5

The last plague was indeed the worst, falling on Egyptians and Israelites alike if they did not follow God's instructions. God, as a just God, was bringing judgment on sin, but as a God of love, he was also *mercifully* providing a way of *escape*.

Take a lamb...

The LORD said to Moses and Aaron in Egypt, "...on the tenth day of this month each man is to take a lamb for his family, one for each household." Exodus 12:1,3

A male, without blemish. It couldn't be deformed or defective in any way. God was asking for a perfect lamb.

"The animals you choose must be year-old males without defect, and you may take them from the sheep or the goats." Exodus 12:5

Kill the lamb at the appointed time.

"Take care of them until the fourteenth day of the month, when all the people of the community of Israel must slaughter them at twilight." Exodus 12:6

Apply the blood to the door posts and the lintel.

"Then they are to take some of the blood and put it on the sides and tops of the doorframes of the houses where they eat the lambs." Exodus 12:7

Stay inside the house until morning.

"Not one of you shall go out the door of his house until morning." Exodus 12:22

Do not break any of the bones.

"It must be eaten inside one house; take none of the meat outside the house. Do not break any of the bones." Exodus 12:46

I will pass over.

> *"On that same night I will pass through Egypt and strike down every firstborn—both men and animals—and I will bring judgment on all the gods of Egypt. I am the LORD.*
>
> *The blood will be a sign for you on the houses where you are; and when I see the blood, I will pass over you. No destructive plague will touch you when I strike Egypt."*
>
> *Exodus 12:12–13*

When God came in judgment to kill the firstborn, He would *pass over* every house where the blood was applied.

> *The Israelites did just what the LORD commanded Moses and Aaron.*　　*Exodus 12:28*

Their obedience was outward evidence that they trusted God, believing what he said was true.

CONSIDER

You can imagine what would have happened if a fellow had reasoned to himself: "This is ridiculous, killing the best lamb. I have an old cripple, it will do."

Or, if one called to his friends, "Hey guys, it's a beautiful night. Let's have our party outside."

Or, if another said, "No way am I going to mess up my door posts with blood—gross! I'll dump it on the ground outside the back door."

Would God have passed over? Obviously not. They may have done it with the best of intentions, but they would not be following God's instructions. They would be *doing their own thing*—just like Cain, and the people of Noah's day. The Lord would judge them along with the Egyptians because they refused to trust him. They would be getting just what they deserved.

On the other hand, what if an Egyptian happened by, and heard that God was going to send a final plague? And that Egyptian got to thinking: "You know, our gods are false. The Israelites worship the only true God. I want that God to be my God. What does the Lord require of me?" And then that same Egyptian, putting his faith solely in God, followed the instructions for the Passover. Would God *pass over* his house that night? Would he escape punishment? Yes, he would—because he believed the Lord and was coming to God in God's way. His faith would be honored by God who would extend to him grace and mercy.

> At midnight the LORD struck down all the firstborn in Egypt, from the firstborn of Pharaoh, who sat on the throne, to the firstborn of the prisoner, who was in the dungeon, and the firstborn of all the livestock as well.
>
> Pharaoh and all his officials and all the Egyptians got up during the night, and there was loud wailing in Egypt, for there was not a house without someone dead.
>
> During the night Pharaoh summoned Moses and Aaron and said, "Up! Leave my people, you and the Israelites! Go, worship the LORD as you have requested. Take your flocks and herds, as you have said, and go. And also bless me."

The Egyptians urged the people to hurry and leave the country. "For otherwise," they said, "we will all die!"

And on that very day the LORD brought the Israelites out of Egypt...　　　　　　　　　　　*Exodus 12:29–33,51*

GOD KEEPS HIS WORD

God had been gracious with Pharaoh. He had given him many chances to let the Israelites go, but Pharaoh had continued to refuse. God said he would judge the Egyptians, and he did just that. God is not like us. We may threaten to discipline our children, but often we never follow through. But God always keeps His Word. The Egyptians were judged.

On the other hand, the Israelites experienced the Lord's kindness because they believed him. When he came in judgment, wherever he saw the blood applied, he passed over. The firstborn lived—but only because a lamb died. It had been this way from the very beginning. God had accepted Abel's sacrifice as a death payment in Abel's place. When Abraham offered Isaac as a sacrifice, the ram died in Isaac's place. Now with the Passover, the lamb died in the place of the firstborn.

These substitutionary sacrifices were visible statements of each person's trust in God as their Savior. Because they believed the Lord, they obeyed him.

This feast was to become a tradition for the Israelites. Every year they were to eat the *Passover* as a reminder of how God had delivered them from slavery.

> *"This is a day you are to commemorate; for the generations to come you shall celebrate it as a festival to the LORD—a lasting ordinance."*　　　　　　　　　*Exodus 12:14*

And so the Israelites were freed from their bondage and thrust out of the land by their former masters. God had kept his promise—it happened just the way he had said it would.

Chapter Eight

1 BREAD, QUAIL AND WATER

The Israelites were a disheveled crowd as they started off on their long journey. The Egyptians sped their departure by loading them down with valuables and, with no time to pack in an orderly fashion, they left in a mighty rush, driving their livestock before them. Multiply those factors with their approximate number—2 ½ million—and you have confusion! Moses was the leader, but how do you yell, "This way!" to such a multitude? Even the best gawkers and rubberneckers couldn't spot Moses! God solved the dilemma.

> *By day the LORD went ahead of them in a pillar of cloud to guide them on their way and by night in a pillar of fire to give them light, so that they could travel by day or night.*
> *Exodus 13:21*

With a trailblazing beacon, all were able to organize themselves immediately. All they had to do was look ahead and follow the special cloud, trusting the Lord to guide them. They could even travel at night, courtesy of God's pillar of fire. This was crowd-control on a grand scale!

> *God did not lead them on the road through the Philistine country, though that was shorter. For God said, "If they face war, they might change their minds and return to Egypt." So God led the people around by the desert road toward the Red Sea.* *Exodus 13:17,18*

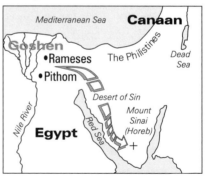

God was watching out for the Israelites. He led them out into the Sinai wilderness where virtually no one lived. This desolate wasteland was devoid of enemies, but there was also very little food. So the people let loose with a massive grumble session.

> *…the whole community grumbled against Moses and Aaron. The Israelites said to them, "If only we had died by the LORD's hand in Egypt! There we sat around pots of meat and ate all the food we wanted, but you have brought us out into this desert to starve this entire assembly to death."* *Exodus 16:2–3*

The people complained and even wanted to return to slavery. Their cynical attitude towards God's provision was saddening, for the Lord had shown vigilant care for them and he wasn't about to abandon them. They should have asked God for food, for he wanted to be their provider. But no, they grumbled!

BREAD AND QUAIL

The LORD said to Moses, "I have heard the grumbling of the Israelites. Tell them, 'At twilight you will eat meat, and in the morning you will be filled with bread. Then you will know that I am the LORD your God.'"

That evening quail came and covered the camp, and in the morning there was a layer of dew around the camp. When the dew was gone, thin flakes like frost on the ground appeared on the desert floor. When the Israelites saw it, they said to each other, *"What is it?" For they did not know what it was.

Moses said to them, "It is the bread the LORD has given you to eat."

Exodus 16:11–15

*What is it? is a literal rendering of the word manna. Some translations use the word manna.

God provided them with meat and bread and they didn't even have to work for it. Every day the bread was available to be gathered and every day they would be reminded: *it is God who provides.* They must have felt a little embarrassed for having griped in the first place. God was teaching the Israelites yet another lesson.

A SIMPLE LESSON

The bread had a purpose greater than food. God said…

"In this way I will test them and see whether they will follow my instructions."

Exodus 16:4

God told Moses to tell the people to gather only as much bread as they could eat in one day. It was an easy instruction…

However, some of them paid no attention to Moses; they kept part of it until morning, but it was full of maggots and began to smell. So Moses was angry with them.

Exodus 16:20

It was a simple lesson and no one was hurt, but through it the people learned that the Lord meant what he said and was to be trusted. Disobedience was fraught with hazards.

GRIPING

> *The whole Israelite community set out from the Desert of Sin, traveling from place to place as the LORD commanded. They camped at Rephidim, but there was no water for the people to drink. So they quarreled with Moses and said, "Give us water to drink. ... Why did you bring us up out of Egypt to make us and our children and livestock die of thirst?"*
>
> *Then Moses cried out to the LORD, "What am I to do with these people? They are almost ready to stone me."*
>
> Exodus 17:1-4

So much for learning from past mistakes. The people were back in the grumble and gripe mode, only this time it had to do with water.

> *The LORD answered Moses, "Walk on ahead of the people. Take with you some of the elders of Israel and take in your hand the staff...I will stand there before you by the rock at Horeb. Strike the rock, and water will come out of it for the people to drink."*
>
> *So Moses did this in the sight of the elders of Israel.*
>
> Exodus 17:5–6

WATER

On occasion you see an artist's rendition of this miracle. Moses is portrayed as standing by a rock holding his staff, and a little stream of water about the size you'd expect from your kitchen faucet is spurting onto the ground. The truth of the matter is, there must have been quite a gush. There was a vast throng of thirsty people to water, plus all their livestock. This was not a trickle, but a mighty torrent! The Bible says:

> *He opened the rock, and water gushed out; like a river it flowed in the desert.*
>
> Psalm 105:41

Again, the Lord provided for the people's needs even though they really didn't deserve it. God, as their Creator-Owner, could have cracked the whip; told them to sit up and behave themselves. After all, sin does have consequences. But God was patient and gentle. He showed them grace—undeserved kindness. As a sinner, man does not deserve God's gracious love, but God cares for man in spite of his sin.

2 Ten Rules

The Lord had said that the Israelites were *His* people, and as such, they were to be an example to the rest of the world of God's relationship to man and man's relationship to God. But the Israelites had a lot to learn about the Lord. God's process of revealing himself was continuing, and the next major revelation of his character was about to begin.

> In the third month after the Israelites left Egypt…they entered the Desert of Sinai, and Israel camped there…in front of the mountain.
>
> Then Moses went up to God, and the LORD called to him from the mountain and said, "This is what you are to say to…the people of Israel: 'You yourselves have seen what I did to Egypt, and how I carried you on eagles' wings and brought you to myself. Now *if* you obey me fully and keep my covenant, **then** out of all nations you will be my treasured possession. Although the whole earth is mine, you will be for me a kingdom of priests and a holy nation.' These are the words you are to speak to the Israelites."
>
> Exodus 19:1–6

If … Then

In simple terms God was saying, "If you obey me, then you will be accepted by me, and you will be a statement to all the other nations of what I am like." The one condition—the big catch phrase was, "*if* you obey me, *then* …"

So far the Israelites had a miserable track record. They gathered more bread than they needed, even when the Lord clearly told them not to. They grumbled rather than trusted. An honest response to God's words would have gone like this: "God, we are failures at following your word. You are holy and we are sinful. If you are looking for us to be holy priests—if you are going to accept us on the basis of how well we obey You—we're in trouble!"

No Problem

But when Moses gathered all the people together and asked them how they felt about God's declaration, he received an enthusiastic green light.

The people all responded together, "We will do everything the LORD has said." So Moses brought their answer back to the LORD.   Exodus 19:8

They all echoed with a hearty, "Sure God, anything you ask us is fine. We will make great priests. Holiness is no problem either. We will make the best holy nation you have ever seen. We can do it!" Well, maybe that is a little exaggerated, but you get the idea. The truth of the matter was that man, at this time, could not fully understand holiness or righteousness, so God was going to spell it out in detail.

VISUAL AIDS

The lesson started with some visual aids.

And the LORD said to Moses, "Go to the people and consecrate them today and tomorrow. Have them wash their clothes and be ready by the third day, because on that day the LORD will come down on Mount Sinai in the sight of all the people."   Exodus 19:10–11

God told Moses they were to be *consecrated*, or separated. This visual aid helped Israel realize the need to be *untouched* by sin. The washing of their clothes demonstrated cleanliness or purity before the Lord. In themselves, these actions had no intrinsic value, but they helped the people to understand that spiritual purity was an important aspect of righteousness.

God wasn't done with his visual aids. He told Moses to...

"Put limits for the people around the mountain and tell them, 'Be careful that you do not go up the mountain or touch the foot of it. Whoever touches the mountain shall surely be put to death.'"   Exodus 19:12

The boundary line was a graphic picture of the separation that exists between God and man because of sin. Man was warned not to approach God, for he is holy, and sinful man cannot live in his presence. It was a reminder that death is the consequence of sin.

On the morning of the third day there was thunder and lightning, with a thick cloud over the mountain, and a very loud trumpet blast. Everyone in the camp trembled. Then Moses led the people out of the camp to meet with God, and they stood at the foot of the mountain.

> *Mount Sinai was covered with smoke, because the*
> *LORD descended on it in fire. ... Then Moses spoke and*
> *the voice of God answered him.*   Exodus 19:16–19

God's final visual aids were frighteningly impressive—
thunder, lightning, a thick cloud, the blast of a loud trumpet,
smoke and fire. All the people shook! As sinful people, man
had good reason to tremble in the presence of a holy God.
The Lord was getting his point across.

In the next few minutes, man would make a quantum leap in
the available knowledge of what God was like. God was about
to define what he meant by the words *holy* and *righteous*.
It was like the Lord was saying, "You have seen with your
own eyes that I am a God who cares for you. Now I have
never done this before—I've never laid things out so clearly
before—but <u>if</u> you will obey the ten rules that I will give
you, <u>then</u> you will be a holy people—a special people with
a special relationship, belonging just to me. You will know
how to live together in a pleasing and orderly fashion. All
other nations will be able to see that fact."[1]

Then God spoke:

Rule # 1

"I am the LORD your God ... You shall have no other
gods before Me."   Exodus 20:2–3

The Lord was telling man not to worship anyone or anything
else. The reason given was clear:

> *"I am the LORD, and there is no other; apart from me*
> *there is no God."*   Isaiah 45:5

There was only one God to be honored. It wasn't just a matter
of trusting *a* god, it had to be *the* God—the true God. Those who
desired to be righteous must only worship the Lord.

People often feel comfortable thinking that they have
kept this rule because they do not worship a *pagan* god.
But the implication of the command is this: If family,
status, work, appearance, money, recreation, retirement
or anything else is more important to you than God, then
you have broken this command.

RULE # 2

"You shall not make for yourself an idol in the form of anything in heaven above or on the earth beneath or in the waters below. **You shall not bow down to them or worship them ..."**
Exodus 20:4–5

The first rule said we should not worship another god. In the second command, man was directed not to worship an image or idol of *any* god, whether it be true or false. God didn't even want mankind bowing down to images, icons, or pictures which represented himself. Since the Lord is a spirit, there is no need for man to form a physical image of him. No man-made image is worthy of worship—only the true God is.

> *"I am the LORD; that is my name! I will not give my glory to another or my praise to idols."*   Isaiah 42:8

Another of God's requirements for holiness—to be accepted by the Creator God—was that one must not worship any image or picture of him or his creation.

RULE # 3

"You shall not misuse the name of the LORD your God, for the LORD will not hold anyone guiltless who misuses his name."
Exodus 20:7

God was telling man that He should always be respected. As the Sovereign God, even his name is not to be used lightly. As the Judge of all the earth, he deserves reverence. As King, he is worthy of our utmost honor. Rule # 3 was clear. To be righteous, one must also esteem the Most High God.

Our culture is permeated with disrespect for God. At every turn he is treated flippantly and his name is used as a verbal punctuation mark. If you have ever used God's name as a swear word, then you have broken this command.

RULE # 4

"Remember the Sabbath day by keeping it holy. Six days you shall labor and do all your work, but the seventh day is a Sabbath to the LORD your God. On it you shall not do any work ..."
Exodus 20:8-10

God was telling the Israelites that they were to keep the seventh day, Saturday, as a rest day. This special day would show the rest of the world that God had established a distinct relationship with them. The Bible says:

> *"Say to the Israelites, 'You must observe my Sabbaths. This will be a sign between me and you for the generations to come, so you may know that I am the LORD, who makes you holy.'"* Exodus 31:13

God wanted the Israelites to know that to be holy they must honor the Sabbath as a special sign of distinction.

RULE # 5

"Honor your father and your mother ..." Exodus 20:12

In this command, God said that children should esteem their parents. God says that the normal family should be a place of peace, not hostility. Children are to be respectful and obedient. In this context, parents are assumed to be looking out for the best interests of their family.

God was telling all children that holiness demands that they have an honorable relationship with their parents. The Lord wanted families to be places of order and respect, not chaos and anger.

Talking back, ignoring, arguing, pouting, the silent treatment, criticism—all are ways of being disrespectful.

RULE # 6

"You shall not murder." Exodus 20:13

God had given life to man, and so it was wrong for one man to take the life of another. But the Lord had more than the action of murder in mind. He was also targeting the intent behind the action.

The Bible tells us that...

> *God ... judges the thoughts and attitudes of the heart.*
>
> *... Nothing in all creation is hidden from God's sight. Everything is uncovered and laid bare before the eyes of him to whom we must give account.* Hebrews 4:12–13

Because God looks on the heart, he interprets murder on a much broader plane than we do. The Lord considers certain types of anger as murder.

> "You have heard that it was said to the people long ago, 'Do not murder, and anyone who murders will be subject to judgment.'
>
> But I tell you that anyone who is angry with his brother will be subject to judgment… anyone who says, 'You fool!' will be in danger of the fire of hell." *Matthew 5:21–22*

To meet God's standard of righteousness, one must not lose his temper, or be angry without just cause.

RULE #7

"You shall not commit adultery." *Exodus 20:14*

God was saying that the only acceptable time to have sex is after you are married, and the only rightful person to share that intimacy with is your marriage partner.

But then the Lord goes one step further. Because he looks at the heart, he knows when someone has sinful thoughts.

> "You have heard that it was said, 'Do not commit adultery.' But I tell you that anyone who looks at a woman lustfully has already committed adultery with her in his heart."
> *Matthew 5:27,28*

To look at someone to whom you are not married with the desire to have sex, means you have broken this law. To be holy means one must have a pure mind as well as pure actions.

RULE #8

"You shall not steal." *Exodus 20:15*

God does not want anyone to take things that belong to others. God is the one who gives each person the right to own property. To steal is to disobey the Lord, and one who has stolen cannot be considered righteous.

Theft includes cheating—whether on an exam or on taxes.

Rule #9

"You shall not give false testimony against your neighbor."

Exodus 20:16

Man should always be honest, for God will have no part in deceitfulness. Earlier we saw that Satan is a liar, that by his very nature he is deceitful. But God is the direct opposite. Truth comes from God's nature—it's his very essence. He is the…

> … God, who cannot not lie … Titus 1:2 NKJV

When the Lord tells us something, we can count on it being true, because…

> … it is impossible for God to lie … Hebrews 6:18

Because God is true, to him all lying is a defiant *slap in the face*. Satan is the *father of lies,* and anyone who tells a lie is following Satan's agenda. False accusations, slander, libel, gossip—all of these are sinful according to his law.

Rule #10

*"You shall **not covet** your neighbor's house. You shall not covet your neighbor's wife, or his manservant or maidservant, his ox or donkey, or **anything that belongs to your neighbor.**"*

Exodus 20:17

Man must not envy other people's possessions, their abilities, their looks, or whatever they may have.

Satan had said, *"I will be like the Most High,"* coveting God's position. To covet, to be greedy or jealous, is sin and totally unacceptable to the Lord. It's the path that Satan followed.

In our society we *bump* the parameters of this law all the time. It's very subtle. Many have a craving to upgrade, a *keep up with the Jones'* mentality. We are told we *deserve it,* which is an appeal to our pride—another sin.

Now I Know

So the giving of the Ten Commands was concluded. God had them written on stone, probably to signify that his law does not change. Over the process of time, man might convince himself that cheating was okay, but the Law would still say it was wrong.

Now man knew what the Lord considered to be sin. One of the biblical writers reflecting on this truth wrote...

> *Indeed I would not have known what sin was except through the law. For I would not have known what coveting really was if the law had not said, "Do not covet."*
>
> Romans 7:7

But questions remained. Just how strict was God about following these rules? Would it be acceptable if a person broke one occasionally? What did God expect?

3 THE COURTROOM

The Ten Commandments might be thought vague unless one knows *how* and *when* the rules need to be obeyed. Are there any exceptions? Suppose a person had committed adultery sometime in the past. Would God hold that against him forever? What would a perfect lawgiver expect?

To begin with, God tells us that to be accepted by him, we must keep all ten of the commandments—every one of them!

> *Again I declare to every man...that **he is obligated to obey the whole law.**[2]*
>
> Galatians 5:3

We can't pick four and ignore the rest. God is very specific. We are required to obey *all* of them. Not only that, but...

> ...*whoever keeps the whole law and yet stumbles at just one point is guilty of breaking all of it.*   James 2:10

If we disobey just one command—only ONCE—it's like we have violated all of them. We are no longer perfect. God cannot accept us into his holy presence.

The Lord is utterly perfect in his holiness, and he can only accept those who are perfect in their righteousness. *Man's righteousness must* <u>*equal*</u> *God's righteousness* or the relationship cannot be restored.

Not only must we keep the whole Law, but God holds us accountable for all sin, even the sin of which we are not aware.

> *If a person sins and does what is forbidden in any of the LORD's commands, even though he does not know it, he is guilty and will be held responsible.*   Leviticus 5:17

Breaking the Law is like cutting a string with ten knots. You only have to cut one knot for the whole string to be broken. In the same way, you only have to break one law to be guilty of violating God's entire standard of right and wrong.

On one occasion I was teaching this subject to a young couple. As I reached this point in the lesson, the fellow banged his fist on the table and swore. (His girlfriend pointed out to him that he had just broken one of God's laws by misusing God's name. It was bad timing!) He said, *"God is not fair! If this is the only way I can be accepted by God, he's made it impossible. There is no way I can keep that list of rules perfectly!"* His frustration was very evident.

THE KNOWLEDGE OF SIN

God knew that man could not keep this list of rules flawlessly. It was no surprise to him. His intention in giving the Ten Commandments is clear.

> *Now we know that whatever the law says, it says...that* **every mouth may be stopped** *[or silenced], and* **all the world may become guilty** *[or accountable] before God.*
> Romans 3:19 NKJV

This verse is saying two things:

1. The Law silences those who say their lives are good enough to be accepted by God. No one can candidly study these ten rules without sensing their sinfulness.

2. The ten commands show us that we are indeed law-breakers. In the beginning man had been God's friend, *innocent* of all evil. But when Adam and Eve disobeyed God's instructions, God laid aside the mantle of friendship and donned the magistrate's cloak. Now, instead of God being a friend of man, He was a judge, summoning man to the courtroom bench. No lawyer rose to defend man's cause. None could. No advocate, no matter how clever, could lead the court into thinking that the condemned was anything but what he was. There would be no hung jury. No bribes. The perfect Judge spoke. The verdict was in. Man was GUILTY of breaking God's Law.

GUILTY

> *Therefore no one will be declared righteous in his sight by observing the law; rather, through the law we become conscious of sin.* Romans 3:20

The purpose of the ten laws is to make us aware or conscious that we are sinners. It shows us God's holiness and our sinfulness. It's a simple measure of what's right and what's wrong. The Ten Commandments are like a thermometer—it can show us that we are sick, but it does not contribute to making us better.

A MIRROR

In many ways, the Ten Commandments are to us as a mirror is to a dirty face. If you are alone, you can't tell whether or not your face is clean. Someone could point at you and say, *"Your face is filthy,"* but you could deny it outright and say, *"My face isn't dirty—I don't see anything!"* and you might truly believe that. But if given a mirror, you could see that your face was indeed grimy and you would no longer be able to deny the fact. Your mouth would be *silenced.* You would realize you were *guilty* of having a dirty face.

It's the same way with sin. We did not really know what *sin* was until God gave us the Law. Just as the mirror exposed the dirt, so the ten rules made us aware of sin.

The ten commands were **not** given as a list of rules to keep in order to make us right with God. That wasn't the Law's purpose. It would be like trying to rub the dirt off your face with a mirror! Mirrors are designed for reflecting, not cleaning. In fact, there's a good chance that, in the process of trying to clean yourself with the mirror, you would smudge the glass, thus hampering its ability to give a clear reflection. People who try to be accepted by God by keeping the Ten Commandments usually modify or minimize the commands so that they will not look so bad.

God's Viewpoint

There is another way of looking at this. Remember how we compared our view of a maggot-infested rat to God's viewpoint on sin? Well, trying to please the Lord by keeping the Ten Commandments is comparable to spraying perfume on the rotten rat—it doesn't make it any more appealing to us. *The rat is still rotten.* In the same way, keeping the Ten Commandments doesn't make us any more acceptable to God. *We're still sinners.*

This brings us back to the reason for the ten commands. God gave the Law...

> ...so that through the commandment sin would become utterly sinful.   Romans 7:13 NASB

God wants us to see all sin, big or small, the way he sees it—utterly sinful, totally destructive, grossly offensive, thoroughly repulsive, appalling, malignant, filthy. He wants us to comprehend that his purity far exceeds any righteousness we might achieve on our own. He wants us to understand that even at the best of times, *our goodness is not equal to his holiness.* It doesn't even come close.

The Gulf

Until this time a man could have boasted that God loved him more than another, because he thought himself to be a better person. But with the giving of the Law, God was bringing everyone to the point of realizing that...

> Surely I was sinful at birth, sinful from the time my mother conceived me.   Psalm 51:5

Now, not only could man know his true sinfulness, but he could catch a glimpse of the Lord's perfection. God's holiness—his righteousness—was beyond man's reach, unattainable. The chasm caused by sin was wider than man expected. Because no one could keep the Law perfectly, the Law could not bridge the gap.

TWO GROUPS

The Israelites' reaction to the first reading of the Ten Commandments undoubtedly reflects the thinking of many people today. The Bible says that all the Israelites shook with fear, but probably the great majority were only terrified by the thunder and lightning. They were caught up in the externals, alarmed only by the tremendous display of power. As for the ten rules, they missed the point—they felt they could obey them just fine. So do many people today. They focus on obeying the commands and miss their purpose.

On the other hand, there were those Israelites who had just gained a deep awareness of God's righteousness. They now knew what God meant when He said *holiness equals sinlessness*. They feared too, but for another reason. They knew they could never keep such a set of laws perfectly.

For whatever reason, the Bible says the Israelites trembled.

> *They...said to Moses, "Speak to us yourself and we will listen. But do not have God speak to us or we will die."*
> Exodus 20:19

The LORD said to Moses, "Come up to me on the mountain and stay here, and I will give you the tablets of stone, with the law and commands I have written for their instruction."

Exodus 24:12

The Ten Commandments were now in force and the Israelites were accountable to keep them as a moral standard. But for those who were honest with themselves, they now knew that if they were going to be *accepted by God,* they would have to come another way.

THE TEN SUGGESTIONS?

The Ten Commandments are sometimes referred to as the Moral Law, as they are concerned with ethical and moral behavior.

Just because the Moral Law is unable to restore the broken relationship with God does not mean it is without value. Just as physical laws create order in the universe, so spiritual laws create order in a nation.

Many countries have rejected the biblical code of conduct at the risk of living in a morally-neutral society. No such society truly exists. No such civilization has ever survived. To take no stand is, in effect, to take a position.

The rejection of biblical absolutes has resulted in a callousness towards wrong, with each generation becoming more comfortable with sin. The Bible teaches that this will eventually lead to chaos.

WHAT KIND ARE YOU?

Most people will agree that they are *sinners*. However, few will readily admit that they are *helpless sinners*. There is a big difference.

❖ *Sinners* believe that there is something they can do to make themselves acceptable to God. They may believe that God wants them to observe the Ten Commandments, keep the Golden Rule, go to church, pray, be baptized, give to charity or be nice to their neighbors. They think that doing any one of these things will make them pleasing to God.

The notion that a person's *good* can outweigh his *bad,* and therefore merit God's acceptance, is totally foreign to the Bible. To do *good* is commendable, but the Bible teaches that none of these deeds can restore our broken relationship with God. We have a deep problem we can't get rid of—it's the *sin condition*.

GOOD   **BAD**

CONCEPT NOT FOUND IN THE BIBLE

❖ On the other hand, *a helpless sinner* knows there is nothing he can do to make himself acceptable to God. He cannot get rid of that dead rat of sin contaminating his life. The Bible says we are totally helpless.

> *All of us have become like one who is unclean, and **all our righteous acts are like filthy rags**; we all shrivel up like a leaf, and like the wind our sins sweep us away.*
> Isaiah 64:6

Even our *goodness* falls far short of God's holiness. For illustrative purposes, one could say **all our righteous acts are like filthy rats**. Just as a rotten rat is repulsive to us, so all sin is offensive to a pure, holy God.

CHAPTER NINE

1 THE TABERNACLE

As we said in the last chapter, no doubt there were those Israelites who thought they could be acceptable to God by keeping the Ten Commandments. Foolishly, they had chosen a path that led into a spiritual wilderness. On the other hand, there were others who were ready for God to show them the only way to acceptance.

LOST

Taking the broad scope of Scripture, let's speculate for a moment. If God was writing a lesson plan to teach man exactly what he must do to be *right* or *righteous* with him, how would he have started? Just what would have been his first point?

LESSON OUTLINE—POINT #1:

> Illustration: A man swimming across a river was caught in the swift-flowing current. Floundering, he called for help! Many people were watching but none were capable of helping the drowning man, except one strong swimmer.

> Those on the bank kept urging this likely rescuer to go to the drowning man's assistance. But he didn't respond. He stood watching while the struggle for survival became more and more desperate. Finally, when the man became utterly exhausted, the strong swimmer dived into the water and pulled him ashore.

> When the people criticized the rescuer for waiting so long, he said, "The drowning man would never have allowed me to help him while he had any strength of his own. I could only save him when he gave up trying to help himself."[1]

> Conclusion: The first step to approaching God is to realize you are a *helpless* sinner, incapable of saving yourself from the eternal consequences of sin.

If the Lord had presented his lesson this way, you could almost have heard the Israelites cry out in frustration, *"But God, you have already made that point. We know that!"*

We could presume that God would reply, "Yes, I know, but that is the very point I want you to understand. The first step to acceptance by me is to realize that you are a helpless sinner. I can only rescue those who have given up trying to save themselves."

The above lesson may be imaginary, but the application is fact. It's what the Bible consistently teaches. Now let's go a step further.

> The LORD said to Moses, "Tell the Israelites to bring me an offering. You are to receive the offering for me from each man whose heart prompts him to give.
>
> Then have them make a sanctuary for me, and I will dwell among them." *Exodus 25:1–2,8*

A Visual Aid

The Israelites were to build a *sanctuary, a sacred place called the *Tabernacle*, where God could live among them. God was *not* asking them to do this because he needed a house. | *Do not confuse this structure with a church. They are unrelated.

Rather, God was creating an elaborate visual aid. As we study, we will slowly gain an understanding of its full meaning. It takes a few pages to explain, so don't get impatient and jump ahead to the next chapter. It's an important piece of the puzzle.

It began with God asking for voluntary contributions for a building project. He only wanted people to give willingly, from the heart. There were no appeals or arm-twisting. What each one gave was up to him. However, God made one thing clear:

> "Make this Tabernacle and all its furnishings exactly like the pattern I will show you." *Exodus 25:9*

Basic layout

The Tabernacle could be disassembled and moved. The tent-like portion had solid walls with rug-like coverings for the roof. It was divided into two parts: one-third forming a room called *The Holy of Holies* or *The Most Holy Place*, and the other two-thirds forming *The Holy Place*. A heavy curtain, sometimes referred to as the *veil*, separated the two areas.

> *"The curtain will separate the Holy Place from the Most Holy Place."*
> Exodus 26:33

The Tabernacle was completed with an external courtyard which, in turn, was surrounded by a fence approximately seven feet (2 m) in height. Access to the entire compound was gained through a single gate.

There were seven primary pieces of furniture inside the *tent* and outside in the *courtyard*.²

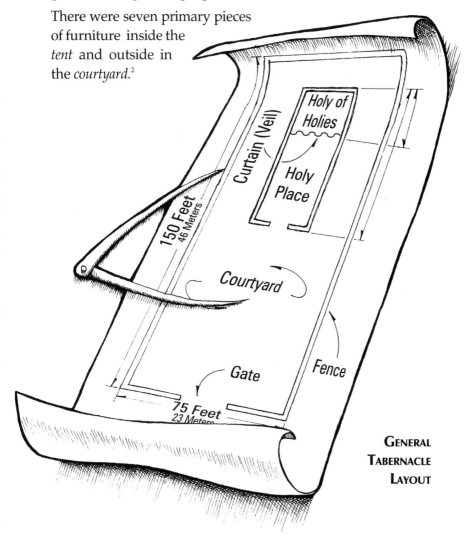

GENERAL TABERNACLE LAYOUT

The Courtyard

❶ THE BRONZE ALTAR:
Just inside the courtyard gate was the first piece of furniture. It was quite large, made of wood overlaid with bronze, having four horns on the corners, and long poles on each side so that it could be carried.

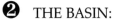

❷ THE BASIN:
This large bronze bowl was situated halfway between the Bronze Altar and The Holy Place. Filled with water, it was used for ceremonial washing, and signified that man must be pure when he approached God.

❸ THE LAMPSTAND:
The size of the lampstand was not defined by God, but we know its shape. It had a main shaft branching into seven arms. The fact that it was made of pure gold undoubtedly limited its size.

❹ THE TABLE WITH THE BREAD:
On this special table were placed twelve loaves of bread, each representing one of the tribes of Israel.

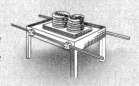

❺ THE ALTAR OF INCENSE:
This altar was placed squarely before the curtain that divided *The Holy of Holies* from *The Holy Place*. Incense was offered on it as the Israelites gathered outside to pray. The scent wafting toward the sky was symbolic of prayers going up to God.

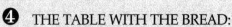

The Curtain (Veil)

**The
Holy Place**

**The Holy
of Holies**

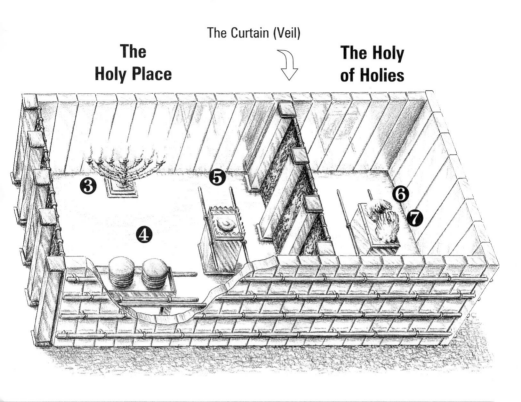

❸

❺

❻

❹

❼

❻ THE ARK OF THE COVENANT:
This small wooden box overlaid with pure gold was designed in part to function as a chest. A couple of the objects it held are already familiar to us—the tablets with the Ten Commandments written on them and a pot containing a sample of the bread God was providing for them in the desert.

❼ THE ATONEMENT COVER:
The Ark of the Covenant had an intricate gold lid or cover comprised of two angels with outstretched wings.

The Ark and its Atonement Cover were the only pieces of furniture placed in the Holy of Holies. God said…

> *"There, above the [atonement] cover between the two cherubim that are over the ark of the Testimony, I will meet with you and give you all my commands for the Israelites."* Exodus 25:22

THE PRIESTS

"Have Aaron your brother brought to you from among the Israelites, along with his sons... so they may serve me as priests."   Exodus 28:1

God asked Moses to appoint Aaron and his sons as *priests* in the Tabernacle with Aaron appointed as the *High Priest.* God set these men apart from the others, not because they were special in themselves, but because the Lord wanted the people to respect His holiness. God didn't want an unorganized rabble taking care of the Tabernacle. The priests were specially trained to perform God's instructions and they functioned as custodians, taking care of the Tabernacle as the nomadic Israelites moved from one place to another.

THE TABERNACLE COMPLETED

The entire structure was finished nine months after the Israelites arrived at Mount Sinai.

Moses inspected the work and saw that they had done it just as the LORD had commanded.   Exodus 39:43

So the Tabernacle was set up on the first day of the first month in the second year.   Exodus 40:17

With the Tabernacle completed, the cloud that led the Israelites moved into position above the Holy of Holies. It signified God's presence in the midst of his people.

Then the cloud covered the Tent of Meeting...

Moses could not enter the Tent of Meeting because the cloud had settled upon it, and the glory of the LORD filled the Tabernacle.   Exodus 40:34–35

THE VISUAL AID IMPLEMENTED

With the Tabernacle in place, it was time to implement this large visual aid. God said to Moses...

"Speak to the Israelites and say to them: 'When any of you brings an offering to the LORD, bring as your offering an animal from either the herd or the flock...'"   Leviticus 1:2

God was telling man to bring a sacrifice to the Tabernacle.

It had to be *"...from the herd..."* *Leviticus 1:3*

It could be a sheep, goat or bullock, but it could not be any other animal such as a pig, horse or camel.

They were to *"...offer a male..."* *Leviticus 1:3*

It was to be *"...without defect..."* *Leviticus 1:3*

There could be no disease nor lameness.

"...He must present it at the entrance to the Tent of Meeting so that it will be acceptable to the LORD..." *Leviticus 1:3*

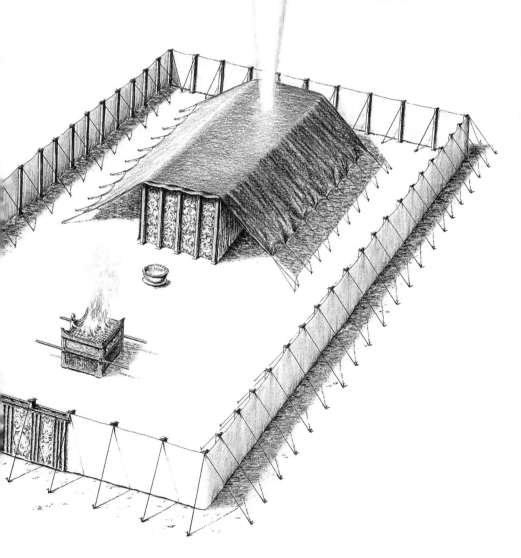

The sacrifice was to be offered just inside the door of the courtyard on the *Bronze Altar. In addition to acknowledging oneself as a helpless sinner, this was the first step in approaching God. The individual bringing it was…

*In the Bible, bronze is commonly associated with judgment on sin.

> "…to lay his hand on the head of the burnt offering, and it [would] be accepted on his behalf to make atonement for him…"
>
> Leviticus 1:4

In placing his hand on the head of the offering, the man identified himself with the sacrifice. The hand on the head symbolized the individual's sin and guilt being moved from the man onto the animal. Because the animal now carried the man's sin, it had to die. *Death is the penalty for sin.* The one offering the sacrifice slit its throat, a final acknowledgment that it was *his* sin that caused the death of the animal. It was a case of *the innocent dying in the place of the guilty*—as a substitute. The Bible says that God accepted the sacrifice on his behalf.

This must have sounded very familiar to the Israelites. Had not their forefathers come to God offering blood sacrifices? Indeed they had.

A RIGHTEOUS SAVIOR

Once again, the Lord was reminding his people that the only way to acceptance was to believe that he is…

> …A righteous God and a Savior…
> Isaiah 45:21 NASB

In offering the animal sacrifice, the people were giving outward evidence of an inner trust in God—it showed they believed the Lord. Because death is the penalty for sin, the sacrifice pictured what was necessary for sin to be forgiven.

> …without the shedding of blood there is no forgiveness.
> Hebrews 9:22

> "For the life of a creature is in the blood, and I have given it to you to make atonement for yourselves on the altar; it is the blood that makes atonement for one's life." Leviticus 17:11

When God saw the death of the animal, he was satisfied that the requirement of *the law of sin and death* had been justly met—there had been a *death payment* for sin. God would not hold man's sin-debt against him; man would not be judged; the eternal consequences would no longer apply. Instead, the Lord would honor the person's trust in him and credit righteousness to his account, just as he had to Abraham.

DEBTOR

> "Abraham believed God, and it was credited to him as righteousness."
> Romans 4:3

Because that righteousness was coming from God, it fully provided man with the perfection needed to live in God's presence.

There was nothing new about this at all. It was the way that Abel, Noah, Abraham, Isaac, Jacob and all the other righteous men down through the ages had come to God.

THE DAY OF ATONEMENT

In fulfilling their duties, the priests had complete freedom within the Tabernacle compound, with one exception. They were absolutely forbidden to enter the Holy of Holies.

The Holy of Holies was where God's presence symbolically lived with man. Sinful man wasn't even to peek into the room. The curtain that hung between the two rooms was thick, shielding all from an inquisitive eye. It protected the most sacred of all places. Even Aaron, as High Priest, was not to enter the Holy of Holies except on the Day of Atonement.[3]

> *But only the high priest entered the inner room, and*
> *that only once a year, and never without blood, which*
> *he offered for himself and for the sins the people had*
> *committed in ignorance.* Hebrews 9:7

Any violation of this instruction would result in his death.

> *The LORD said to Moses: "Tell your brother Aaron not*
> *to come whenever he chooses into the Most Holy Place*
> *behind the curtain in front of the atonement cover on*
> *the ark, or else he will die, because I appear in the cloud*
> *over the atonement cover."* Leviticus 16:2

The Day of Atonement offering was a yearly ceremony, a constant reminder of man's need to have his sin hidden from the eyes of a holy God. This ceremony was repeated each year because, although God did not hold man's sin against him, the blood of animals did not remove the sin-debt. The blood was only a temporary covering.

The Tabernacle, the furniture, the priests, the sacrifices, the Day of Atonement—all were part of God's elaborate visual aid. These *visuals* helped to explain what the Lord was planning to do for mankind.

2 Unbelief

The Israelites were learning more and more about the Lord. God was faithfully providing them with food and water. The Bible tells us that God even made their shoes especially durable—they didn't wear out. The Israelites now had a moral code by which to live. Although observing the Ten Commandments did not result in acceptance with God, it did provide a standard of right living that united the nation. They knew what was right, and what was wrong. God had also shown his love by providing a way to be accepted—by faith—as evidenced through the blood sacrifice. You would think the Israelites would have been eternally grateful for all that the Lord was doing for them. If they were grateful, their outward actions didn't demonstrate it. They began to grumble—again.

In case we should take a self-righteous attitude and think that it was only the Israelites who were hardheaded, we must remember that we are made out of the same flesh and blood.

In a very real sense, the Israelites were functioning as representatives of the entire human race. As such they were becoming much better acquainted with God each year, but the knowledge they gained also brought additional responsibility. The Bible says...

> From everyone who has been given much, much will be demanded; and from the one who has been entrusted with much, much more will be asked. Luke 12:48

Collectively, the Israelites now knew more about God than any other nation on earth.

> They traveled from Mount Hor along the route to the Red Sea, to go around Edom. But the people grew impatient on the way; they spoke against God and against Moses, and said, "Why have you brought us up out of Egypt to die in the desert? There is no bread! There is no water! And we detest this miserable food!" Numbers 21:4,5

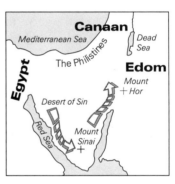

These accusations were not true—God, the Great Provider, *was* meeting their needs. But instead of thanking the Lord for his daily care, they accused him of neglect. They ignored God's Law, telling lies and dishonoring his name.

As we have seen before, to break a law has consequences. Just as defying God's law of gravity results in fractured bones, so violating God's Moral Law has ramifications.

In the past, God had repeatedly *overlooked their sin—he had been gracious. But the Israelites were no longer beginners in their relationship with their Creator-Owner. They had learned many things about God. They now knew the Ten Commandments and that knowledge made them accountable. God could not condone

*God only overlooks sin for a period of time. He does judge all sin. Compare Acts 17:30

the people's sin and say, *"Oh forget it. We'll pretend it never happened."* No, sin has its consequences. It always does.

> *…the LORD sent venomous snakes among them; they bit the people and many Israelites died.*   Numbers 21:6

From the very beginning, God had said that sin would lead to death—physical, relational and eternal. Now that truth was graphically illustrated as many died.

The Israelites were desperate and realized that only God could save them from his punishment. They were helpless.

> *The people came to Moses and said, "We sinned when we spoke against the LORD and against you. Pray that the LORD will take the snakes away from us."* Numbers 21:7

God's purpose in judgment is to bring about a change of attitude—a change of mind. In the Bible, this change is described by the word *repent*. Only during this life on earth can people repent and be heard by God. After physical death, when the sinner is facing judgment in the Lake of Fire, it is too late to have *a change of mind.*

The Israelites recognized that they had sinned, so they repented and asked God to deliver them. They were trusting God again.

> *So Moses prayed for the people.*
>
> *The LORD said to Moses, "Make a snake and put it up on a pole; anyone who is bitten can look at it and live."*

So Moses made a bronze snake and put it up on a pole.
Then when anyone was bitten by a snake and looked at
the bronze snake, he lived.   Numbers 21:7–9

The serpent on the pole was not some sort of *mind-over-matter* gimmick. God was simply giving the Israelites an opportunity to demonstrate that they believed Him. When an Israelite was bitten, all he had to do was turn and look at the bronze serpent and he would be healed. With that look, the individual expressed his faith in the Lord, trusting him to be true to his word.

Let's suppose one fellow was bitten and did not look at the bronze serpent. Instead he told his neighbors, "Old Moses is really demented. If he thinks looking at that ridiculous snake is going to heal a venomous bite, he's got to be crazy. I don't believe it." Such a person would have died, not only because of his snake bite, but also because he did not believe God. God honors faith, but judges unbelief.

It is important to understand that God holds us responsible for all that we understand of him. We are accountable for what we know.

Years later the original serpent made by Moses was destroyed by King Hezekiah because the people were worshiping it, violating another one of the Ten Commandments.

See 2 Kings 18:4

REVIEW: DEATH

The Bible speaks about death in three different ways:

1. Death of the body: Separation of man's spirit from his body
2. Death to a relationship: Separation of man's spirit from God
3. Death to a future joy: Separation of man's spirit from God forever

   … the wages of sin is death …   Romans 6:23

3 Judges, Kings and Prophets

We have now come to a lesson that compresses centuries of events into just a few pages. For those of you who are allergic to history, be assured that it's a painless study and, even if you don't understand it all, you will pick up needed tidbits of background information. It will help if you compare the titles at the head of each section with the time line on pages 162–163.

Forty years passed from the time the Israelites left Egypt until the time they entered Canaan. Moses died before he entered the promised country and was replaced by an able general named Joshua.

After entering the land, it took years before the Israelites were able to fully settle it. The land was divided according to *tribes*, each tribe equating with, for the most part, one of Jacob's (or Israel's) twelve sons.

TIME OF THE JUDGES

For a period of time the Israelites trusted God, but then they began to drift from the truth, and ended up believing in idols. The Lord punished Israel for worshiping false gods by allowing them to be overrun by foreign nations who forced Israel to serve them and pay tribute. After a time the Israelites would repent and call on God to deliver them from their oppressors. God would raise up a leader, called a *Judge,* and the Israelites would throw out the foreign conquerors. So began a cycle that was to last approximately 300 years. This cycle occurred over and over again. During this time there were fifteen Judges.

Some people believe that if you *trust in God* then you're okay. But in the back of their minds they believe that all roads—all beliefs—ultimately lead to the same God. This is not what the Bible teaches. The Scripture tell us that there are many false gods, but only one true God. The Israelites were judged when they trusted a false god.

TIME OF THE KINGS

Of all the nations of the world, Israel was the most fortunate, for God himself was their Leader and King. But as time passed and the Israelites observed other nations, they rejected God and demanded a human king. God granted their request, but their propensity to wander off and trust false gods remained.

Israel was to have many kings, but only a few believed and obeyed the Lord. Because of this, the cycle of earlier years continued, only instead of a *Judge*, they now had a *King*.

Several of the kings were especially noteworthy. Probably the greatest and best known of Israel's monarchs was David. Unlike many of the other kings who ruled over Israel, King David truly trusted God. He believed that only God could save him from the consequences of sin. David called the Lord, *"my Savior."*

King David was also a great Prophet, inspired by God to write down Scripture. He is noted for the songs he wrote, praising God for his love and mercy. David wrote specifically about THE PROMISED DELIVERER, and God made a pledge to him that THE ANOINTED ONE would be one of his descendants.[4] King David had a great ambition to replace the portable tabernacle with a permanent structure of a similar design. It would be called the *Temple*. He wanted to build it in Jerusalem, which had become the capital of the country during his reign. Although David gathered the building materials, it was his son, Solomon, who actually saw the task accomplished.

King Solomon is known for two things: his great wisdom and the Temple he built. This magnificent structure was constructed in Jerusalem on Mount Moriah, possibly on the same site where Abraham was prepared to offer Isaac.

After Solomon's death, the nation split in two: the northern ten tribes retained the name *Israel*, while the southern two tribes became the nation of *Judah*. This division seemed to be the Israelites' first step towards a semi-permanent distance from God. The northern tribes led the way. The people went through the motions of doing what the Lord said, but their hearts were far from God.

Prophets

God sent prophets, men who not only preached against the wandering morals of the people, but also warned of judgment to come.

 Many of these prophets were also prompted by God to write Scripture. Some of them gave specific information about the coming Promised Deliverer.

Generally speaking, the prophets were not well received by the Israelites or their respective kings. There was a reason. The prophets were giving them a message they did not want to hear. For example, the prophet Isaiah told the people…

> The Lord says: "These people come near to me with their mouth and honor me with their lips, but their hearts are far from me. Their worship of me is made up only of rules taught by men." Isaiah 29:13

The majority despised the prophets' message and refused to trust God. They persecuted and killed them. To complicate matters further, false prophets inspired by Satan churned the spiritual scene. Even though God provided clear instructions to enable his people to discern the difference between truth and error, the false prophets were much more popular, for they were telling the people the very things they wished to hear.

Dispersal of Israel

Eventually the Lord did send judgment. The Assyrians invaded the ten northern tribes in 722 BC and took them into captivity. The Bible does not record an organized return of these people to the land of Israel.

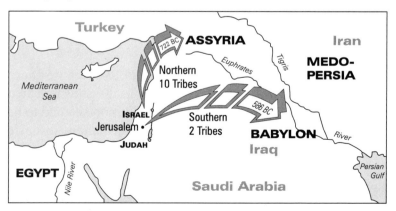

JUDAH TAKEN CAPTIVE

The two southern tribes continued as a distinct political entity until 586 BC, when the *Babylonians ravished the city of Jerusalem, demolished the great temple of Solomon and took them into exile.

While in exile, the people began to be called *Jews*, a reference to the fact that most of them were from the tribe of Judah. With the temple no longer available as the center of worship, the Jews introduced the **synagogue as a place for social interaction, teaching and the study of the Scriptures.

*People from the area where the tower of Babel was built.

**Greek for the word *assemblies*.

The exile continued for 70 years, but in 536 BC the two southern tribes began to trickle back to their homeland to settle in and around Jerusalem, in the area formerly occupied by the tribe of Judah. The temple was rebuilt, though not in the grandeur of Solomon's day, and the sacrificial system was reinstituted.

THE INFLUENCE OF THE GREEKS

Around 400 BC, the biblical record pauses and remains silent for a period of some four centuries. History didn't stand still though. Alexander the Great, the brilliant general of the Greeks, swept through the Middle East engulfing the Jews in the process. His emissaries introduced **Greek** as the trade language and the Hellenistic culture became a status symbol for centuries to follow.

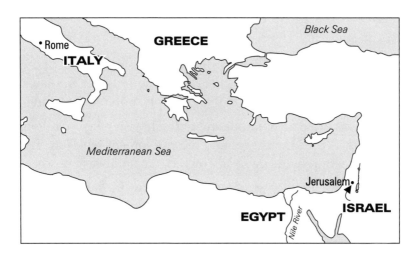

Some Jews freely embraced the Greek culture, combining it with their beliefs about God. These people were called *Sadducees*. Though small in number, they were people of wealth and influence. They tended to control the high priest, a position that had come to be bought and sold. Unfortunately, they also denied parts of the Bible as being true. **The Sadducees *took away* from God's Word.**

For about two hundred years, the Jews knuckled under a succession of Greek occupying forces and then in 166 BC they revolted. Judas Maccabeus led the people into a period of autonomy.

During this time a party of Jewish religious zealots, called *Pharisees*, came to the forefront. The Pharisees fought the influence of the Greek culture and clung to the *law* given to Moses. In their zeal, they created a protective ring of other laws around Moses' law so that none of the *real law* would be broken. These additional laws became an authority of their own, assuming equal weight with *the law of Moses*. **The Pharisees *added* to God's Word.**

Another significant social force in Jewish life was the *Scribes*, the human equivalent to photocopiers. Long before the advent of printing presses, these men copied with extreme care the Word of God over and over again. The term *Scribe* implied education and religious fervor. It was more of a job description than a religious or political party.

The Romans

The Jews' liberty under the Maccabean leadership lasted barely 100 years. The iron heel of Rome crushed the Jews' freedom in 67 BC when General Pompey entered Jerusalem.

Rome was quite accommodating of the Jewish religion as long as the Jews paid their taxes and did not foment rebellion. The civilized world of the day had entered into an uneasy peace.

The Roman empire was far too large to be administered effectively from Rome, so local leaders were selected to rule the different regions. In Judea, now a province of Rome, a man named Herod was appointed as a puppet king. He would come to be known as *Herod the Great*. Cruel beyond belief, Herod was a follower of the Jewish religion in name only. Under Rome's authority, he and his descendants would rule the resentful Jewish world for the next one hundred years. The people yearned for rescue—for one who could give them relief.

More than two thousand years had passed since God first promised Abraham that one of his descendants would be THE PROMISED DELIVERER. Throughout the centuries God had those people, sometimes only a few, who believed His Word and were *right* with him. They had waited in eager anticipation for THE ANOINTED ONE to come. In these early years of the Roman empire, those who clung tenaciously to God's promises were still waiting to see them fulfilled. The time had come, but they were unaware of it. The stage was now set. The angels of Heaven must have hushed. Satan must have shuddered. Who would this PROMISED DELIVERER be?

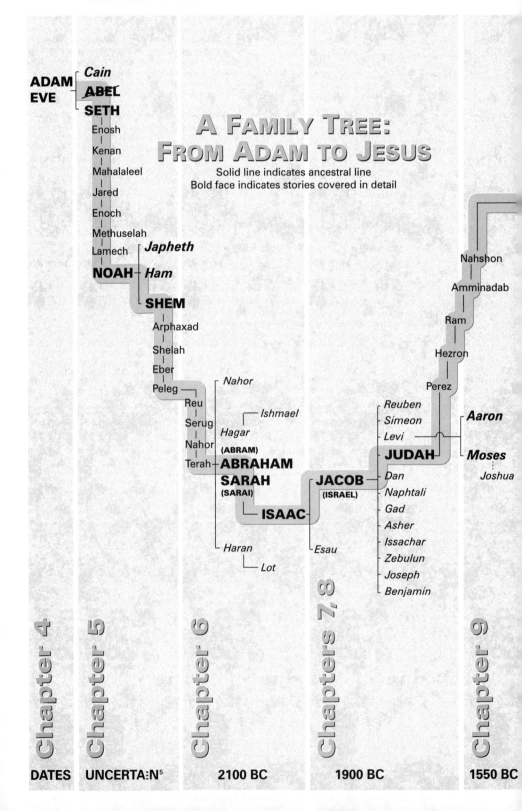

A FAMILY TREE:
FROM ADAM TO JESUS

Solid line indicates ancestral line
Bold face indicates stories covered in detail

ADAM
EVE

Cain
ABEL
SETH
Enosh
Kenan
Mahalaleel
Jared
Enoch
Methuselah
Lamech

Japheth
NOAH — Ham
SHEM
Arphaxad
Shelah
Eber
Peleg
Reu
Serug
Nahor
Terah

Nahor

Ishmael
Hagar
(ABRAM)
ABRAHAM
SARAH
(SARAI)
ISAAC

Haran
Lot

JACOB
(ISRAEL)

Esau

Reuben
Simeon
Levi
JUDAH
Dan
Naphtali
Gad
Asher
Issachar
Zebulun
Joseph
Benjamin

Nahshon
Amminadab
Ram
Hezron
Perez

Aaron
Moses
Joshua

Chapter 4
Chapter 5
Chapter 6
Chapters 7,8
Chapter 9

DATES   UNCERTAIN⁵   2100 BC   1900 BC   1550 BC

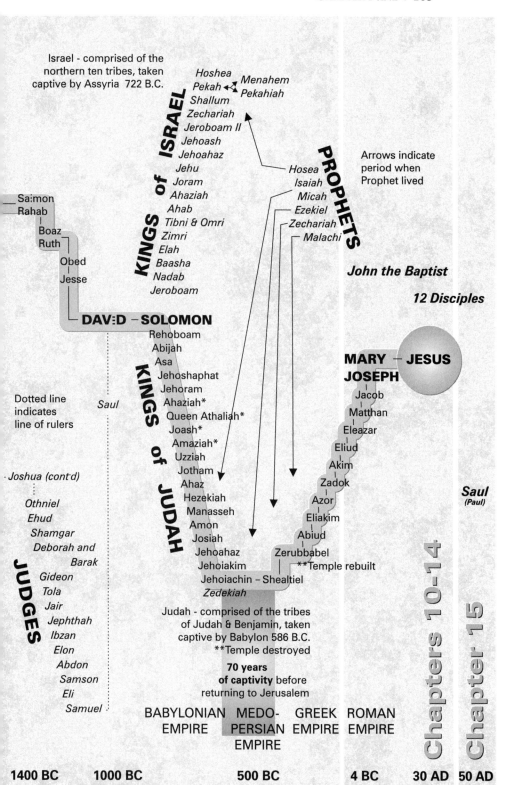

Israel - comprised of the northern ten tribes, taken captive by Assyria 722 B.C.

KINGS of ISRAEL

Hoshea
Pekah ◄ Menahem
Shallum Pekahiah
Zechariah
Jeroboam II
Jehoash
Jehoahaz
Jehu
Joram
Ahaziah
Ahab
Tibni & Omri
Zimri
Elah
Baasha
Nadab
Jeroboam

PROPHETS

Hosea
Isaiah
Micah
Ezekiel
Zechariah
Malachi

Arrows indicate period when Prophet lived

John the Baptist

12 Disciples

Salmon
Rahab
Boaz
Ruth
Obed
Jesse

DAVID – SOLOMON

Rehoboam
Abijah
Asa
Jehoshaphat
Jehoram
Ahaziah*
Queen Athaliah*
Joash*
Amaziah*
Uzziah
Jotham
Ahaz
Hezekiah
Manasseh
Amon
Josiah
Jehoahaz
Jehoiakim
Jehoiachin – Shealtiel
Zedekiah

KINGS of JUDAH

Saul

Dotted line indicates line of rulers

MARY – JESUS
JOSEPH
Jacob
Matthan
Eleazar
Eliud
Akim
Zadok
Azor
Eliakim
Abiud
Zerubbabel
**Temple rebuilt

Saul
(Paul)

· Joshua (cont'd)

Othniel
Ehud
Shamgar
Deborah and
    Barak
Gideon
Tola
Jair
Jephthah
Ibzan
Elon
Abdon
Samson
Eli
Samuel

JUDGES

Judah - comprised of the tribes of Judah & Benjamin, taken captive by Babylon 586 B.C.
**Temple destroyed

70 years of captivity before returning to Jerusalem

BABYLONIAN   MEDO-   GREEK   ROMAN
EMPIRE   PERSIAN   EMPIRE   EMPIRE
    EMPIRE

Chapters 10-14

Chapter 15

1400 BC   1000 BC   500 BC   4 BC   30 AD   50 AD

*Rulers that do not appear in Matthew's account of Jesus' ancestral line.

CHAPTER TEN

1 ELIZABETH, MARY AND JOHN

Before THE PROMISED DELIVERER arrived on the scene, God was going to prepare the Jewish people by sending a special messenger to announce the impending event. One can't help but wonder if the angels were in deep discussion over who this select bearer of good tidings might be. *Would it be one of them?* But then news of a different kind leaked through— news having to do with the identity of THE DELIVERER. It must have left all of heaven gasping.

> *In the time of Herod king of Judea there was a priest named Zechariah, ... his wife Elizabeth was also a descendant of Aaron. Both of them were upright in the sight of God, observing all the Lord's commandments and regulations blamelessly. But they had no children, because Elizabeth was barren; and they were both well along in years.*
>
> *Once when Zechariah's division was on duty and he was serving as priest before God, he was chosen by lot, according to the custom of the priesthood, to go into the temple of the Lord and burn incense. And when the time for the burning of incense came, all the assembled worshipers were praying outside.*
>
> *Then an angel of the Lord appeared to him, standing at the right side of the altar of incense. When Zechariah saw him, he was startled and was gripped with fear. But the angel said to him: "Do not be afraid, Zechariah; your prayer has been heard. Your wife Elizabeth will bear you a son, and you are to give him the name John. He will be a joy and delight to you, and many will rejoice because of his birth, for he will be great in the sight of the Lord. ... Many of the people of Israel will he bring back to the Lord their God. And he will go on before the Lord, ... to turn the hearts of the fathers to their children and the disobedient to the wisdom of the righteous—to make ready a people prepared for the Lord."* Luke 1:5-17

The angel had told Zechariah that his son, John, would be the messenger to prepare the way for the coming of the Lord. That was news alright, but it was that last tidbit of information that had heaven all astir. *God Himself—the LORD—was coming to earth.* HE would be The Promised Deliverer. The news must have stunned Satan.

No doubt Zechariah was floundering as he tried to absorb all of this. Seeing an angel was unheard of in his day. And the news of Elizabeth having a son at their age was enough to give an old man pause. But then to be informed that the Creator God was coming as The Promised Deliverer—well, it was simply unbelievable! However, Zechariah was familiar with the writings of the prophets.

 Four hundred years before his time, the prophet Malachi had written about this event.

> "See, I will send my messenger, who will prepare the way before me. Then suddenly the Lord you are seeking will come to his temple; the messenger of the covenant, whom you desire, will come," says the LORD Almighty.
>
> Malachi 3:1

There it was in plain words. Zechariah must have wondered why he had not seen it before. It was obvious! The LORD Almighty had said, *"I will send a messenger to prepare the way before me!"* God himself would be coming as The Anointed One. Moreover, the angel had said that the messenger who would prepare his way would be the priest's own son—John.

Elizabeth

Zechariah went home dumbfounded. And God kept his word; it happened just as the angel said it would.

> After this his wife Elizabeth became pregnant and for five months remained in seclusion. "The Lord has done this for me," she said. "In these days he has shown his favor and taken away my disgrace among the people."
>
> Luke 1:24,25

But a question must have nagged away at the back of Zechariah's mind. Just how would the Creator come to earth? Would he come in a golden chariot driving seven white steeds, surrounded with legions of angels all dressed in brilliant light? Would he unseat the Roman rulers—dump Herod off his throne? The angel had not said.

MARY

The scene now shifts. The angel made another visit, this time to a young lady by the name of Mary.

> *In the sixth month, God sent the angel Gabriel to Nazareth, a town in Galilee, to a virgin pledged to be married to a man named Joseph, a descendant of David. The virgin's name was Mary.*   Luke 1:26,27

Joseph and Mary were engaged to each other according to their Jewish customs. The Bible says that both Joseph and Mary were direct descendants of King David who had lived 1000 years earlier.

> *The angel went to her and said, "Greetings, you who are highly favored! The Lord is with you."*
>
> *Mary was greatly troubled at his words and wondered what kind of greeting this might be. But the angel said to her, "Do not be afraid, Mary, you have found favor with God. You will be with child and give birth to a son, and you are to give him the name Jesus."*   Luke 1:28–31

What!? Now it was Mary's turn to be speechless. When Mary finally found her tongue, she asked a very logical question.

> *"How will this be," Mary asked the angel, "since I am a virgin?"*
>
> *The angel answered, "The Holy Spirit will come upon you, and the power of the Most High will overshadow you. So the holy one to be born will be called the Son of God."*
>   Luke 1:34,35

Mary was to be the mother of THE PROMISED DELIVERER!

It all made sense now. Mary knew the stories well. Way back in the garden of Eden, God had promised Eve that THE PROMISED DELIVERER would be *her offspring.* It did not say *their offspring,* referring to both man and woman. Now the promise was about to be fulfilled, and the child would be born of a virgin—it would be her offspring only. *The baby would not have a human father.* What had seemed to be an insignificant choice of phrasing now carried tremendous weight.

But this little notation in the footsteps of history had greater ramifications. Because the Baby would not be conceived by the seed of the man, the Baby would not be part of Adam's bloodline. All descendants of Adam had inherited his nature—the sin nature.[1] But Jesus would not be a *son of Adam.* Rather, he was the *Son of God.* He would have the nature of the God Most High. No wonder the angel referred to the Baby as *the Holy One.* The child would be sinless, just as God is sinless. Jesus would be perfect from conception.

So, God would *not* be coming with all of Heaven's pomp and grandeur. Rather, he would arrive on the planet as all mankind had and ever will—as a baby! The angel said...

> *"Even Elizabeth your relative is going to have a child in her old age, and she who was said to be barren is in her sixth month. For nothing is impossible with God."*
>
> *"I am the Lord's servant," Mary answered. "May it be to me as you have said." Then the angel left her.* Luke 1:36–38

Mary knew Elizabeth was too old to have a child. Surely if it was possible for Elizabeth to conceive, then it was just as believable for a virgin to give birth. Mary chose to trust God.

JOHN

> *When it was time for Elizabeth to have her baby, she gave birth to a son.* Luke 1:57

John was born just as God had promised. The Bible says it was quite an occasion, and well it should have been, for in that day and age a stigma was attached to those who could not bear children. Zechariah was so thrilled he burst into a speech, a benediction of praise to God. What he had to say was really a mini-tour of the world's history, punctuated with the repeated promises God had given over the centuries—the promise to send a DELIVERER. You can see the elderly Zechariah holding the child high, fixing his eyes on baby John's face as he said:

> *"And you, my child, will be called a prophet of the Most High; for you will go on before the Lord to prepare the way for him..."* Luke 1:76

John would be the messenger who would announce the arrival of THE PROMISED DELIVERER to the world.

THE MEANING OF A NAME

The Bible records many instances of prophets who lived long before the birth of Jesus, who wrote with unerring accuracy about his coming. Isaiah recorded this 700 years before the birth of Jesus...

> For to us a child is born, to us a son is given, and the government will be on his shoulders. And he will be called Wonderful Counselor, Mighty God, Everlasting Father, Prince of Peace.　　　Isaiah 9:6

Note how the *child* is called *Mighty God.* There are many other names that describe aspects of the Lord's character:

Son of God: This name is a metaphor with no physical implications. It simply means Jesus had the nature of God, in contrast to a *son of Adam* who had a sin nature.

> The Son is the radiance of God's glory and the exact representation of his [God's] being...　　　Hebrews 1:3 NASB

Son of Man: This name was used to emphasize Jesus' humanity and declare his identity. For centuries, scholars recognized this term as referring to THE ANOINTED ONE.[2]

When the above two names are combined, they find their complete expression in the fact that...

> He [God] was made visible in human flesh...
> 1 Timothy 3:16 The Amplified New Testament

The Word: God didn't just *tell* us about himself, he *showed* himself to us. The spoken word became the living *Word.*

> In the beginning was the Word,...and the Word was God. ...The Word became flesh and made his dwelling among us.　　　John 1:1,14

God came to earth to personally explain how man could be saved from eternal death. Think of it this way. You see a bull-dozer clearing a road, but in its path lies an anthill. You know the ants are about to be destroyed, but what can you do about it? The only answer would be to become an ant and warn them in the way ants warn each other of impending danger.

> ...Jesus came into the world to save sinners...
> 1 Timothy 1:15 NASB

2 Jesus

This is how the birth of Jesus Christ came about: His mother Mary was pledged to be married to Joseph, but before they came together, she was found to be with child through the Holy Spirit. Because Joseph her husband was a righteous man and did not want to expose her to public disgrace, he had in mind to divorce her quietly.

Matthew 1:18,19

A Jewish pledge to be married implied a much stronger tie than our western concept of engagement. In almost every sense the couple was considered married. Joseph was called Mary's husband, and vice versa, except they had not lived together nor had sexual union. According to the customs of that day, to break the engagement a divorce was required.

Imagine for a moment how Joseph felt. He must have been in anguish. Mary was pregnant and the child wasn't his. To reveal the truth publicly would label Mary for what she must be, an adulteress, unless Mary's preposterous explanation about an angel appearing to her was right. No, that was absurd. The poor girl must be losing her mind. Joseph loved her, but he could not marry a girl who had cheated on him and was obviously trying to cover it up with an insane story. What Joseph thought about it all we don't really know, but we do know that he painfully decided to quietly divorce her.

But after he had considered this, an angel of the Lord appeared to him in a dream and said, "Joseph son of David, do not be afraid to take Mary home as your wife, because what is conceived in her is from the Holy Spirit. She will give birth to a son, and you are to give him the name Jesus, because he will save his people from their sins."

All this took place to fulfill what the Lord had said through the prophet: "The virgin will be with child and will give birth to a son, and they will call him Immanuel"—which means, "God with us." Matthew 1:20-23

Joseph could not have heard it any more plainly. Mary was still a virgin, and she was going to have a child! The child's name would be *Jesus* which means *Deliverer* or *Savior*. He would *deliver*, or *save*, people from the consequences of their sin. The angel said that another of Jesus' names would be

Immanuel, meaning *God with us.* Jesus would be God living in human flesh among men.

 The prophet Isaiah had written about this event 700 years before.

> *Therefore the Lord himself will give you a sign: The virgin will be with child and will give birth to a son, and will call him Immanuel.*   Isaiah 7:14

Joseph must have bolted upright in bed. So Isaiah had been right! It was happening just as God said it would. But what would everyone think? No matter! There was only one thing to do—he would believe God and do what he said.

> *When Joseph woke up, he did what the angel of the Lord had commanded him and took Mary home as his wife. But he had no union with her until she gave birth to a son.*
> Matthew 1:24–25

THE CENSUS

> *In those days Caesar Augustus issued a decree that a census should be taken of the entire Roman world.*   Luke 2:1

Caesar Augustus was ruler of the Roman empire.

Caesar needed money, and if the Romans got an accurate census, more people would have to pay taxes. It's doubtful that Joseph was happy. His wife was almost due. Being a carpenter by trade, he'd probably been working on a crib and had arranged with the local midwife for a clean, safe place for the baby's delivery. Now he was required to take his wife to Bethlehem, which a thousand years before had been King David's ancestral home. A seventy mile (120 km) trip with a wife who might give birth any day was not a welcome thought when you had to travel by donkey or on foot. Why did the Romans have to come up with this idea now? Why not take the census in Joseph's home town, Nazareth? This was very awkward. But the Romans weren't giving people any choice. He would have to take Mary to Bethlehem.

> *And everyone went to his own town to register. So Joseph also went up from the town of Nazareth in Galilee to Judea, to Bethlehem the town of David, because he belonged to the house and line of David.*

He went there to register with Mary, who was pledged to be married to him and was expecting a child. While they were there, the time came for the baby to be born, and she gave birth to her firstborn, a son. She wrapped him in cloths and placed him in a manger, because there was no room for them in the inn. Luke 2:3–7

So Jesus was born in Bethlehem, far from Joseph and Mary's home. The town was so crowded that the only place where they could find lodging was in a stable. Jesus' first crib was a manger, a trough for feeding cattle. As Joseph looked at his wife, it must have seemed like his careful plans had all gone wrong. *Bethlehem!* Of all places! And in a musty stable! But as he looked at the child, he must also have sensed that everything was right. Very much right.

And he gave him the name Jesus. Matthew 1:25

THE SHEPHERDS

*And there were shepherds living out in the fields nearby, keeping watch over their flocks at night. An angel of the Lord appeared to them, and the glory of the Lord shone around them, and they were terrified. But the angel said to them, "Do not be afraid. I bring you good news of great joy that will be for all the people. Today in the town of David **a Savior has been born** to you; **he is Christ the *Lord.** This will be a sign to you: You will find a baby wrapped in cloths and lying in a manger."*

Suddenly a great company of the heavenly host appeared with the angel, praising God and saying, "Glory to God in the highest, and on earth peace to men on whom his favor rests." Luke 2:8–14

*The term LORD, in and of itself, was used by the ancient prophets to refer to THE DELIVERER.

The shepherds had been minding their own business, tending their sheep as they always had. Often sheep from their flocks were used in the temple sacrifices in Jerusalem only a few miles north of Bethlehem. Life continued as usual. But now the angels had come, and their whole world was askew. The shepherds must have excitedly queried each other, "Did you hear what I heard? The Christ is the LORD!"

CHRIST / MESSIAH

The Greek word *Christ* is the same as the Hebrew word *Messiah*. The word means, *the anointed one.* For centuries the name *Messiah* had been applied to THE PROMISED DELIVERER.

Now the angels were saying that THE ANOINTED ONE—the Messiah/Christ—was the Lord.[3] He was God Himself.

> *When the angels had left them and gone into heaven, the shepherds said to one another, "Let's go to Bethlehem and see this thing that has happened, which the Lord has told us about."*
>
> *So they hurried off and found Mary and Joseph, and the baby, who was lying in the manger. When they had seen him, they spread the word concerning what had been told them about this child…*   Luke 2:15–17

The shepherds were poor men, not the sort of folks that one would normally expect to be invited to the birth of a King. But there were others on their way to see Jesus.

WISE MEN

> *After Jesus was born in Bethlehem in Judea, during the time of King Herod, *Magi from the east came to Jerusalem and asked, "Where is the one who has been born king of the Jews? We saw his star in the east and have come to worship him."*
>
> Matthew 2:1–2

*Christmas scenes often depict three Magi, but the Bible does not say how many there actually were. The Magi were probably non-Jewish experts in the study of the stars, coming from Arabia or further east.

The Magi were men of status and wealth. Such men could be expected to visit a king. The king enthroned in Judea at this time was Herod the Great who, no doubt, had been alerted to this rather prestigious company. They could hardly have escaped the notice of the sentries guarding Judea's borders.

Their visit could not have been perceived as a threat as they were not leading armies. All they had was a question: "Where's the newborn King?"

> *When King Herod heard this he was disturbed, and all Jerusalem with him.*
> Matthew 2:3

That single question really rocked Herod. He held his authority as king in a tightly clenched fist, and he would crush anyone who dared try to wrench it from him. No doubt the whole city was a little shaken as well. Herod was known to be cruel to his citizens, especially when he was upset. Who knew what he might do. Herod called his religious advisors.

> *When he had called together all the people's chief priests and teachers of the law, he asked them where the Christ was to be born.*
> Matthew 2:4

THE PROPHECY

You can see an agitated scribe blowing dust off a small scroll. His fellow sages bend over the papyrus and with rheumy eyes scan the text. They are a little rattled. They want Herod to understand that *they* are not the ones who had said these things. A prophet by the name of Micah had written it over 700 years earlier. A shaky finger points to a well-worn part of the document. Herod disdains to look. A scribe clears his raspy throat and reads:

> *"But you, Bethlehem Ephrathah,⁴ though you are little among the thousands of Judah, yet out of you shall come forth to Me the One to be Ruler in Israel, whose goings forth are from of old, from everlasting."*
> Micah 5:2 NKJV

The baby *must* be born in Bethlehem. (That information would have raised the eyebrows of a distraught Joseph.) Herod wanted to see if the Prophet Micah had recorded more. He had! It clearly said that the *One* to be born had lived *from everlasting*. Herod must have been ashen. It couldn't be. Only God was eternal. God would never come to earth as an infant, especially to be born in the backwoods of Bethlehem. He would arrive with trumpets and chariots—in Jerusalem. Aha! Perhaps the scribes were intentionally trying to alarm him, to manipulate him. It wouldn't hurt to humor them. He would show them what sort of worship new kings could expect. He shooed out his priests...

> Then Herod called the Magi secretly and found out from them the exact time the star had appeared. He sent them to Bethlehem and said, "Go and make a careful search for the child. As soon as you find him, report to me, so that I too may go and worship him."
>
> After they had heard the king, they went on their way, and the star they had seen in the east went ahead of them until it stopped over the place where the child was. When they saw the star, they were overjoyed. On coming to the house, they saw the child with his mother Mary, and they bowed down and worshiped him. Then they opened their treasures and presented him with gifts of gold and of incense and of myrrh.[5]   Matthew 2:7–11

WORSHIP

These men of wealth and status worshiped Jesus. The law was very specific—only the God Most High was to be worshiped. Joseph and Mary knew the Ten Commandments well and yet they did not intervene. They must have known deep inside that the Magi were worshiping God—God who had come in human flesh.

> And having been warned in a dream not to go back to Herod, they returned to their country by another route.
>
> When they had gone, an angel of the Lord appeared to Joseph in a dream. "Get up," he said, "take the child and his mother and escape to Egypt. Stay there until I tell you, for Herod is going to search for the child to kill him."
>
> So he got up, took the child and his mother during the night and left for Egypt, where he stayed until the death of Herod.   Matthew 2:12–15

Consistent with what secular history records of him, Herod did make an all-out effort to kill Jesus, but the child remained safe in Egypt. Eventually Herod died, and so Joseph, Mary and Jesus moved back to Nazareth where Joseph worked as a carpenter.

> And the child grew and became strong; he was filled with wisdom, and the grace of God was upon him.   Luke 2:40

Jerusalem and Surrounding Area

To Nazareth
and Galilee

Damascus Gate

Roman Fortress

Garden of
Gethsemane

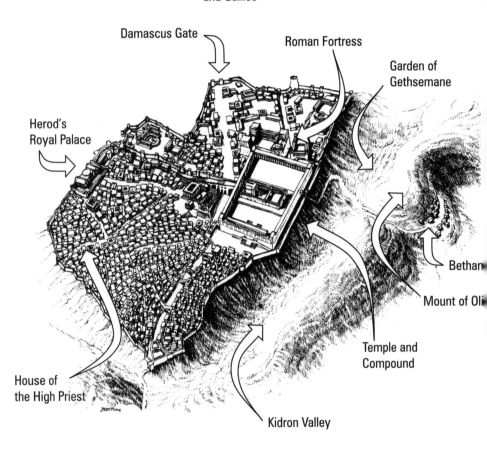

Herod's
Royal Palace

Bethan

Mount of Oli

Temple and
Compound

House of
the High Priest

Kidron Valley

To the
Mediterranean

To the Jordan River
and the Dead Sea

3 AMONG THE SAGES

Although Jesus was God himself, he chose to enter the human race as a baby. It must have been quite an experience for Joseph and Mary to raise this child. Jesus was sinless. Even as a youngster, he never became impatient, never talked back or threw a temper tantrum. Little is told of Jesus' younger years, but one story was recorded about him at the age of twelve.

> Every year his parents went to Jerusalem for the Feast of the **Passover**. When he was twelve years old, they went up to the Feast, according to the custom.   Luke 2:41–42

According to Jewish culture, at puberty a boy became a *full member of the religious community. As such, he had all the privileges and responsibilities accorded to a young man. As Joseph and Mary took the customary trip to Jerusalem, Jesus' *coming of age* could not have been far from their minds.[6]

*A boy became a *son of the covenant,* a custom continued in the present *bar mitzvah* ceremony.

GOING HOME

With the feast over, everyone headed home. Though we don't know all the details of the trip, we can imagine how the events unfolded. Probably the folks from Nazareth all traveled together for company and mutual safety. Because the children walked slower, they, along with the women and some of the men, left early in the morning to get a head start. The rest of the men would have stayed behind for last-minute visiting and then would have headed out to catch up with the rest of the group at dusk.

> After the Feast was over, while his parents were returning home, the boy Jesus stayed behind in Jerusalem, but they were unaware of it. Thinking he was in their company, they traveled on for a day.   Luke 2:43–44

You can picture Mary leaving at sunrise. Jesus was nowhere in sight, but she wasn't alarmed. Jesus was at the age when he was expected to be a man. He would be hanging back with the others as they visited in the temple complex. No doubt he was with Joseph. At the very thought Mary smiled with satisfaction. And what a wonderful young man he was! She was glad he could take the extra time to listen to the wise men in the temple.

Dusk fell as Joseph arrived at the prearranged spot along with the other men. They'd had a good day too, filled with learning. They had spent extra time listening to the scholarly men of the temple teach God's Word; then they had discussed the teaching en route as they hurried to catch up with the women. His only regret was that Jesus hadn't remained with him. After all, he was at the age when he was expected to shoulder the responsibilities of a young man. He could have learned so much. But obviously he had gone on ahead with Mary and the rest of the children. He must remind Jesus that he was growing up. It wasn't often that he had to do that. Come to think of it, he couldn't remember ever reminding Jesus about anything. Then Joseph spotted Mary. Both were all smiles:

"Did you have a good day?"

"Yeah, great!"

"Did Jesus enjoy himself?"

"Jesus?"

The smiles disappeared. "I thought...!"

"Yes, but I thought..."

Then they began looking for him among their relatives and friends. When they did not find him, they went back to Jerusalem to look for him.   Luke 2:44–45

THE SEARCH

The search must have been frantic. "Oh no! We've lost the Son of God!" They searched all the places a normal boy might be found. The sweets section of the market was thoroughly checked and local construction sites were turned inside out to see if he had lingered to watch. In desperation Joseph retraced his footsteps. The last he had seen of Jesus was in the temple.

After three days they found him in the temple courts, sitting among the teachers, listening to them and asking them questions. Everyone who heard him was amazed at his understanding and his answers.   Luke 2:46–47

Jesus was right where he was supposed to be, doing what both Joseph and Mary had wished him to do. There was only one difference. Instead of being instructed by the temple wise men, Jesus was doing the teaching. No, he wasn't delivering a lecture—but the penetrating questions, the profoundness of his own understanding, the depth of his answers, did not go unnoticed. Indeed, the temple sages were hanging on to every word. The Bible says the learned men were *amazed!* No wonder. They were listening to God Himself. Who wouldn't be dumbfounded in a discussion with the Creator of the universe?!

The learned men weren't the only ones speechless. Joseph and Mary were flabbergasted and, no doubt, much relieved. They found their tongues quick enough.

> When his parents saw him, they were astonished. His mother said to him, "Son, why have you treated us like this? Your father and I have been anxiously searching for you."   Luke 2:48

Jesus asked them a question. (You'd sort of expect that of God.)

> "Why were you searching for me?" he asked. "Didn't you know I had to be in my Father's house?"   Luke 2:49

A GENTLE REMINDER

This wasn't a sassy retort. Jesus was simply saying that he was right where a child should be—at home in his Father's house. *But what did he mean by Father? Who was this Father he was referring to?* We will study this more in the next section. For now, all you need to know is that Jesus used this phrase as a gentle reminder to his earthly parents of who he really was.

> But they did not understand what he was saying to them. Then he went down to Nazareth with them and was obedient to them. But his mother treasured all these things in her heart. And Jesus grew in wisdom and stature, and in favor with God and men.   Luke 2:50–52

4 BAPTISM

Jesus did not officially begin his life's work until he was about thirty years of age. John, the son of Zechariah, had already started to prepare the way for him by telling everyone who would listen that THE ANOINTED ONE had arrived. It created quite a stir.

> In those days John the Baptist came, preaching in the Desert of Judea and saying, "Repent, for the kingdom of heaven is near."
> Matthew 3:1–2

John was being referred to as *the Baptist* because he was *baptizing* people. The ritual of baptism was not uncommon to the Middle Eastern people of that day. It was full of meaning. Today, however, much confusion surrounds this word.

This uncertainty is a result of not having a word in the English language that precisely translates the Greek word *baptizo*. The translators resolved the problem by creating the word *baptism*. That's okay, but it doesn't help the average person understand its original meaning.

IDENTIFICATION

Baptism implies *identification*. A common meaning of the word *baptizo* originated in the early Greek textile industry. In the process of dying fabric, a piece of cloth was plunged into a vat of dye, whereby it took on the color of the pigment. The cloth was totally identified with the dye.

John taught that the Jews had strayed from the Scripture, embracing man's ideas. He said they needed to *change their mind* about their wandering ways and return to God; in short, repent. The Jews who were baptized showed that they identified (or agreed personally) with his message of repentance.

> People went out to him from Jerusalem and all Judea and the whole region of the Jordan. Confessing their sins, they were baptized by him in the Jordan River.
>
> But when he saw many of the Pharisees and Sadducees coming to where he was baptizing, he said to them: "You brood of vipers! Who warned you to flee from the coming wrath? Produce fruit in keeping with repentance."
> Matthew 3:5–8

REPENT

John the Baptist saw that some in his audience were Pharisees and Sadducees. Remember, they were the ones who *added to* or *took away* from the Bible. These two sects did not have much use for each other, but they had one thing in common—they both thought they were a *cut above* the ordinary. They were proud. John called them a *bunch of snakes* because they enforced unbearably strict rules on others, but did not practice what they preached. He told them to repent, to have a change of mind.

JESUS' BAPTISM

Then Jesus came from Galilee to the Jordan to be baptized by John. But John tried to deter him, saying, "I need to be baptized by you, and do you come to me?" Matthew 3:13–14

John recognized who Jesus was—he was God. Jesus did not need to repent of anything because he was perfect. John knew that *he* was the one who needed to be baptized, not Jesus.

Jesus replied, "Let it be so now; it is proper for us to do this to fulfill all righteousness." Then John consented.
Matthew 3:15

Jesus insisted on being baptized because he wanted to be identified with John's message of righteous living. He wanted to affirm John's message as being true.

As soon as Jesus was baptized, he went up out of the water. At that moment heaven was opened, and he saw the Spirit of God descending like a dove and lighting on him. And a voice from heaven said, "This is my Son, whom I love; with him I am well pleased." Matthew 3:16–17

In a moment, we will look at this verse in more depth, but first, let's finish the story.

THE LAMB OF GOD

The next day John saw Jesus coming toward him and said, "Look, the Lamb of God, who takes away the sin of the world! This is the one I meant when I said, 'A man who comes after me has surpassed me because he was before me.'" John 1:29–30

John identified Jesus as THE PROMISED SAVIOR, the one who would take away the sin of the world. He said that Jesus had lived before him—eternally. John said...

> *"I have seen and I testify that this is the Son of God."*
>
> John 1:34

On one occasion, I was teaching a young couple, step by step through the Bible. Upon reading this verse, *"Look, the Lamb of God, who takes away the sin of the world!"*, the lady came alive! In an excited, animated voice she said, *"The Lamb, the Lamb! Does this have anything to do with all the lambs we have been reading about in the old part of the Bible!?"*

I told her, "Yes, it does...and when the time comes, it will all fit together in a way that will make incredible sense."

I had the opportunity to visit a tribe in Papua New Guinea who had been exposed to fragments of biblical thought. They had adopted baptism, believing that their sins were washed away. They were so convinced of its literal nature that they would not go into the river after a baptism for fear they would take on the sin.

The Bible is clear that baptism does not make us acceptable to God. It is only an outward picture of what has transpired inwardly. In this instance, it demonstrated that these Jews were believing John's message and identifying with it.

Today, many "theologians" would give baptism much more meaning than the Bible warrants.

Does God Talk to Himself?

Beginning in the first pages of the Bible, we noticed an unusual way that God speaks, as if he was talking to himself. For example, when he created man...

> God said, "Let **Us** make man in **Our** image, according to **Our** likeness..."
> *Genesis 1:26 NKJV*

When Adam sinned, we find God in conversation...

> And the LORD God said, "The man has now become like one of **us**, knowing good and evil." *Genesis 3:22*

When God dispersed the people of Babel, he said...

> "Come, let **us** go down and confuse their language so they will not understand each other." So the LORD scattered them... *Genesis 11:7–8*

Who is God talking to? Who are the *Us* and *Our*?

When the angel talked to Mary, he said...

> "**The Holy Spirit** will come upon you, and the power of **the Most High** will overshadow you. So the holy one to be born will be called **the Son of God**."
> *Luke 1:35*

Here we see *the Holy Spirit, the Most High,* and *the Son of God* all mentioned in one verse. We know that the *Most High* is God. We have just been reading a score of verses that say *Jesus* is God come in human flesh. Are they one and the same? What about the *Holy Spirit*? What does the Bible say? We come now to the verse we just read:

> As soon as Jesus was baptized, he went up out of the water. At that moment heaven was opened, and he saw **the Spirit of God** descending like a dove and lighting on him. And **a voice from heaven** said, "This is my **Son**, whom I love; with him I am well pleased."
> *Matthew 3:16–17*

We have three entities here: *Jesus, the Spirit of God* and a *voice from heaven.* Confusing? It can be if you don't understand some basic biblical concepts. Here are some more pieces to the puzzle.

Continued next page

First of all, we know that there is only one God. That is emphasized repeatedly in the Bible.

> *Jesus answered him… "Hear, O Israel; The Lord our God is one Lord."* Mark 12:29 NKJV

That is reasonably straightforward. However, there are things about God that are beyond our scope of reason; incredible complexities that are difficult for us to fathom. For example, the whole concept of an *eternal* God is not easy to digest. In the same vein, trying to conceptualize a God who is *everywhere at the same time* is totally baffling. Getting a solid handle on just these two truths is impossible for our finite minds. Now we are faced with a revelation about God that is equally difficult to grasp, yet nonetheless clearly taught in the Bible. The Scripture reveals to us a God, who is *at the same time* Father, Son, and Holy Spirit—three eternal and co-equal persons that comprise the being of God. These three persons form a *tri-unity* or *trinity*, but comprise the one and only God.

Over the years, various attempts have been made to explain the Trinity:
1. The egg: Each egg has a shell, a white and a yolk; three distinct parts, but only one egg.
2. Dimensions: A box has height, width and length; though not the same, they cannot be separated.
3. Multiplication: 1 x 1 x 1 = 1

Although some of these illustrations may be helpful, they still fall short of giving us a full understanding. We need to be careful that we don't try to drag God down to our level and view him as one like ourselves. God says part of the reason we don't understand him is because…

> *You thought that I was just like you…* Psalm 50:21 NASB

As children, there were many things we didn't understand and yet we accepted them at face value. *"What is electricity? Why doesn't it run out onto the floor when I pull the plug out of the socket? I can't see it. What do you mean it will hurt me if I stick tweezers in the outlet?"* Just because we failed to understand electricity didn't make it any less real.

As adults, we are somewhat smug in our ability to comprehend the world about us. Over the centuries, things that puzzled the ancients have become commonplace to our understanding. Yet, we need to be humble. Much of the known universe still contains great mysteries. People living 100 years from now may look back on us as being blind to what they will consider obvious. The time may come when the concept of a *trinity* will make perfect sense.

Even if that day does come, we need to recognize that our limited ability to reason cannot fit an infinite God into our finite minds. Rightly understood, God, as revealed in the Bible, is a God who leaves us astonished.

Think for a moment: an eternal God; all-knowing, everywhere present at the same time; Creator of the whole universe; *a Trinity, one, yet comprised of three persons—Father, Son and Holy Spirit—who are all equal in character and ability.* Unfathomable! Though these concepts may be hard to grasp, the Bible says all are true.

> *The secret things belong unto the LORD our God: but those things which are revealed belong unto us...*
> Deuteronomy 29:29 KJV

The very word *God* is a statement about the Trinity. The Hebrew language has *singular* (one), *dual* (two only) and *plural* (three or more) noun forms. The word *God*, in Hebrew *Elohim*, is grammatically plural, allowing for three, but has a singular meaning.

Though it is correct to refer to any member of the Trinity as God, a distinction can be made as follows:

> *The Most High = The Father*
> *Jesus Christ   = The Son*
> *The Spirit   = The Holy Spirit*

The accompanying diagram has been used for centuries to explain the Trinity.

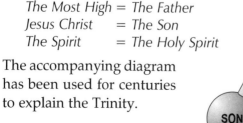

CHAPTER ELEVEN

1 TEMPTED

At the beginning of creation, Lucifer defiantly rebelled against God, grasping after His position. Now God the Son, though still fully God, had set aside all his visible glory and majesty to leave Heaven and come to earth as a human being. Jesus must have appeared very vulnerable to Satan. If he could only entice Jesus to do his bidding, it would be a great victory. From God's perspective, it was time to reveal something more about himself.

> Then Jesus was led by the Spirit into the desert to be tempted by the devil. After fasting forty days and forty nights, he was hungry. *Matthew 4:1–2*

| *Devil* means false accuser, slanderer.

Jesus had just completed a lengthy time without food. Although he is God, he also was a real man with real physical needs.

> The tempter came to him and said, "If you are the Son of God, tell these stones to become bread." *Matthew 4:3*

A SUGGESTION

Satan was suggesting that Jesus do something that everyone would understand, namely, take care of his physical well-being. It also seemed like a prime opportunity for Jesus to prove who He really was. If he was God, then he had created the world simply by speaking it into existence. To turn stones into bread would be a simple matter. But there was a catch. To do so, he would be following Satan's orders.

> Jesus answered, "It is written: 'Man does not live on bread alone, but on every word that comes from the mouth of God.'" *Matthew 4:4*

JESUS QUOTES THE BIBLE

Christ responded to Satan by quoting the Bible, God's written Word. He said that it was more important to follow God than to take care of physical needs. This is a significant statement, as many people are so concerned about this physical life that they ignore their spiritual well-being.

> For what will it profit a man if he gains the whole world, and loses his own soul? *Mark 8:36 NKJV*

Satan "Quotes"

> *Then the devil took him to the holy city [or Jerusalem] and had him stand on the highest point of the temple. "If you are the Son of God," he said, "throw yourself down. For it is written: 'He will command his angels concerning you, and they will lift you up in their hands, so that you will not strike your foot against a stone.'"* Matthew 4:5–6

Now the challenge was brazen. "Prove it! Prove that you are God's Son! If God is truly your Father, then he will save you!"

Satan was quoting a passage found in the Book of Psalms. Satan loves religion and quoting the Bible is a favorite trick of his. The problem was that Satan was not quoting Scripture accurately. He was selecting only the portion that suited his purposes. He had done this with Adam and Eve in the garden of Eden and now he was trying it on Jesus.

Jesus Quotes the Bible

Once again, Jesus answered Satan's temptation by quoting the Bible, only he quoted it correctly. He didn't need to prove Himself.

> *Jesus answered him, "It is also written: 'Do not put the Lord your God to the test.'"* Matthew 4:7

An Offer Resisted

> *Again, the devil took him to a very high mountain and showed him all the kingdoms of the world and their splendor. "All this I will give you," he said, "if you will bow down and worship me."* Matthew 4:8–9

Satan was offering Jesus the nations of the world, *if* Jesus would only worship him. After all, wasn't that what Jesus wanted—for people to follow him? What Satan did not mention was that if Jesus worshiped him, then Jesus would also be serving him. Worship and service always go together. You can't divide the two. But Satan's ploy didn't work. Again Jesus quoted Scripture:

Satan means adversary, or enemy.

> *Jesus said to him, "Away from me, Satan! For it is written: 'Worship the Lord your God, and serve him only.'"*
>
> *Then the devil left him, and angels came and attended him.*
> Matthew 4:10–11

Satan had not succeeded in entrapping Jesus in his treacherous web of deceit. Jesus was above reproach, uncompromising in his resistance to temptation. The Devil retreated temporarily, still determined to destroy Jesus.

From Satan's perspective, he did have a measure of success. John the Baptist had been thrown into jail.[1]

> When Jesus heard that John had been put in prison, he returned to Galilee. Leaving Nazareth, he went and lived in Capernaum, which was by the lake...
> Matthew 4:12–13

SINLESS

The struggle between good and evil is not a balanced one. Jesus, the Creator God, is far more powerful than Satan, a created being. Though Jesus was tempted, he did not give in to temptation. He was perfect.

True and false prophets have come and gone, but none have claimed to be sinless. The Bible records the lives of many people who were either revealed as sinners, or confessed their sinfulness. But Jesus never did. You will search the Scripture in vain, looking for one reference where Jesus sinned or asked for forgiveness. Even those who were closest to him, and were most likely to know of any character flaws, wrote that Jesus...

> ...committed no sin, Nor was any deceit found in His mouth.
> 1 Peter 2:22 NKJV

Jesus' temptation was just one more way in which he identified with humanity. When God finally judges all mankind, no one will be able to stand before him and say, "God, you don't understand! You were born in a palace; I, in dirt. You were never tempted; I was. How can you judge me when you never faced what I faced." No, the Bible says we don't have a God...

> ...who is unable to sympathize with our weaknesses, but we have one who has been tempted in every way, just as we are—yet was without sin.
> Hebrews 4:15

Jesus' righteousness was revealed for all to see.

2 Power and Fame

After John was put in prison, Jesus went into Galilee, proclaiming the good news of God. "The time has come," he said. "The kingdom of God is near. Repent and believe the good news!" Mark 1:14–15

Jesus came offering the Jewish people a new identity, a kingdom led by God. Initially, the people must have been somewhat nonplused by this offer. Here was Jesus, dressed in homespun clothes. *"Were not his kin from Nazareth? His father was a carpenter, I believe."* And he was on foot. Kings don't walk! A real king would come on a horse—a steed, with chariots and armies—and he would ride right up to Herod's palace. A king would issue a challenge, a royal proclamation of independence. You could never read that into Jesus' message even at the best of times. He said *repent*. What sort of king would say that? The local gossips were having a heyday. Even the most serious folk were twitching with laughter.

But not everyone was scoffing. Repentance was something that happened inwardly, and the heart was the place where Christ intended to begin his rule. For those who actually met Jesus… well, he was different. His words made you pause and think.

As Jesus walked beside the Sea of Galilee, he saw Simon and his brother Andrew casting a net into the lake, for they were fishermen. "Come, follow me," Jesus said, "and I will make you fishers of men." At once they left their nets and followed him.

When he had gone a little farther, he saw James son of Zebedee and his brother John in a boat, preparing their nets. Without delay he called them, and they left their father Zebedee in the boat with the hired men and followed him. Mark 1:16–20

AUTHORITY

They went to Capernaum, and when the Sabbath came, Jesus went into the synagogue and began to teach. The people were amazed at his teaching, because he taught them as one who had authority, not as the teachers of the law. Mark 1:21–22

Those who heard Jesus knew there was something very unusual about him. His teaching commanded attention, and no wonder, they were listening to God Himself. But Jesus not only spoke with authority, he also demonstrated it.

> *Just then a man in their synagogue who was possessed by an evil spirit cried out, "What do you want with us, Jesus of Nazareth? Have you come to destroy us? I know who you are—the Holy One of God!"* Mark 1:23–24

This was a case of demon possession. One of Satan's angels was living inside this man, with the man's consent. The demon knew who Jesus was, calling him the *Holy One of God!*

> *"Be quiet!" said Jesus sternly. "Come out of him!"* Mark 1:25

Because demons always twist the truth for their own purposes, Jesus did not want them telling others who he was. Christ himself validated that he was God by ordering the demon out.

> *The evil spirit shook the man violently and came out of him with a shriek.*

> *The people were all so amazed that they asked each other, "What is this? A new teaching—and with authority! He even gives orders to evil spirits and they obey him." News about him spread quickly over the whole region of Galilee.*
> Mark 1:26–28

Now the tongues were wagging to a different tune. Jesus' incredible power must have made headline news in the local gossip sessions and this was only the beginning!

> *A man with leprosy came to him and begged him on his knees, "If you are willing, you can make me clean."*

> *Filled with compassion, Jesus reached out his hand and touched the man. "I am willing," he said. "Be clean!" Immediately the leprosy left him and he was cured.* Mark 1:40–42

In ancient times, leprosy was a dreaded disease—a horribly mutilating, slow death. The Bible says Jesus healed all kinds of nasty ailments, where the person was obviously ill or severely crippled. No man was ever sent away because his disease was incurable. He even raised the dead!

It's important to understand that Jesus wasn't putting on a show for the entertainment of the local populace. Jesus not only felt genuine compassion for the people he helped, but he was also establishing that both he and his message were from Heaven. No, he didn't need a horse, a chariot, or an army. All he needed to do was speak. He was God.

3 Nicodemus

Now there was a man of the Pharisees named Nicodemus, a member of the Jewish ruling council. He came to Jesus at night and said, *"Rabbi, we know you are a teacher who has come from God. For no one could perform the miraculous signs you are doing if God were not with him."

In reply Jesus declared, "I tell you the truth, no one can see the kingdom of God unless he is born again."   John 3:1–3

*Rabbi is the name for a Jewish religious teacher. To call a person Rabbi implied respect.

Born again?

Nicodemus was a man of status. He was a member of the Sanhedrin, the Jewish ruling council that advised the Romans. As a Pharisee, he kept Moses' law meticulously. As a Jew, descended from Abraham, Nicodemus was part of the people chosen to be His own. Nicodemus had a privileged ancestry; everything was *right* about his birth. But Jesus found fault with it and said, *"You must be born again."* Jesus was supposed to be giving good news—but this was bad news. Besides, how was it possible to be born again?

"How can a man be born when he is old?" Nicodemus asked. "Surely he cannot enter a second time into his mother's womb to be born!"

Jesus answered, "I tell you the truth, no one can enter the kingdom of God unless he is born of water and the Spirit. Flesh gives birth to flesh, but the Spirit gives birth to spirit. You should not be surprised at my saying, 'You must be born again.'"   John 3:4–7

So that was it. Jesus wasn't talking about Nicodemus' birth as an infant—when he was *born of water* or *born of the flesh*. The second birth was about a spiritual birth, a spiritual beginning. Well, that was straightforward enough. To go to Heaven you not only needed a physical birth, but you also needed to be born a second time with a spiritual birth. But how could one be born spiritually? Jesus continued:

"Just as Moses lifted up the snake in the desert, so the Son of Man must be lifted up, that everyone who believes in him may have eternal life."   John 3:14–15

Jesus was saying that to be born again, Nicodemus needed to have *a change of mind*. He needed to stop thinking that his birth, his status and good living would make him acceptable with God, and instead trust Jesus to provide a way of acceptance. If he put his faith in Jesus, the Lord would provide Nicodemus with eternal life.

FAITH AND TRUST

The word *believe* in this context implies more than intellectual assent. An Israelite could have acknowledged that looking at Moses' bronze serpent would heal him, but if he did not demonstrate faith in God by actually *looking* at the pole, then he would have died. The biblical meaning of the word includes an act of the will, and is synonymous with faith and trust.

The *object* of one's faith is also important—it's critical! A number of years ago, someone with a twisted mind placed deadly poison in the capsules of a pain reliever. Subsequently, several people, sincerely believing the medicine to be what was advertised, took the medication and died. They were honestly trusting, but inadvertently trusting in the wrong thing.

A man might devoutly believe that a UFO could save him from his sin, but sincerity based on an erroneous belief is meaningless. However, if the object of his faith is God, such trust will have a very different effect. We've seen that God keeps His Word.

> "For God so loved the world that he gave his one and only Son, that whoever believes in him shall not perish but have eternal life."   *John 3:16*

EVERLASTING LIFE

Jesus was promising eternal life, not just to Nicodemus, but to *whoever believes* in him! The angel had instructed Mary and Joseph to name their son Jesus because that name meant DELIVERER or SAVIOR. And now Jesus was saying he would deliver man from the consequence of sin—eternal punishment in the Lake of Fire.

ETERNAL LIFE

> "For God did not send his Son into the world to condemn the world, but to save the world through him."   *John 3:17*

Jesus had not come to earth to judge it. Rather he had come to save the world from all the tragedy that sin, Satan and death had brought.

> *"Whoever believes in him is not condemned, but whoever does not believe stands condemned already because he has not believed in the name of God's one and only Son."*
> John 3:18

NO MIDDLE GROUND

Jesus said that those who put their faith in him would not be judged as sinners. But those who did *not* trust in him were already under judgment. There was no middle ground; you couldn't get around it. One could not say, *"I'll think about it,"* and comfortably remain in a gray zone. You had to choose to believe, otherwise you remained an unbeliever. To make no choice was, in effect, to make a choice.

ETERNAL JUDGMENT

Also, you didn't need to wait until death to find out your eternal destiny. Jesus was stating it in black and white terms. A man was under judgment, bound for the Lake of Fire, until he put his trust in Jesus to deliver him. Then he would have eternal life. This was the promise Jesus was making.

> *"I tell you the truth, whoever hears my word and believes him who sent me has eternal life and will not be condemned; he has crossed over from death to life."* John 5:24

Jesus wasn't ignoring the judgment of sin. He knew that not everyone would trust in him. Many would choose not to do so for their own reasons.

> *"This is the verdict: Light has come into the world, but men loved darkness instead of light because their deeds were evil. Everyone who does evil hates the light, and will not come into the light for fear that his deeds will be exposed."*
> John 3:19–20

Jesus was talking about spiritual light versus spiritual darkness. He said that many hate the light because light exposes their self-righteousness. People don't like being revealed as sinners. They'd rather hide or blame their sin on someone else, just as Adam and Eve did. The Bible says such people prefer darkness. But what is this *light*?

> *When Jesus spoke again to the people, he said, "**I am the light of the world**."* John 8:12

At the time of creation, God made light so we could see our way along a physical path. Now he had come to earth to be the *light* for our spiritual path.

> *Whoever follows me will never walk in darkness, but will have the light of life."*
>
> John 8:12

4 REJECTION

> *A few days later, when Jesus again entered Capernaum, the people heard that he had come home. So many gathered that there was no room left, not even outside the door, and he preached the word to them. Some men came, bringing to him a paralytic, carried by four of them.*
>
> Mark 2:1–3

THE PARALYZED

This was a familiar scenario wherever Jesus went. As soon as he put in an appearance, the sick and lame began to arrive. In this case four men brought a paralyzed friend.

> *Since they could not get him to Jesus because of the crowd, they made an opening in the roof above Jesus and, after digging through it, lowered the mat the paralyzed man was lying on.*
>
> Mark 2:4

The houses of the time were typically flat-roofed. Stairs led to the top, making it a cool place to relax in the evening. When the four men could not get close to Jesus, they simply went up on the roof, tore it open and lowered the paralyzed man down in front of Jesus. I say "simply," but that only applies to getting up on the housetop. Tearing up the roof must have been an ordeal. You can imagine the dust and chunks of packed earth that rained down on those inside. Of course, Jesus' lesson was interrupted. Everyone stared at the ceiling wondering what was going on. As the faces of the determined men came into view, probably Jesus' audience took to yelling and carrying on: *"For crying out loud! Where's your respect?! We're covered in dust! You're wrecking the house!"* But Jesus saw something different.

> *When Jesus saw their faith, he said to the paralytic, "Son, your sins are forgiven."*
>
> Mark 2:5

The heart

Jesus was first concerned about the inward man, the heart. It was no problem for him to forgive sin. He's God. But some of his audience had trouble accepting that. Though they didn't say anything out loud, their thoughts were hostile.

> *Now some teachers of the law [or the Scribes] were sitting there, thinking to themselves, "Why does this fellow talk like that? He's blaspheming! Who can forgive sins but God alone?"* Mark 2:6–7

They were right—only God *can* forgive sin!

> *Immediately Jesus knew in his spirit that this was what they were thinking in their hearts, and he said to them, "Why are you thinking these things?"* Mark 2:8

Jesus knew what they were reasoning, and he told them so. You can imagine the Scribes' mortification. They probably reeled back in their minds trying to remember what they had been thinking during the previous ten minutes. One thing was certain—Jesus could read their thoughts! But Jesus wasn't trying to impress them. He had a question.

> *"Which is easier: to say to the paralytic, 'Your sins are forgiven,' or to say, 'Get up, take your mat and walk'?"* Mark 2:9

Questions, Questions

A lawyer could not have framed a more difficult question. You can see the Scribes straining their brains. "The man was obviously paralyzed. To restore the crippled limbs to use was impossible. Only God could heal such an infirmity. But if Jesus could give life to withered limbs, then that meant he was…no, that was unthinkable. God would never come to earth and live a life like Jesus did. He was a nobody, living on the dusty outskirts of the empire. The audacity to ask such a loaded question! Who did he think he was anyway? God!?" Jesus answered their query without them asking…

> *"…But that you may know that the Son of Man has authority on earth to forgive sins…" He said to the paralytic, "I tell you, get up, take your mat and go home." He got up, took his mat and walked out in full view of them all. This amazed everyone and they praised God, saying, "We have never seen anything like this!"* Mark 2:10–12

The purpose of the miracles was not to create something equivalent to a vaudeville act or a circus side show. The miracles authenticated who Jesus said he was—that he was God.

HELPLESS SINNERS

Once again Jesus went out beside the lake. …As he walked along, he saw Levi son of Alphaeus sitting at the tax collector's booth. "Follow me," Jesus told him, and Levi got up and followed him.   Mark 2:13–14

Although Levi was a Jew, he worked as a tax collector for the Romans. These money-grubbers gained their shekels from a hidden surcharge on the tax, and often grossly overcharged the people in order to comfortably line their own pockets. They were hated for their corrupt power and for their willingness to work as bloodsuckers for the Romans. Nevertheless, as Jesus passed the tax office, he invited Levi to follow him.

While Jesus was having dinner at Levi's house, many tax collectors and "sinners" were eating with him and his disciples, for there were many who followed him.

When the teachers of the law who were Pharisees saw him eating with the "sinners" and tax collectors, they asked his disciples: "Why does he eat with tax collectors and 'sinners'?"

On hearing this, Jesus said to them, "It is not the healthy who need a doctor, but the sick. I have not come to call the righteous, but sinners."   Mark 2:15–17

Jesus affirmed that he could only help those who recognized their own sinfulness.

WORKING ON THE SABBATH

Jesus' constant rebukes must have been galling to the Pharisees. They were losing face. Hoping to catch Jesus in some act of blatant sin, they began to keep a close eye on him.

Another time he went into the synagogue, and a man with a shriveled hand was there. Some of them were looking for a reason to accuse Jesus, so they watched him closely to see if he would heal him on the Sabbath.   Mark 3:1–2

According to the Law, no one was to work on the Sabbath. To work was to break God's Law and that would be sin. In the

Pharisees' minds, *work* included such things as performing the service of a doctor. The Law didn't say it was wrong to heal on this day, but the Pharisees had encircled the Ten Commandments with their own list of rules, and those precepts had taken on the authority of Scripture. So they watched to see if Jesus would heal the man, if he would "work" on the Sabbath. But Jesus was fully aware of the purpose for which God had given the Law. Knowing the Pharisees' scheme to entrap him, Christ could have avoided a confrontation but he didn't back off.

Jesus said to the man with the shriveled hand, "Stand up in front of everyone." Mark 3:3

You can see Jesus slowly turn and gaze at those who had plotted to accuse him. The moment is frozen…

Then Jesus asked them, "Which is lawful on the sabbath: to do good or to do evil, to save life or to kill?" Mark 3:4

There he went again, asking loaded questions! The Pharisees were in a huff—seething with anger and resentment. As the religious answer-men, their credibility was being tarnished.

But they remained silent.

He looked around at them in anger and, deeply distressed at their stubborn hearts, said to the man, "Stretch out your hand." He stretched it out, and his hand was completely restored. Mark 3:4–5

PLOTTING

Jesus had done it. He had "worked" on the Sabbath! The Pharisees' had caught him in the act.

Then the Pharisees went out and began to plot with the Herodians how they might kill Jesus. Mark 3:6

Normally such an alliance would have been unthinkable. The Herodians were a political party which supported the rule of Herod and the Romans. On the other hand, the Pharisees despised the Romans—but they hated Jesus even more. If they were going to kill him, they would need Rome's help.

The religious leaders had rejected Jesus. As far as they were concerned, he could not be THE PROMISED DELIVERER.

THE TWELVE DISCIPLES

Jesus withdrew with his disciples to the lake, and a large crowd from Galilee followed. When they heard all he was doing, many people came to him...

Jesus went up on a mountainside and called to him those he wanted, and they came to him. He appointed twelve—designating them apostles...

Simon (to whom he gave the name Peter); James, son of Zebedee and his brother...John (to them he gave the name Boanerges, which means Sons of Thunder); Andrew, Philip, Bartholomew, Matthew, Thomas, James son of Alphaeus, Thaddaeus, Simon the Zealot and... Judas Iscariot, who betrayed him.   Mark 3:7–8, 13–14, 16–19

From those who followed him, Jesus selected twelve disciples with whom he would spend extra time. They were a mixed lot comprised of a Rome-employed tax collector on one end of the social spectrum and, on the other end, a zealot pledged to overthrow the Romans. Among the remaining were an assortment of fishermen. Only God could have maintained peace between these rugged men! Regardless of their background, these twelve were all committed to following Jesus through thick and thin. That is, all but one.

5 THE BREAD OF LIFE

Some time after this, Jesus crossed to the far shore of the Sea of Galilee (that is, the Sea of Tiberias), and a great crowd of people followed him because they saw the miraculous signs he had performed on the sick. Then Jesus went up on a mountainside and sat down with his disciples. The Jewish Passover Feast was near.

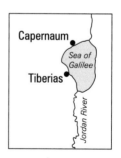

When Jesus looked up and saw a great crowd coming toward him, he said to Philip, "Where shall we buy bread for these people to eat?"   John 6:1–5

Jesus was asking questions again.

He asked this only to test him, for he already had in mind what he was going to do.

> *Philip answered him, "Eight months' wages would not buy enough bread for each one to have a bite!"*
>
> *Another of his disciples, Andrew, Simon Peter's brother, spoke up, "Here is a boy with five small barley loaves and two small fish, but how far will they go among so many?"*
>
> John 6:6–9

You can't help wondering if Andrew was like a small boy hinting to his father, hoping that Jesus could do something.

> *Jesus said, "Have the people sit down." There was plenty of grass in that place, and the men sat down, about five thousand of them. Jesus then took the loaves, gave thanks, and distributed to those who were seated as much as they wanted. He did the same with the fish.*
>
> John 6:10–11

The biblical account is stated so matter-of-factly that you almost miss what happened. Jesus had just fed a massive crowd with a boy's lunch. This is not a lesson in exponential multiplication. Jesus divided the bread and fish among his twelve disciples, and they apportioned it to five thousand men—the women and children would have been in addition to this number. This was reproduction of an unheard of magnitude, and Jesus wasn't being miserly. They had enough leftovers for each disciple to take a basketful home.

> *After the people saw the miraculous sign that Jesus did, they began to say, "Surely this is the Prophet who is to come into the world."*
>
> John 6:14

MAKE JESUS A KING

The men who had benefited from this miracle were so impressed that they decided they would forcibly install Jesus as their king. But Jesus wasn't interested in starting an earthly kingdom, though there would be a time for that in the future. For now he was seeking to rule peoples' hearts.

> *Jesus, knowing that they intended to come and make him king by force, withdrew again to a mountain by himself.*
>
> *When they found him on the other side of the lake, they asked him, "Rabbi, when did you get here?"*
>
> *Jesus answered, "I tell you the truth, you are looking for me, not because you saw miraculous signs but because you ate the loaves and had your fill."*
>
> John 6:15,25–26

Wrong Motives

Well, there you have it. Jesus could see that the people only wanted him to be king so that they could get free food. They weren't interested in the fact that these miracles revealed that he was The Promised Savior. Jesus said …

> "Do not work for food that spoils, but for food that endures to eternal life, which the Son of Man will give you. On him God the Father has placed his seal of approval." *John 6:27*

The food they ate could only sustain life for a short time. Sooner or later, they would all die. Therefore, Jesus said their all-consuming goal in life should be to pursue that which would give them eternal life.

> Then they asked him, "What must we do to do the works God requires?"
>
> Jesus answered, "The work of God is this: to believe in the one he has sent." *John 6:28–29*

The people wanted to know what sort of *work* they would have to do to earn everlasting life. Jesus said that they only needed to *believe*; they only needed to trust in him to be their Savior. That was all. It seemed so simple.

> So they asked him, "What miraculous sign then will you give that we may see it and believe you?" *John 6:30*

What was that? They were asking Jesus for a sign to prove that he was God, as if feeding the five thousand with a boy's lunch wasn't enough?! What they were really asking for was another free meal, another loaf of bread.

The Bread of Life

> Jesus said to them, "I tell you the truth, …it is my Father who gives you the true bread from heaven. For the bread of God is he who comes down from heaven and gives life to the world."
>
> "Sir," they said, "from now on give us this bread."
>
> Then Jesus declared, "**I am the bread of life.** He who comes to me will never go hungry, and he who believes in me will never be thirsty." *John 6:32–35*

CHAPTER TWELVE

1 FILTHY RAGS

Jesus was a master storyteller, often using parables to make a point. A parable is a story that contains one simple message. In this case, he directed the story to those who thought they were *right* with God because they trusted in themselves.

> *To some who were confident of their own righteousness and looked down on everybody else, Jesus told this parable: "Two men went up to the temple to pray, one a Pharisee and the other a tax collector."* Luke 18:9–10

In the Jewish culture of that day, Pharisees were viewed as meticulous keepers of Moses' law. In contrast, the tax collectors were considered to be crooks. Now here were two people from opposite ends of the moral spectrum, praying in the same place.

THE PHARISEE

> *"The Pharisee stood up and prayed about himself: 'God, I thank you that I am not like other men—robbers, evildoers, adulterers—or even like this tax collector. I *fast twice a week and give a tenth of all I get.'"* Luke 18:11–12

*His fasting, or doing without food, was presumably for giving time to prayer. He also gave a tenth of his income to a charitable cause.

In patting himself on the back, the Pharisee mentioned only a couple of things that he did or did not do. His list could have been lengthy. But that didn't matter. The *way* he prayed showed the attitude of his heart. He was relying on his own right living (or good works) to make himself righteous before God.

THE TAX COLLECTOR

> *"But the tax collector stood at a distance. He would not even look up to heaven, but beat his breast and said, 'God, have mercy on me, a sinner.'"* Luke 18:13

The tax collector was overwhelmed by the awareness that he was a sinner and that he desperately needed God's help. He begged God for mercy, asking him to provide a way to escape the rightful punishment for his sin. Jesus continued:

> *"I tell you that this man, rather than the other, went home justified before God. For everyone who exalts himself will be humbled, and he who humbles himself will be exalted."* Luke 18:14

Justified means *to be declared righteous.*

Repentance

It is interesting that Jesus tied repentance to humility. The Bible makes it very clear that pride is what caused Satan to fall. It is also pride which causes man to hold back from admitting that he is a sinner, needing to trust God. The Pharisee was convinced that, if he was diligent in observing all the Law and performing good deeds, God would be pleased. He was proud to the point that he was blind to his own need. Jesus said:

> *"Isaiah was right when he prophesied about you hypocrites;*
> *as it is written: 'These people honor me with their lips,*
> *but their hearts are far from me. They worship me in vain;*
> *their teachings are but rules taught by men.' You have let*
> *go of the commands of God and are holding on to the*
> *traditions of men."*   Mark 7:6–8

Blind

Outwardly, the Pharisees went through the motions of appearing righteous, but inwardly, they were sinful. They also undercut the intent of the Ten Commandments by adding their own man-made rules. Jesus said:

> *"Thus you nullify the word of God by your tradition that*
> *you have handed down."*   Mark 7:13

The Pharisees believed that their *religious* observances, their *good works* and their Jewish *birth* would make them right with God.

Jesus said that these things do nothing to make a person acceptable, because evil...

> "...come[s] from inside and make[s] a man 'unclean.'"
>
> Mark 7:23

The Bible is clear on this point: good deeds do not earn a right standing with God. Indeed it says...

> ...all our righteous acts are like filthy rags...   Isaiah 64:6

SLAVES

Sometimes folk view themselves as models of perfection, but the Bible states quite the opposite. It says that all people...

> ...are slaves to sin, which leads to death...   Romans 6:16

Sin has wrapped its chains around the life of every human.

> "I tell you the truth, everyone who sins is a slave to sin."
>
> John 8:34

We often get frustrated because the harder we try to do that which is right, the more we seem to fail. Just as we get one area of life under control, we find ourselves falling short in another. In every way, the sin nature works against our efforts to live right. It's no wonder New Year resolutions rarely succeed.

In addition, the Bible speaks of Satan making man his SLAVE. This doesn't necessarily mean that a person has been dabbling in the occult; rather, the Devil manipulates man by temptation and pride to accomplish his ends. Indeed, Satan works very hard to convince man that he is inherently good. The Scripture says that people need to...

SLAVE

> ...come to their senses and escape from the trap of the devil,
> who has taken them captive to do his will.   2 Timothy 2:26

Just because man is a slave to sin and Satan, does not justify a devilish lifestyle. God still holds everyone responsible for the choices they make. But being slaves does create a dilemma. The sort of perfection man needs to enter the presence of a perfect God is far beyond man's capability to achieve.

The age-old question still remains. "How can we get rid of our *sin* and gain a *righteousness <u>equal</u> to God's righteousness* so we can be accepted in his presence?"

I was born a Christian...

The word *Christian* implies *Christ-one* or *belonging to the household of Christ.* The biblical meaning has been distorted and confused beyond belief. But even in the original sense of the word, to say that one has been *born a Christian* is not accurate. Being born in a *Christian home* no more makes you a Christian than being born in a hospital makes you a doctor. Physical birth has nothing to do with our relationship with God or our future destiny.

Though the term is used of entire nations, rightly understood it can only apply to an individual. Some supposedly *Christian nations* have perpetrated terrible crimes in the name of Christ. Others are morally corrupt.

---

2 The Way

Often Jesus used common day to day experiences to illustrate spiritual truth. In this story, Jesus began by reminding his listeners of the sort of pen in which sheep were kept. The enclosure was constructed using stones, upon which thorny vines were encouraged to grow. The purpose of these brambles was to dissuade wild animals or thieves from crawling over the wall. The pen had only one entrance.

During the day, the shepherd would lead his flock out to the pasture for grazing. At night, the flock would be returned to the fold and the shepherd would sleep in the entrance. No one could enter and the sheep could not leave without disturbing the guardian. The shepherd's body literally became the door to the pen.

> *Therefore Jesus said again, "I tell you the truth, I am the gate for the sheep."*
> John 10:7

Jesus compared those who trust him as being sheep, safely secured in the sheep pen.

> *"I am the gate; whoever enters through me will be saved."*
> John 10:9

Jesus said that *he* alone was the gate—there were no other doors. It was only through *him* that one could be *saved* from the terrible consequences of sin. It was only through him that one could have eternal life.

> *"The thief comes only to steal and kill and destroy; I have come that they may have life, and have it to the full."*
> John 10:10

Thieves do not care about the welfare of sheep. The Bible calls them false teachers. Often they use the Bible to feed a power trip or thicken their wallets. These *thieves* fabricate a way to earn eternal life—a way that appears good, but still ends in spiritual death.

> *There is a way that seems right to a man, but in the end it leads to death.*
> Proverbs 14:12

On the other hand, Jesus came to give a full life to those who trust in Him, a life abundant with joy. Jesus said …

> *"I am the way and the truth and the life. No one comes to the Father except through me."* John 14:6

Jesus said: He is the *only* **way** to God.

His Word is the *only* **truth**.

Eternal **life** can *only* be found in Him.

Jesus emphasized that no one can come to God any other way. Just as the shepherd was the only gate to the sheepfold, so Jesus is the only way to God.

3 Lazarus

> *Now a man named Lazarus was sick. He was from Bethany, the village of Mary and her sister Martha. So the sisters sent word to Jesus, "Lord, the one you love is sick."* John 11:1,3

Lazarus, Mary and Martha were close friends of Jesus who lived a couple of miles from Jerusalem. At the time of this event, Jesus was on the other side of the Jordan River, a full day's journey from Bethany.

> *Jesus loved Martha and her sister and Lazarus. Yet when he heard that Lazarus was sick, he stayed where he was two more days.* John 11:5–6

Now that doesn't make sense. In this day of quick-response rescue teams, everyone knows that when someone is seriously ill, you don't dawdle. But Jesus stayed where he was for another two days! What was going on in his mind?

> *Then he said to his disciples, "Let us go back to Judea."*
>
> *"But Rabbi," they said, "a short while ago the Jews tried to stone you, and yet you are going back there?"*
>
> *So then he told them plainly, "Lazarus is dead, and for your sake I am glad I was not there, so that you may believe. But let us go to him."* John 11:7–8, 14–15

DEAD FOUR DAYS

On his arrival, Jesus found that Lazarus had already been in the tomb for four days. Bethany was less than two miles from Jerusalem, and many Jews had come to Martha and Mary to comfort them in the loss of their brother. When Martha heard that Jesus was coming, she went out to meet him, but Mary stayed at home.

"Lord," Martha said to Jesus, "if you had been here, my brother would not have died. But I know that even now God will give you whatever you ask."   John 11:17–22

We are not told what Martha thought Jesus might ask God for, but one thing is abundantly clear—she had faith in him.

Jesus said to her, "Your brother will rise again."
Martha answered, "I know he will rise again in the resurrection at the last day."   John 11:23–24

Martha wasn't surprised at Jesus' statement. She knew that the Bible says that all people will come back to life, but *that* would occur at the end of the world when everyone will be judged by God. Until then, a person only dies once.

Jesus said to her, "I am the resurrection and the life. He who believes in me will live, even though he dies; and whoever lives and believes in me will never die. Do you believe this?"   John 11:25–26

These were potent words. Jesus told Martha that Lazarus did not have to wait until the day of judgment to be raised back to life. Jesus was the one who gave life, and therefore had the power to restore life to Lazarus at any moment. Did she believe him?

"Yes, Lord," she told him, "I believe that you are the Christ, the Son of God, who was to come into the world."
          John 11:27

Martha not only believed Jesus; she also affirmed that he was the Christ—the Messiah, God Himself.

"Where have you laid him?" he asked.
"Come and see, Lord," they replied.
Jesus wept.   John 11:34–35

There has been much speculation about why Jesus cried. Some have conjectured that Jesus grieved at the thought of bringing Lazarus back to life—back from all the joy and perfection of

Heaven—back to the earth with all its sin and sorrow. The Bible doesn't tell us why, but the fact that he wept does show us that Jesus experienced human feelings, even though he was sinless.

> Then the Jews said, "See how he loved him!"
>
> But some of them said, "Could not he who opened the eyes of the blind man have kept this man from dying?"
>
> Jesus, once more deeply moved, came to the tomb. It was a cave with a stone laid across the entrance.   John 11:36–38

The traditional Jewish burial of the day often involved placing the body in a tomb which, over time, became the last resting place of successive generations. A natural cave was commonly used, though sometimes the sepulcher was hewn out of solid rock. These tombs were large; you could stand upright in the ❶ weeping chamber.

Inside, ❷ shelves were carved on which to lay the ❸ bodies. A ❹ wheel-shaped rock, weighing several tons, was hewn to tightly seal the entrance. Resting in a ❺ trench, this door could be rolled back and forth. When closed, the door rested in a small hollow in front of the entrance, preventing the stone from rolling open.

> "Take away the stone," he said.
>
> "But, Lord," said Martha, the sister of the dead man, "by this time there is a bad odor, for he has been there four days."
>
> Then Jesus said, "Did I not tell you that if you believed, you would see the glory of God?"
>
> So they took away the stone. Then Jesus looked up and said, "Father, I thank you that you have heard me. I knew that you always hear me, but I said this for the benefit of the people standing here, that they may believe that you sent me."

When he had said this, Jesus called in a loud voice, "Lazarus, come out!" The dead man came out, his hands and feet wrapped with strips of linen, and a cloth around his face.

Jesus said to them, "Take off the grave clothes and let him go."
John 11:39–44

It was a good thing that Jesus said, "Lazarus..." If he had simply said "come forth!" the whole cemetery would have emptied its dead! Lazarus was alive! His friends had to unwind the long strips of burial clothes before Lazarus could walk away. There was no doubt that Jesus had performed a tremendous miracle.

Therefore many of the Jews who had come to visit Mary, and had seen what Jesus did, put their faith in him. But some of them went to the Pharisees and told them what Jesus had done. Then the chief priests and the Pharisees called a meeting of the *Sanhedrin.

*The Sanhedrin was the Jewish ruling council.

"What are we accomplishing?" they asked. "Here is this man performing many miraculous signs. If we let him go on like this, everyone will believe in him, and then the Romans will come and take away both our place and our nation."

So from that day on they plotted to take his life. John 11:45–48, 53

Some believed, but others plotted. Not even a resurrection could convince the chief priests and Pharisees. They had too much at stake—their power and their pride. It sort of sounds like Lucifer. No doubt it was!

REINCARNATION

Reincarnation is the belief that, after death, a departed spirit returns to the earth to live again in the form of another human or animal.

Not only is this concept *not* taught in the Bible, but the Bible clearly teaches the opposite. Each person has only one life.

... man is destined to die once, and after that to face judgment...
Hebrews 9:27

As a cloud vanishes and is gone, so he who goes down to the grave does not return. He will never come to his house again; his place will know him no more. Job 7:9–10

4 HELL

For three years Jesus taught all who would listen. It seems an incredibly brief span of time, considering everything that happened. His teaching ranged from comforting to provoking, from parables to accounts of real people, each suited to the need of the listener. On this occasion, Jesus related the following true story:

> *"There was a rich man who was dressed in purple and fine linen and lived in luxury every day. At his gate was laid a beggar named Lazarus, covered with sores and longing to eat what fell from the rich man's table. Even the dogs came and licked his sores."* Luke 16:19–21

THE BEGGAR DIES

> *"The time came when the beggar died and the angels carried him to Abraham's side."* Luke 16:22

ETERNAL
LIFE

For the intent of this study, *Abraham's side* is equivalent to Heaven and is sometimes referred to as *paradise.* The man in question here was a different person than the Lazarus in the last story. This Lazarus went to *paradise,* not because he was poor, but because he trusted the Lord.

THE RICH MAN DIES

> *"The rich man also died and was buried. In hell, where he was in torment, he looked up and saw Abraham far away, with Lazarus by his side. So he called to him, 'Father Abraham, have pity on me and send Lazarus to dip the tip of his finger in water and cool my tongue, because I am in agony in this fire.'"* Luke 16:22–24

ETERNAL
JUDGMENT

The rich man had gone to Hell, not because he was wealthy, but because he ignored God and lived only for himself while on earth. He begged Abraham for help.

> *"But Abraham replied, 'Son, remember that in your lifetime you received your good things, while Lazarus received bad things, but now he is comforted here and you are in agony. And besides all this, between us and you a great chasm has been fixed, so that those who want to go from here to you cannot, nor can anyone cross over from there to us.'"* Luke 16:25–26

IT'S FINAL

The Bible makes it clear that one can only repent—have a change of mind—while here on earth. After a person dies, there is no second chance, no opportunity to escape Hell for Heaven. Those who die and are not in a right relationship with God remain separated from him forever. Nowhere does the Scripture suggest that one can escape this place of suffering. Even though the rich man cried out for a measure of relief from his torment and misery, there was none. Mercy can only be received during this lifetime. The rich man continued...

> "He answered, 'Then I beg you, father, send Lazarus to my father's house, for I have five brothers. Let him warn them, so that they will not also come to this place of torment.'"
>
> Luke 16:27–28

Even though this man was in terrible agony, he could remember his life on earth. He knew that his five brothers were not right with God and wanted them to be warned.

The idea of partying with one's friends in Hell is foreign to the Bible. Those in Hell wouldn't wish it on their worst enemies.

> "Abraham replied, 'They have Moses and the Prophets; let them listen to them.'
>
> 'No, father Abraham,' he said, 'but if someone from the dead goes to them, they will repent.'
>
> [Abraham] said to him, 'If they do not listen to Moses and the Prophets, they will not be convinced even if someone rises from the dead.'"
>
> Luke 16:29–31

Earlier, we read of one whom Jesus raised from the dead. Yet in spite of this great demonstration of power, many still would not accept Jesus. Instead, they plotted to kill him. The Bible says that if people refuse to believe God's written Word, then...

> "...they will not be convinced even if someone rises from the dead."
>
> Luke 16:31

The description of Hell is almost synonymous with that of the Lake of Fire.[1] The Bible says that those who enter Hell have already entered everlasting punishment.

5 Acceptance and Betrayal

As they approached Jerusalem and came to Bethphage and Bethany at the Mount of Olives, Jesus sent two of his disciples, saying to them, "Go to the village ahead of you, and just as you enter it, you  *will find a colt tied there, which no one has ever ridden. Untie it and bring it here."*
Mark 11:1–2

When they brought the colt to Jesus and threw their cloaks over it, he sat on it. Many people spread their cloaks on the road, while others spread branches they had cut in the fields. Those who went ahead and those who followed shouted, "Hosanna!" "Blessed is he who comes in the name of the Lord!" "Blessed is the coming kingdom of our father David!" "Hosanna in the highest!"
Mark 11:7–10

The word *hosanna* means *save now.* The crowd was giving Jesus an impromptu version of a Roman parade normally used to welcome a triumphant conqueror. They were applauding and praising him in hopes that he would oust their Roman oppressors.

 Unbeknown to them, they were fulfilling a 500 year old prophecy. The Prophet Zechariah had written that Jesus would receive just such a welcome.

> *Rejoice greatly, O Daughter of Zion! Shout, Daughter of Jerusalem! See, your king comes to you, righteous and having salvation, gentle and riding on a donkey, on a colt, the foal of a donkey.*
> Zechariah 9:9

This is the only time Jesus ever allowed such a momentous reception on his behalf. He had a reason. Jesus was forcing the hand of those who were out to kill him. He wanted them to act now, without delay.

> *Now the Passover and the Feast of Unleavened Bread were only two days away, and the chief priests and the teachers of the law were looking for some sly way to arrest Jesus and kill him. "But not during the Feast," they said, "or the people may riot."*
> Mark 14:1–2

From the perspective of the shouting crowd, it was time for Jesus to announce that he was the true King of Israel. But for the religious leaders who were plotting his death, it was an awkward situation. If Jesus needed to be put off the stage, now was the time, but they were afraid of the public reaction. Jesus was obviously very popular.

The city was crammed with people for the Passover, many of whom were expectantly watching Jesus in the hope that he would evict the Romans. But as the hours passed with no official proclamation of his kingship, his hero-status was fast fading.

THE PASSOVER MEAL

Jesus instructed two disciples to arrange a room for the Passover.

> *When evening came, Jesus arrived with the Twelve. While they were reclining at the table eating, he said, "I tell you the truth, one of you will betray me—one who is eating with me."*
>
> *They were saddened, and one by one they said to him, "Surely not I?"*
>
> *"It is one of the Twelve," he replied, "one who dips bread into the bowl with me."* Mark 14:17–20

When Jesus chose his twelve disciples three years earlier, he knew that one was a traitor.

 1000 years before this time, King David, in speaking of this betrayal, had written from THE SAVIOR'S perspective...

> *"Even my close friend, whom I trusted, he who shared my bread, has lifted up his heel against me."* Psalm 41:9

BETRAYED

The traitor was Judas Iscariot. Though he was treasurer for the disciples, he was also a thief. Apparently, he oiled his ambitions and lined his pockets without the disciples being any the wiser. But Jesus knew, and apparently Satan knew it too. He had been watching for a weak link in Jesus' armor, a time and place to crush THE PROMISED SAVIOR forever. Now Satan saw his opportunity. Judas was willing. As the Passover bread was being served, the Devil made his move.

As soon as Judas took the bread, Satan entered into him.

"What you are about to do, do quickly," Jesus told him, but no one at the meal understood why Jesus said this to him.   John 13:27–28

And Judas went to the chief priests and the officers of the temple guard and discussed with them how he might betray Jesus. They were delighted and agreed to give him money.   Luke 22:4–5

The Broken Bread And The Cup

This scenario with Judas happened in the middle of the meal. While the traitor went about his diabolical mission, Jesus continued with the supper. It has great significance.

While they were eating, Jesus took bread, gave thanks and broke it, and gave it to his disciples, saying, "Take it; this is my body."   Mark 14:22

Obviously they weren't eating Jesus' flesh, and yet Jesus was saying that the broken Passover loaf represented his body. The disciples must have been rather perplexed. Did this have to do with his earlier reference to himself as the Bread of Life?

Then he took the cup, gave thanks and offered it to them, and they all drank from it.

"This is my blood of the covenant, which is poured out for many," he said to them.   Mark 14:23–24

Again the symbolism was similar—Jesus' blood would soon be poured out *for many* people. We will see the significance of this later on.

When they had sung a *hymn, they went out to the Mount of Olives.   Mark 14:26

*a song praising God.

Thursday Night:
Jesus and his disciples celebrate the Passover together. After singing a hymn they depart for the Garden of Gethsemane, located at the foot of the Mount of Olives.

❸

❷ Monday to Wednesday:
Jesus and his twelve disciples spend time in and around Jerusalem and Bethany.

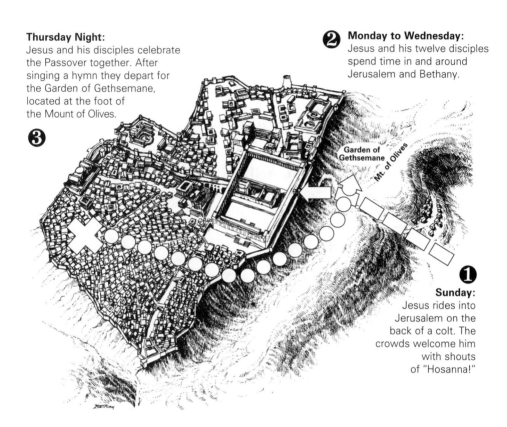

Garden of Gethsemane

Mt. of Olives

❶
Sunday:
Jesus rides into Jerusalem on the back of a colt. The crowds welcome him with shouts of "Hosanna!"

CHAPTER THIRTEEN

1 THE ARREST

They went to a place called Gethsemane, and Jesus said to his disciples, "Sit here while I pray." He took Peter, James and John along with him, and he began to be deeply distressed and troubled. "My soul is overwhelmed with sorrow to the point of death," he said to them. "Stay here and keep watch."

Going a little farther, he fell to the ground and prayed that if possible the hour might pass from him. *"Abba, Father," he said, "everything is possible for you. Take this cup from me. Yet not what I will, but what you will."   Mark 14:32–36

*A term of endearment similar to *daddy* or *papa*.

HIS HUMANITY

Sometimes in emphasizing that Jesus was truly God, it's easy to forget that he was also human. Suffering was not foreign to Jesus—he knew and felt pain. Being God, he knew the future agony he was about to face. He felt overwhelmed with the prospect that faced him. In the intimate language that only a son could have with his dear father, Jesus cried out, *Abba—Daddy—please find another way.* But then he submitted his human will to his heavenly Father and prayed, *Your will be done.*

Just as he was speaking, Judas, one of the Twelve, appeared. With him was a crowd armed with swords and clubs, sent from the chief priests, the teachers of the law, and the elders.

Now the betrayer had arranged a signal with them: "The one I kiss is the man; arrest him and lead him away under guard."   Mark 14:43–44

Jesus, knowing all that was going to happen to him, went out and asked them, "Who is it you want?"

"Jesus of Nazareth," they replied.   John 18:4–5

HE SPOKE

"I am {he}," Jesus said. (And Judas the traitor was standing there with them.)   John 18:5

The word {*he*} does not appear in the original Greek text. It was supplied to help the English rendering flow better, but in this case it distracts from the significance of what Jesus said.

Jesus answered the question with an emphatic *"I AM!"* It could be translated[1] literally, *"I am **right now,** GOD!"* As we have seen, I AM is God's name, meaning *the One who exists by his own power.* And it wasn't just anyone saying it; it was God himself. The effect is worth noting.

> When Jesus said, **"I am** he," they drew back and fell to the ground.
> John 18:6

They didn't simply drop to the ground; they drew back and fell down. Jesus *blew them off their feet* with a mini-burst of his majesty. After the stunned group had gotten up and dusted themselves off...

> Again he asked them, "Who is it you want?"
> And they said, "Jesus of Nazareth."
> John 18:7

You can almost sense the crowd's respect and fear. Jesus had unsettled the mob. This was not shaping up to be a typical arrest. Their wall of confidence cracked even more when Jesus revealed that he knew the agreed-upon sign of betrayal.

> ...Jesus asked him, "Judas, are you betraying the Son of Man with a kiss?"
> Luke 22:48

> Going at once to Jesus, Judas said, "Rabbi!" and kissed him.
> Mark 14:45

The other eleven disciples were galvanized into action. Simon Peter had a weapon...

> With that, one of Jesus' companions reached for his sword, drew it out and struck the servant of the high priest, cutting off his ear.
> Matthew 26:51

A Healing

> But Jesus answered, "No more of this!" And he touched the man's ear and healed him.
> Luke 22:51

What can you say? Even in the midst of all the tension, Jesus was thinking of others; he healed the High Priest's servant. It was a short-sighted effort on Peter's part anyway—zeal without knowledge. On a human level, the disciples were greatly outnumbered. You can't help admiring Peter's efforts. At least he tried! But obviously Peter was better with nets than swords. When you aim at the head and get an ear, it tells you something.

QUESTIONS, QUESTIONS

Then Jesus asked a question—an uncomfortable question.

> *"Am I leading a rebellion," said Jesus, "that you have come out with swords and clubs to capture me? Every day I was with you, teaching in the temple courts, and you did not arrest me. But the Scriptures must be fulfilled."*
>
> Mark 14:48–49

God's questions always expose a person's true thoughts, and if the rabble had taken a moment to think, they would have realized the inconsistency of their actions. But they were so fixated in their determination to do away with Christ, even another encounter with the miraculous power of this man didn't deter them the least bit.

Fearing for their lives, the disciples fled into the night.

> *Then everyone deserted him and fled. Then the detachment of soldiers with its commander and the Jewish officials arrested Jesus. They bound him.*
>
> Mark 14:50; John 18:12

One can hardly read this without feeling some sense of incongruity. Jesus was only one individual. The detachment sent to arrest him would have numbered between 300 and 600 soldiers. In addition, there were Jewish officials, priests and servants. It was an overkill for sure, but you can't help wondering if deep down inside they felt a poverty of power. They rushed Jesus and bound him. Satan must have chortled with delight.

IN COURT

> *They took Jesus to the high priest, and all the chief priests, elders and teachers of the law came together.*
>
> Mark 14:53

Temple courts were not held at night. The fact that the Sanhedrin, consisting of seventy-one men, could be assembled so quickly tells you something about the plot. Their willingness to convene in the middle of the night reveals even more. What they were doing was strictly illegal according to their own law. Even for those not familiar with the judicial system of that day, the irregularities of the trial are painfully obvious. No matter. Forget the rules. They wanted Jesus dead.

The chief priests and the whole Sanhedrin were looking for evidence against Jesus so that they could put him to death, but they did not find any. Many testified falsely against him, but their statements did not agree.

Then the high priest stood up before them and asked Jesus, "Are you not going to answer? What is this testimony that these men are bringing against you?" But Jesus remained silent and gave no answer.   Mark 14:55–56, 60–61

ARE YOU GOD?

Again the high priest asked him, "Are you the Christ, the Son of the Blessed One?"   Mark 14:61

The question was black and white: "Are you God or not?"

"I am," said Jesus. "And you will see the Son of Man sitting at the right hand of the Mighty One and coming on the clouds of heaven."

The high priest tore his clothes. "Why do we need any more witnesses?" he asked. "You have heard the blasphemy. What do you think?"

They all condemned him as worthy of death.   Mark 14:62–64

The High Priest, Caiaphas, knew exactly what Jesus had said. Jesus was claiming to be God Himself. Blasphemy was anything that was considered injurious to God's character, and for a mere man to call himself *God* was sacrilege. But Jesus wasn't a mere man—he was God! However, neither Caiaphas nor the other Jewish leaders believed him. So they condemned Him to die. But there was a problem: the Sanhedrin did not have the authority to pass a death sentence; only the Romans could do that.

2 THE CRUCIFIXION

Because night courts were illegal, the Sanhedrin met again just after sunrise to go through the legal motions of trying Jesus. He must have been exhausted. He hadn't slept all night, and they had given him a severe beating just to make sure he knew who was in control.

Then the whole assembly rose and led him off to Pilate.
Luke 23:1

PONTIUS PILATE

Pontius Pilate, governor of Judea, had all the authority of imperial Rome behind him. Since in most cases the Jewish courts could not impose the death penalty, they needed Roman sanction. Pilate was their man. The temple leaders knew he was weak-kneed, so a little persuading was in order.

> *And they began to accuse him, saying, "We have found this man subverting our nation. He opposes payment of taxes to Caesar and claims to be Christ, a king."* Luke 23:2

Jesus had never prohibited his followers from paying taxes. In fact, Jesus had said quite the opposite. This was a deliberate lie. But with so many legalities having already been ignored, who was keeping track? On the other hand, it was true that Jesus claimed to be the Messiah!

> *So Pilate asked Jesus, "Are you the king of the Jews?"* Luke 23:3

> *Jesus said, "My kingdom is not of this world. If it were, my servants would fight to prevent my arrest by the Jews. But now my kingdom is from another place."* John 18:36

Jesus' reign began in the heart. He had no political ambitions.

> *"You are a king, then!" said Pilate.*

> *Jesus answered, "You are right in saying I am a king. In fact, for this reason I was born, and for this I came into the world, to testify to the truth. Everyone on the side of truth listens to me."*

> *"What is truth?" Pilate asked.* John 18:37–38

People still ask the same question today. But Pilate was in no mood for listening; he didn't even wait for the answer.

> *With this he went out again to the Jews and said, "I find no basis for a charge against him."* John 18:38

Pilate mistrusted the priests. As Roman governor, he knew he was hated by the Jews, and he had reason to believe that the priests did not have Caesar's best interests in mind. The Sanhedrin must have some other motive for wanting Jesus dead.

> *Then Pilate announced to the chief priests and the crowd, "I find no basis for a charge against this man."*

> *But they insisted, "He stirs up the people all over Judea by his teaching. He started in Galilee and has come all the way here."*

On hearing this, Pilate asked if the man was a Galilean. When he learned that Jesus was under Herod's jurisdiction, he sent him to Herod, who was also in Jerusalem at that time.

Luke 23:4–7

Pilate had the authority to hear Jesus' case, but the situation was getting uncomfortable. Jesus was being accused of inciting the people to insurrection. How would he explain to his superiors in Rome if Jesus did provoke a riot? It would be easier to dump the whole sorry mess in Herod's lap. Besides, Herod was no friend of his, so Pilate passed the buck.

HEROD ANTIPAS

Herod Antipas was a son of Herod the Great. As a puppet of Rome, he had been given jurisdiction over Jesus' home province of Galilee. He had traveled to Jerusalem for the yearly Passover festivities.

③④ Friday Morning Early: Jesus taken to Roman Fortress to appear before Pontius Pilate.

Thursday Night Late: Jesus arrested in the Garden of Gethsemane and taken to the house of the High Priest. It is thought they traveled around the northern wall to avoid Temple traffic. ❶❷

Friday Morning: Pilate sends Jesus to Herod who returns him to Pilate. ❹❺❹

Garden of Gethsemane

High Priest's House

❷❸ Friday Sunrise: After appearing before Annas, Caiaphas the High Priest, and the Sanhedrin in a middle of the night session, Jesus is taken to the Temple for a quick court before the Sanhedrin, to formalize accusations.

When Herod saw Jesus, he was greatly pleased, because for a long time he had been wanting to see him. From what he had heard about him, he hoped to see him perform some miracle. He plied him with many questions, but Jesus gave him no answer.   Luke 23:8–9

SILENT

Jesus knew that Herod had no interest in determining the truth. He only wished to be entertained by a miracle, showing his flagrant disrespect for Jesus' character. Jesus didn't indulge Herod. Instead, he remained quiet.

The chief priests and the teachers of the law were standing there, vehemently accusing him. Then Herod and his soldiers ridiculed and mocked him. Dressing him in an elegant robe, they sent him back to Pilate. That day Herod and Pilate became friends—before this they had been enemies.   Luke 23:10–12

CRUCIFY HIM!

Since his arrest, Jesus had been in five court sessions: three Jewish, and two Roman. This sixth trial would be his last. By this time, word had spread throughout the city. No longer were the High Priest and Sanhedrin the only ones accusing Jesus. They had been joined by a fickle multitude, who only a few days before had shouted, *"Hosanna,"* but who now vehemently roared, *"Crucify him!"* Pilate was in a dilemma. The more he dealt with Jesus, the more convinced he was that there was something uncommon about this man!

*Pilate called together the chief priests, the rulers and the people, and said to them, "You brought me this man as one who was inciting the people to rebellion. I have examined him in your presence and have found no basis for your charges against him. Neither has Herod, for he sent him back to us; as you can see, he has done nothing to deserve death. Therefore, I will **punish** him and then **release** him."*   Luke 23:13–16

Neither Herod nor Pilate could find Jesus guilty of anything deserving the death penalty. Indeed, it seemed no one could accuse him of any crime. So hoping to appease the crowd, Pilate offered a weak-kneed compromise. It had two parts:

1. He would whip Jesus:

This was no ordinary beating. The whip was comprised of a stick with leather thongs affixed to one end. Each thong had butterfly-shaped slivers of bone or metal attached to it. The condemned man would have his arms bound and tied above his head to a pole which fully exposed his back to the scourge. As the whip came down, the bone and metal would sink into the flesh. Pulling the whip away virtually stripped the flesh off the back. This type of beating was so severe that often the victim died.

By law a scourging could only be given to a convicted prisoner. Pilate himself had just said that Jesus was innocent. Because a Roman flogging was such a horrible ordeal, it can be assumed that Pilate hoped the whipping would appease Jesus' accusers so that they would accept his next offer.

2. He would release Jesus:

It was the local Roman custom to release one convicted criminal at the Passover as a gesture of goodwill. Pilate suggested that Jesus be released—after he had been beaten. The crowd was unanimous in their response:

> *With one voice they cried out, "Away with this man!"* ... *Wanting to release Jesus, Pilate appealed to them again. But they kept shouting, "Crucify him! Crucify him!"*
>
> *For the third time he spoke to them: "Why? What crime has this man committed? I have found in him no grounds for the death penalty. Therefore I will have him punished and then release him."* Luke 23:18,20–22
>
> *Then Pilate took Jesus and had him flogged.* John 19:1

The soldiers were not satisfied with the cruelty of a flogging. They decided to add a little jest.

> *The soldiers twisted together a crown of thorns and put it on his head. They clothed him in a purple robe and went up to him again and again, saying, "Hail, king of the Jews!" And they struck him in the face.* John 19:2–3

Humiliation was not part of Pilate's sentence. A purple robe was normally worn by royalty. The thorns were a cruel parody of an imperial crown. This was mockery at its worst.

700 years before this time, the prophet Isaiah had written:

> *He was despised and rejected by men, ... and we esteemed him not.* Isaiah 53:3

> *Once more Pilate came out and said to the Jews, "Look, I am bringing him out to you to let you know that I find no basis for a charge against him." When Jesus came out wearing the crown of thorns and the purple robe, Pilate said to them, "Here is the man!"* John 19:4–5

Deep in his heart, Pilate must have known that he was setting aside all justice. No doubt he had hopes that this lacerated, thorn-crowned, bleeding man might evoke some pity.

> *As soon as the chief priests and their officials saw him, they shouted, "Crucify! Crucify!"*

> *But Pilate answered, "You take him and crucify him. As for me, I find no basis for a charge against him."* John 19:6

Pilate knew very well that they could do no such thing. The Jewish courts could not impose the death sentence.

THE SON OF GOD

> *The Jews insisted, "We have a law, and according to that law he must die, because **he claimed to be the Son of God**."*

> *When Pilate heard this, he was even more afraid, and he went back inside the palace. "Where do you come from?" he asked Jesus ...* John 19:7–9

Pilate had just heard that Jesus was from Galilee, thus the reason for having sent him to Herod. Now, again, he was asking Jesus where he was from. No doubt he was feeling a little nervous about someone who claimed to be God! The Greeks believed the gods came down from

Mount Olympus to fraternize with man. Perhaps Pilate was wondering if Jesus fit that category. Certainly this was no ordinary criminal. Just the way he handled himself in court demonstrated a peace and confidence that was disconcerting. *Jesus, where are you really from?*

> ...Jesus gave him no answer. "Do you refuse to speak to me?" Pilate said. "Don't you realize I have power either to free you or to crucify you?"
>
> Jesus answered, "You would have no power over me if it were not given to you from above..."
>
> From then on, Pilate tried to set Jesus free, but the Jews kept shouting, "If you let this man go, you are no friend of Caesar. Anyone who claims to be a king opposes Caesar."
>
> When Pilate heard this, he brought Jesus out and sat down on the judge's seat at a place known as the Stone Pavement (which in Aramaic is Gabbatha). It was the day of Preparation of Passover Week... *John 19:9–14*

The *Day of Preparation* was when the Passover lamb was killed.

> "Here is your king," Pilate said to the Jews.
>
> But they shouted, "Take him away! Take him away! Crucify him!"
>
> "Shall I crucify your king?" Pilate asked.
>
> "We have no king but Caesar," the chief priests answered. *John 19:14–15*

This was Israel's final rejection of Jesus as their King. They had chosen the Roman Caesar in place of God.

> Finally Pilate handed him over to them to be crucified.
>
> So the soldiers took charge of Jesus. Carrying his own cross, he went out to the place of the Skull (which in Aramaic is called Golgotha).[2] Here they crucified him, and with him two others—one on each side and Jesus in the middle. *John 19:16–18*

CRUCIFIXION

Crucifixion was a Roman form of capital punishment used only for slaves and criminals of the lowest order. It was a common method of execution, and secular history records hundreds being crucified at one time. Research has indicated that there were several different forms:

Standing tree: The victim was simply backed up to a tree and tacked onto it, in whatever shape the branches flowed. Josephus, the first century Jewish historian, records the Roman soldiers entertaining themselves by crucifying captives in unusual positions.[3]

I-shaped: A simple post in the ground. Hands were nailed over the head.

X-shaped: Basically two logs planted at angles. The body was splayed out with the hands and feet fixed at four corners.

T-shaped: A pole with a cross bar on the top. This was probably the most common, next to the tree. The arms were stretched out along the bar.

†-shaped: Usually reserved for criminals of some notoriety. A certificate disclosing one's crime would be tacked to the topmost part of the cross. This was the type on which Jesus was crucified.

The victim was usually stretched out naked. Hands and feet were held in place by nails driven through the wrist and ankle bones.

 1000 years earlier, God had instructed King David to write a complete Psalm about the way Jesus would die. In it, David records[4] God as saying…

> …they have pierced my hands and my feet. I can count all my bones; people stare and gloat over me.
> Psalm 22:16–17

This was written long before the Romans had come to power, and about 800 years before the Romans adopted crucifixion as one of their official forms of capital punishment.

To this day crucifixion is considered to be the most brutal form of execution. Death was slow. Sometimes it took days. Ultimately, one died of asphyxiation. Hanging on out-stretched arms, the pressure on the diaphragm made it impossible for one to breathe. One could inhale only by lifting oneself up, by pulling on the arms and pushing with the feet to allow room for the diaphragm to work. Of course, this pulling and pushing was done against the excruciating restraint of the nails. Death came when exhaustion and shock left one unable to lift the body.

The nails and tormented gasping for air were not the only sources of anguish. One also suffered from thirst and exposure. People came to stare and, in Jesus' case, to mock.

> *Pilate had a notice prepared and fastened to the cross. It read: JESUS OF NAZARETH, THE KING OF THE JEWS. Many of the Jews read this sign, for the place where Jesus was crucified was near the city, and the sign was written in Aramaic, Latin and Greek.* John 19:19–20

> *When the soldiers crucified Jesus, they took his clothes, dividing them into four shares, one for each of them, with the undergarment remaining. This garment was seamless, woven in one piece from top to bottom.*

> *"Let's not tear it," they said to one another. "Let's decide by lot who will get it."* John 19:23–24

Gambling was a distraction from a gory task. As the soldiers sat beneath Jesus' cross, perhaps rolling dice in a helmet, they had no way of knowing they were fulfilling an ancient prophecy.

> *This happened that the scripture might be fulfilled which said, "They divided my garments among them and cast lots for my clothing." So this is what the soldiers did.* John 19:24 compare Psalm 22:18

> *The people stood watching, and the rulers even sneered at him. They said, "He saved others; let him save himself if he is the Christ of God, the Chosen One."* Luke 23:35

 Ten centuries earlier, King David had prophetically written that THE PROMISED DELIVERER would be mocked.

> *But I am a worm and not a man, scorned by men and despised by the people. All who see me mock me; they hurl insults, shaking their heads.* Psalm 22:6–7

Even the words of the ridicule were recorded by David.

> *"He trusts in the LORD; let the LORD rescue him. Let him deliver him, since he delights in him."* Psalm 22:8

> *The soldiers also came up and mocked him. They offered him wine vinegar and said, "If you are the king of the Jews, save yourself."*

> *One of the criminals who hung there hurled insults at him: "Aren't you the Christ? Save yourself and us!"*

> *But the other criminal rebuked him. "Don't you fear God," he said, "since you are under the same sentence?*

We are punished justly, for we are getting what our deeds deserve. But this man has done nothing wrong."

Then he said, "Jesus, remember me when you come into your kingdom."

Jesus answered him, "I tell you the truth, today you will be with me in paradise." Luke 23:36–37,39–43

Jesus assured the thief that as soon as they both died, their spirits would meet each other in Paradise. Jesus could say this because he knew that this man was trusting in Him to deliver him from the consequences of sin—from eternal punishment.

It was now about the sixth hour, and darkness came over the whole land until the ninth hour… Luke 23:44

And at the ninth hour Jesus cried out in a loud voice, "Eloi, Eloi, lama sabachthani?"—which means, "My God, my God, why have you forsaken me?" Mark 15:34

Once again, a 1000 years before, King David had written that THE MESSIAH would say just those words.

> *"My God, my God, why have you forsaken me?"*
> Psalm 22:1

It wasn't without reason that Jesus cried this out loud. We will look at its meaning in a following chapter.

The significance of Jesus' final moments on the cross cannot be emphasized enough. The Bible says...

> *Jesus called out with a loud voice, ... "It is finished... Father, into your hands I commit my spirit." When he had said this, he breathed his last... he bowed his head and gave up his spirit.* Luke 23:46 and John 19:30

> *The curtain of the temple was torn in two from top to bottom.* Mark 15:38

Jesus was dead. It's not hard to imagine the whole realm of evil being ecstatic.[5] Satan and his demons had succeeded beyond their wildest dreams. From their perspective, they had killed God. THE PROMISED DELIVERER was dead! But a couple of things did not sit well with Satan. Why had the temple curtain torn—from top to bottom? And why had Jesus shouted *It is finished!* with such intensity?

THE TORN CURTAIN

Remember, the Temple was a permanent replica of the original Tabernacle. The curtain in question separated the Holy Place from the sacred Holy of Holies. It was no small matter for this veil to be torn.

First of all, the Bible says that the curtain shielded the Most Holy Place from man's view. To look behind the curtain was to die. God had told Moses centuries before...

> *"Tell your brother Aaron not to come whenever he chooses into the Most Holy Place behind the curtain in front of the atonement cover on the ark, or else he will die, because I appear in the cloud over the atonement cover."* Leviticus 16:2

Second, to tear the curtain in any way would have been a monumental task. It is said that the curtain was sixty feet in height (18 m) and thirty feet in width (9 m), being the thickness of a man's hand—about four inches (10 cm).[6]

Third, to be torn from the top to the bottom could only mean one thing: God had rent the curtain, not man.

By Jewish reckoning, Jesus died at the ninth hour, which would have been 3:00 p.m. The temple would have been full of priests performing their sacred duties. This was the time of the evening sacrifice, when a lamb was killed. It was also the Passover. News of the torn curtain could not have been concealed. Too many people were present, and the event was too staggering to be forgotten.

The significance of this whole incident will be explained shortly.

IT IS FINISHED!

The phrase "It is finished" is translated from a single Greek word *tetelestai*. *Tetelestai* had many different usages, but the following three have significance to the story:[7]

> 1. *Tetelestai* was used by a servant reporting to his or her master upon completing a task: "The job you gave me is finished."

> 2. *Tetelestai* was also a familiar term in Greek commercial life. It signified the completion of a transaction when a debt was paid in full. When the final payment was made, one could say *"tetelestai,"* that is, "The debt is finished." Ancient receipts for taxes have been found with *tete-lestai*—paid in full—written across them.

3. The selection of a lamb for sacrifice in the temple was always an important time. The flock would be searched and, upon finding an unblemished lamb, one would say *tetelestai*—the job was finished.

Quite literally Jesus shouted: "The work you gave me is completed, the debt is paid, the sacrificial lamb is found." The Scripture says Jesus cried out in a *loud* voice, "*It is finished.*"

> *The centurion, seeing what had happened, praised God and said, "Surely this was a righteous man."*   Luke 23:47

It is noteworthy that it was the centurion, an officer in charge of 100 soldiers, who immediately commented upon Jesus' cry. Surely he, a military man, knew the difference between a gasp of defeat and a shout of victory.

> *Now it was the day of Preparation, and the next day was to be a special Sabbath. Because the Jews did not want the bodies left on the crosses during the Sabbath, they asked Pilate to have the legs broken and the bodies taken down.*   John 19:31

BREAK THE LEGS

It was Passover week and this day was the climax, when the lamb was to be killed. The chief priests wanted this crucifixion business over and done with, so as not to contaminate the feast. They asked that Jesus' legs be broken. This would mean that the one being crucified could no longer lift himself up to breathe, resulting in quick asphyxiation, unless the shock of his bones being broken killed him first.

> *The soldiers therefore came and broke the legs of the first man who had been crucified with Jesus, and then those of the other. But when they came to Jesus and found that he was already dead, **they did not break his legs.** Instead, one of the soldiers pierced Jesus' side with a spear, bringing a sudden flow of blood and water.*
>
> *The man who saw it has given testimony, and his testimony is true. He knows that he tells the truth, and he testifies so that you also may believe. These things happened so that the scripture would be fulfilled: "Not one of his bones will be broken," and, as another scripture says, "They will look on the one they have pierced."*
>   John 19:32–37

3 THE BURIAL AND RESURRECTION

FRIDAY: LATE AFTERNOON

Later, Joseph of Arimathea asked Pilate for the body of Jesus. Now Joseph was a disciple of Jesus, but secretly because he feared the Jews. With Pilate's permission, he came and took the body away. He was accompanied by Nicodemus, the man who earlier had visited Jesus at night. Nicodemus brought a mixture of myrrh and aloes, about seventy-five pounds. Taking Jesus' body, the two of them wrapped it, with the spices, in strips of linen. This was in accordance with Jewish burial customs. At the place where Jesus was crucified, there was a garden, and in the garden a new tomb, in which no one had ever been laid. Because it was the Jewish day of Preparation and since the tomb was nearby, they laid Jesus there.

John 19:38–42

The women who had come with Jesus from Galilee followed Joseph and saw the tomb and how his body was laid in it. Then they went home and prepared spices and perfumes. But they rested on the Sabbath in obedience to the commandment.

Luke 23:55–56

Though Joseph and Nicodemus were part of the Sanhedrin, it seems they did not reject the evidence that Jesus was truly God. According to their traditional custom, they wrapped Jesus in long burial cloths, intermingled with seventy-five pounds (34 kg) of aromatic spices and laid him in a tomb. A large wheel-like stone, possibly weighing as much as two tons (1.8 tonne), was rolled across the front of the sepulcher. The women watched and then went home to prepare additional spices for the final burial. It was now Friday night.

SATURDAY

The next day, the one after Preparation Day, the chief priests and the Pharisees went to Pilate. "Sir," they said, "we remember that while he was still alive that deceiver said, 'After three days I will rise again.' So give the order for the tomb to be made secure until the third day. Otherwise, his disciples may come and steal the body and tell the people that he has been raised from the dead. This last deception will be worse than the first."

"Take a guard," Pilate answered. *"Go, make the tomb as secure as you know how."* So they went and made the tomb secure by putting a seal on the stone and posting the guard.*

Matthew 27:62–66

This was no rag-tag band of soldiery that was sent to guard the tomb. A Roman guard consisted of four to sixteen men, each man trained to protect six feet of ground. Together they were capable of defending themselves against an entire battalion.[8]

Pilate instructed the chief priests and Pharisees to seal the tomb. Ropes would have been stretched across the large stone door and fixed in place with moist clay. The clay would then be imprinted with a signet ring. Any tampering with the rock would be immediately apparent.

Sunday

The guard was set in place on Saturday, the Jewish Sabbath. On Sunday while it was still dark...

There was a violent earthquake, for an angel of the Lord came down from heaven and, going to the tomb, rolled back the stone and sat on it. His appearance was like lightning, and his clothes were white as snow. The guards were so afraid of him that they shook and became like dead men.

Matthew 28:2–4

It took only a glance for these rough and rugged soldiers to know they were no match for this one angel. The last phrase in the above passage is a first century way of saying they passed out from fear! But they weren't the only ones shaking. The whole realm of evil must have been in chaos. It's not hard to imagine what it was like—Satan in confusion, shouting jumbled orders as demons scrambled in disarray. What a shock! Who would have dreamed that the tomb could be empty. Jesus had obviously come back to life. Impossible!

IN THE MEANTIME ...

...Mary Magdalene, Mary the mother of James, and Salome bought spices so that they might go to anoint Jesus' body. Very early on the first day of the week, just after sunrise, they were on their way to the tomb and they asked each other, "Who will roll the stone away from the entrance of the tomb?"

But when they looked up, they saw that the stone, which was very large, had been rolled away.   Mark 16:1–4

Mary Magdalene apparently turned away in shock and dismay at the initial sight of the open tomb. She probably assumed the obvious—Jesus' body had been vandalized. Sobbing, she turned and ran to tell the disciples. But Mary and Salome pushed forward and entered the tomb.

As they entered the tomb, they saw a young man dressed in a white robe sitting on the right side, and they were alarmed.

"Don't be alarmed," he said. "You are looking for Jesus the Nazarene, who was crucified. He has risen! He is not here. See the place where they laid him."

"But go, tell his disciples and Peter, 'He is going ahead of you into Galilee. There you will see him, just as he told you.'"   Mark 16:5–7

So the women hurried away from the tomb, afraid yet filled with joy, and ran to tell his disciples.

Suddenly Jesus met them. "Greetings," he said. They came to him, clasped his feet and worshiped him. Then Jesus said to them, "Do not be afraid. Go and tell my brothers to go to Galilee; there they will see me."   Matthew 28:8–10

He has Risen

Reading the record,[9] you can sense the confusion and excitement of the early morning news. For those who had seen Jesus die, the report from the elated women was met with a great deal of skepticism. Initially...

> ...they did not believe the women, because their words seemed to them like nonsense.　　　　　*Luke 24:11*

Peter ran to check out the tomb. John ran too, passing Peter on the way, but then waited outside the entrance.

> Then Simon Peter, who was behind him, arrived and went into the tomb. He saw the strips of linen lying there, as well as the burial cloth that had been around Jesus' head. The cloth was folded up by itself, separate from the linen.　　　　　*John 20:6–7*

This was not the scene of a plundered grave. The long strips of cloth used to shroud the body were still wrapped as though around a corpse, but they were collapsed—empty! The body had passed right through them. The head napkin was folded too, as if someone had tidied up before leaving. The Bible says Peter saw, but John saw and believed. For John there was no doubt that Jesus was alive! But Peter's head was spinning. He needed time to think.

It still must have been early morning when Mary Magdalene returned and...

> ...stood outside the tomb crying. As she wept, she bent over to look into the tomb and saw two angels in white, seated where Jesus' body had been, one at the head and the other at the foot.
>
> They asked her, "Woman, why are you crying?"
>
> "They have taken my Lord away," she said, "and I don't know where they have put him."　　　　　*John 20:11–13*

The tomb was located in a garden, so perhaps she supposed these angels were gardeners. Mary was so distressed that she did not think to identify the men. We must remember that Mary was grieving intensely and that the entire conversation was carried on through her sobbing.

> At this, she turned around and saw Jesus standing there, but she did not realize that it was Jesus.

"Woman," he said, "why are you crying? Who is it you are looking for?"

Thinking he was the gardener, she said, "Sir, if you have carried him away, tell me where you have put him, and I will get him."

Jesus said to her, "Mary." John 20:14–16

If one can say a name in such a way that it brings back all the memories of every previous encounter with a loved one, then Jesus did just that. Mary recognized the voice immediately.

She turned toward him and cried out in Aramaic, "Rabboni!" (which means Teacher). John 20:16

Now she had a different reason to weep. She must have flung her arms around him, perhaps embracing his feet in keeping with the custom of that day.

Jesus said, "Do not hold on to me, for I have not yet returned to the Father. Go instead to my brothers and tell them..."

Mary Magdalene went to the disciples with the news: "I have seen the Lord!" John 20:17–18

The Guards

While all this was happening, the guards were hunting down the chief priests. There was no way they were going back to face Pilate.

> While the women were on their way, some of the guards went into the city and reported to the chief priests everything that had happened. When the chief priests had met with the elders and devised a plan, they gave the soldiers a large sum of money, telling them, "You are to say, 'His disciples came during the night and stole him away while we were asleep.' If this report gets to the governor, we will satisfy him and keep you out of trouble." So the soldiers took the money and did as they were instructed. And this story has been widely circulated among the Jews to this very day.
> Matthew 28:11–15

It took an immense sum of money to persuade these proud soldiers to say that they had been sleeping. But it wasn't true. Once again you can see the hand of Satan behind it all, rushing around doing damage control. After all, he is the *father of lies*. It was an anemic effort to save face. No doubt, Satan realized that he was defeated. Jesus, The Anointed One, had crushed Satan's head, just as God had promised way back in the Garden of Eden.

Alive

Jesus had come back to life! He was truly alive—physically! For three days his body had laid lifeless in the tomb, separated from his spirit. But then in a dramatic demonstration of supernatural power, Jesus had been resurrected with a new body.

Jesus had foretold his own death during his ministry.

> "The reason my Father loves me is that I lay down my life—only to take it up again. No one takes it from me, but I lay it down of my own accord. I have authority to lay it down and authority to take it up again…" John 10:17–18

Why Did Jesus Have To Die?

Jesus' death had not been an ordinary one. For mankind, death is a consequence of sin—of breaking God's law. But Jesus had kept the ten commands perfectly. He was sinless, so he did not need to die. According to the *law of sin and death*,

Jesus could have lived forever. So why did he die? Satan hadn't killed Jesus against His will; nor had the Jews or the Romans. Jesus had chosen to die, willingly. But why? The succeeding chapters will answer that question.

The events of that early morn were just a beginning. Over the next forty days, Jesus appeared to many of those who knew him best. But before we leave the resurrection day, there is one more account that must be shared.

72 HOURS THAT CHANGED HISTORY

THU Disciples prepare Passover
Passover Supper
Walk to Garden of Gethsemane
Jesus arrested in Garden; disciples flee

FRI 1st Trial — before Chief Priest's father-in-law, Annas
2nd Trial — before Chief Priest and Sanhedrin
3rd Trial — before Sanhedrin (to make it legal)
6:30 am 4th Trial — before Pilate
5th Trial — before Herod (Jesus mocked)
6th Trial — before Pilate (Jesus scourged)

9:00 am Crucifixion

NOON

3:00 pm Jesus cries, "It is finished;" Temple curtain torn
Legs of two thieves broken; Jesus' side pierced
Joseph of Arimathea requests Jesus' body for burial
Jesus buried in tomb

SAT

Roman guard requested and placed at tomb

Tomb sealed

SUN Earthquake - stone rolled away by angels; guards flee
Women go to tomb
Jesus appears to Mary and Salome
Jesus appears to Mary Magdalene
Jesus appears to Peter

Jewish Friday

Jewish Saturday

Jewish Sunday

*Jewish days begin at sundown, continue through the night into the next day until the following sundown.

CHAPTER FOURTEEN

1 THE STRANGER

2 THE EMMAUS ROAD MESSAGE
— ADAM TO NOAH —

3 THE EMMAUS ROAD MESSAGE
— ABRAHAM TO THE LAW —

4 THE EMMAUS ROAD MESSAGE
— THE TABERNACLE TO THE BRAZEN SERPENT —

5 THE EMMAUS ROAD MESSAGE
— JOHN THE BAPTIST TO THE RESURRECTION —

1 The Stranger

Now that same day two of them were going to a village called Emmaus, about seven miles from Jerusalem. They were talking with each other about everything that had happened. As they talked and discussed these things with each other, Jesus himself came up and walked along with them; but they were kept from recognizing him.

He asked them, "What are you discussing together as you walk along?"

They stood still, their faces downcast. Luke 24:13–17

These disciples were not part of the inner circle, but they too, were followers of Jesus.

One of them, named Cleopas, asked him, "Are you only a visitor to Jerusalem and do not know the things that have happened there in these days?"

"What things?" he asked.

"About Jesus of Nazareth," they replied. "He was a prophet, powerful in word and deed before God and all the people. The chief priests and our rulers handed him over to be sentenced to death, and they crucified him; but we had hoped that he was the one who was going to redeem [or set free] Israel. And what is more, it is the third day since all this took place. In addition, some of our women amazed us. They went to the tomb early this morning but didn't find his body. They came and told us that they had seen a vision of angels, who said he was alive. Then some of our companions went to the tomb and found it just as the women had said, but him they did not see." Luke 24:18–24

The two disciples gave a brief synopsis of the day. Of course, all of this was not news to Jesus, but he quietly waited for them to finish. He had news for them too.

He said to them, "How foolish you are, and how slow of heart to believe all that the prophets have spoken! Did not the Christ have to suffer these things and then enter his glory?" And beginning with Moses and all the Prophets, he explained to them what was said in all the Scriptures concerning himself. Luke 24:25–27

Jesus told them that THE MESSIAH *had to* suffer, die and then come back to life. He said it was necessary. You can be sure this raised some eyebrows. But Jesus didn't stop there. He went back into the Jewish Scriptures and taught them about himself, starting at the very beginning. He then progressed step by step, story by story, through the entire Bible. It must have been quite a lesson.

> *As they approached the village to which they were going, Jesus acted as if he were going farther. But they urged him strongly, "Stay with us, for it is nearly evening; the day is almost over." So he went in to stay with them.*
>
> *When he was at the table with them, he took bread, gave thanks, broke it and began to give it to them. Then their eyes were opened and they recognized him, and he disappeared from their sight. They asked each other, "Were not our hearts burning within us while he talked with us on the road and opened the Scriptures to us?"* Luke 24:28–32

God himself had lit a fire of understanding in their minds. They were excited!

> *They got up and returned at once to Jerusalem.* Luke 24:33

You can imagine the trip back to the city as these elated men discussed what they would say to the eleven disciples. The journey was all uphill, but they must have pushed themselves. They had good news!

> *There they found the *Eleven and those with them, assembled together and saying, "It is true! The Lord has risen and has appeared to Simon." Then the two told what had happened on the way, and how Jesus was recognized by them when he broke the bread.*
>
> *Judas Iscariot had committed suicide.
>
> *While they were still talking about this, Jesus himself stood among them and said to them, "Peace be with you."*
>
> *They were startled and frightened, thinking they saw a ghost. He said to them, "Why are you troubled, and why do doubts rise in your minds? Look at my hands and my feet. It is I myself! Touch me and see; a ghost does not have flesh and bones, as you see I have."*
>
> *When he had said this, he showed them his hands and feet. And while they still did not believe it because of joy*

and amazement, he asked them, "Do you have anything here to eat?" They gave him a piece of broiled fish, and he took it and ate it in their presence.

He said to them, "This is what I told you while I was still with you: Everything must be fulfilled that is written about me in the Law of Moses, the Prophets and the Psalms."

Luke 24:33–44

Just as he had done earlier with the two men on the road to Emmaus, Jesus used the Bible to explain all the events surrounding his death, burial and resurrection. The Jews divide the Scriptures into three sections—the Law, the Writings (or Psalms) and the Prophets. Jesus took each of those segments and showed the disciples how it all applied to him.

Then he opened their minds so they could understand the Scriptures. He told them, "This is what is written: The Christ will suffer and rise from the dead on the third day, and repentance and forgiveness of sins will be preached in his name to all nations, beginning at Jerusalem. You are witnesses of these things."

Luke 24:45–48

Jesus said his death, burial and resurrection, **must happen** to fulfill Scripture. He went on to say this was such good news that it would be told everywhere, beginning at Jerusalem.

Before we go on with the story we want to stop and go back to the beginning, just as Jesus did with his disciples. We want to see what Jesus said about himself in the Law, the Prophets and the Psalms.

Exactly why did Jesus come to the earth, and why did he *have to* suffer and die, when all along he planned to come back to life?

Why didn't he simply tell people to believe in him and skip the entire crucifixion?

What were these events all about—this death, burial and resurrection?

The last piece of the puzzle is about to be put in place. When you understand this, you will have the whole picture.

2 The Emmaus Road Message

— Adam to Noah —

To answer this question…Why did Jesus have to die?…we will go back in time, and start at the very beginning.

Adam and Eve

Remember the unique friendship that existed between God and man at the onset of creation? The Lord made man, not as a robot, but with a will, so that by the obedient choices he made he would honor God, just as an obedient son honors his father.

You will recall that through obedience man enjoyed tremendous benefits from this relationship, for the Lord of the universe was committed to Adam and Eve's well-being, walking and talking with them as their friend.

But then Adam and Eve deliberately ignored God's instructions and experimented with forbidden knowledge. Since the events surrounding this incident contain critical elements of the puzzle, the Scripture uses some powerful word pictures to help us understand what happened.

LOST

The Bible says that man felt he knew *better than God* what was good for him. He chose his own path, to do his own thing, but that path led into a spiritual wilderness. Man was LOST.

ENEMY

Instead of listening to God, man trusted and believed Satan. Man joined Satan's rebellious ranks, thus becoming an ENEMY of God.

But such a choice had ramifications. The Scripture teaches us that sin's effects are very costly.

ESTRANGED

Because there was no trust, there was no relationship. Immediately, the unique friendship between God and man ended. Separated by sin, man was ESTRANGED from the perfect, holy God. God was no longer close. He seemed remote and distant.

SLAVE

Satan was not the benevolent friend God had been. Rather, the Devil manipulated man with lies to do his satanic will. Man became a SLAVE to Satan and a slave to sin.

In choosing his own way, man disobeyed the one command that God had given him. This wasn't without hurt or harm, for whenever you break a law, you also face a consequence.

GUILTY

God took off his mantle of friendship and donned a magistrate's cloak. As man's judge, God found man GUILTY of a crime—of breaking his law, of sinning against a holy God.

DEBTOR

In essence, God wrote out a verdict, *a Certificate of Debt.* Man was now a DEBTOR with a price to pay. The penalty for sin was death.

DEAD

SEPARATED

ETERNAL JUDGMENT

Every human being would now DIE physically. The spirit would be *separated* from the body; the life *separated* from family and friends.

Because the stench of sin corrupted man's total being, God *separated* himself from mankind. Man's relationship with God was over—it was DEAD.

After physical death, there would be a SECOND DEATH. Man would be *separated* forever from God and his expressions of love. He would be confined in the Lake of Fire, the place that had been prepared for Satan and his demons.

Death in its three aspects ruled man's life, and he could do nothing about it. Man had no choice as to whether he wanted to die or not. It was a bitter, potent reality that all faced; that all shared; that all who thought soberly, feared. With absolute, utter finality, the Scripture clearly states…

> …*a person shall die for his own sin.*   2 Chronicles 25:4 NKJV

These word pictures help us understand just how far removed from God mankind had become as a result of Adam and Eve's sin. Man was faced with that age-old question: **How can we get rid of our *sin with all its consequences* and gain a *righteousness equal to God's righteousness* so we can be accepted back into his presence?**

A DESPERATE ATTEMPT

Remember how Adam and Eve tried to cover up their sin by clothing themselves in fig leaves? We saw that, though the Lord rejected their efforts, he did not leave them in a lurch. Rather, he…

> …devises ways so that a banished person may not remain estranged from him. 2 Samuel 14:14

The Lord used these events to teach Adam and Eve, as well as us, universal principles that apply to all mankind.

ACCEPTANCE

Just as Adam and Eve could not make themselves acceptable to God by fixing up their outward appearance, neither can we be accepted based on our externals. We may impress others with what we are on the outside, but God knows what we are really like.

We saw that God provided Adam and Eve with a way of acceptance, but on different terms. The Bible says that…

> The LORD God made garments of skin for Adam and his wife and clothed them. Genesis 3:21

The significance of this little verse would be overlooked if it wasn't for other parts of the Bible explaining it. So what does it mean? What would Jesus have told the disciples? Very simply this: Just as an animal had to die to clothe Adam and Eve in acceptable clothing, *so Jesus had to die to make us acceptable in the presence of God.* This was and is God's idea. It's God's way to acceptability.

As the disciples struggled to comprehend what Jesus was saying, there must have been a torrent of questions.

Why would God require an animal to die for Adam and Eve? Why didn't God simply clothe them with his choice of leaves? And why would Jesus have to die for us? Was there not another way?

We can suppose that Jesus continued with the next story.

CAIN AND ABEL

Remember how the children of Adam and Eve brought sacrifices to God? Why did they do that? We saw that the escape route God devised had two dimensions.

There was an *inward* aspect—something they had to work through in their hearts, a choice Cain and Abel each had to make on their own.

There was also an *outward* aspect—a visual aid to help them understand what it would take to remove sin.

Remember how we saw that when Cain and Abel brought their sacrifices to God, Cain brought vegetables from his garden but Abel brought the firstborn of his flock? God rejected Cain's sacrifice, but he accepted Abel's. Why?

CAIN

Inward: Cain did not believe God. He had his own ideas about how to get rid of sin and be made right with the Lord.

In the same way, our world is full of people who have their own notions about God and how to please him. It's become fashionable to have a personally tailored theory. A custom-designed god is in vogue. Cain would have felt right at home.

Outward: Based on his thinking, Cain did his own thing. He brought a sacrifice that did not illustrate God's way of dealing with the sin problem. Vegetables do not shed blood. Cain ignored the fact that...

> ...*without the shedding of blood there is no forgiveness.*
> Hebrews 9:22

His sacrifice did not provide an *atonement-covering* for sin. The Bible tells us...

> *Do not be like Cain, who belonged to the evil one... his own actions were evil and his brother's were righteous.*
> 1 John 3:12

Abel

On the other hand, God accepted Abel's sacrifice.

Inward: Abel was trusting the Lord to be his Savior. This is what God wanted. God still wants people to trust him. We are told repeatedly throughout the pages of Scripture, that we are to trust the Lord Jesus Christ as our Savior.

Outward: God accepted Abel's sacrifice because it illustrated what Jesus accomplished on the cross.

❖ It pictured **substitution**: Just as an innocent animal died in Abel's place, so Jesus, innocent of all sin, died in our place, paying the death penalty for us.

For Christ died for sins once for all, the righteous for the unrighteous, to bring you to God.   1 Peter 3:18

❖ It pictured **atonement**: Just as an animal shed its blood so Abel might have a covering for sin, in the same way Jesus offered himself as the ultimate blood sacrifice so we might have forgiveness of sin.

The Bible says that the relationship that was broken by disobedience is now restored through Jesus' death on the cross.

*Once you were alienated from God and were **enemies**…*

*But now he has **reconciled** you by Christ's physical body through death…* Colossians 1:21–22

As children of Adam and Eve, we were born into this world as *enemies* of God…

ENEMY

…but now because of Jesus' physical death on the cross, we are *reconciled*. We can be friends again. The broken relationship has been restored.

RECONCILED

Some may say, "Okay, I can see how Jesus' death took care of our sin problem, but how do we gain *a righteousness equal to God's righteousness* so we can be accepted back into his presence?"

As we said many chapters ago, this question has two facets, like opposite sides of the same coin. They are related. You can't divide them. When God took care of our sin problem, he also addressed the lack of righteousness. We will understand this more in just a few pages.

NOAH

In the days of Noah the people ignored God's Word. Perhaps they thought the old man was crazy. Whatever the case, they persuaded themselves that life existed only for the here and now. God did not withhold his judgment just because they had the wrong philosophy of life. They perished in their foolishness.

God was saying this: just as the people of Noah's day were judged for their sin, so God will judge all men, regardless of how they think.

> The fool says in his heart, "There is no God." Psalm 53:1; 14:1

> He who trusts in his own heart is a fool … Proverbs 28:26 NKJV

God will let us ignore him and even reject his way of escape for a time, but eventually we must face the inescapable conclusion: we must pay our sin-debt with our eternal death.

Remember how Noah and his sons were kept safe in the Ark? There was only one boat, and only one door to enter and gain refuge from the flood. There was no other option.

In the same way, Jesus Christ is the only way to eternal life. Just as safety could only be found inside the Ark, so only in Jesus can we find safety from everlasting punishment.

> Jesus answered, "I am the way and the truth and the life. No one comes to the Father except through me." John 14:6

There is only one way to God. Those who ignore or reject *the way* face the same fate as those who didn't heed Noah's warnings of the coming flood: eternal death with all its implications.

The Bible is very explicit. Jesus is the only way to God.

Babel

Remember how we saw that Babel was the first incident of organized religion in the Bible? The people tried to build a tower to reach the heavens. We said that a definition for the word religion is this: *man's efforts to reach God.* At Babel, man slaved away with brick and tar. In the same way, religion is a taskmaster that requires constant struggle. It demands ever-increasing efforts to please God, gods, spirits or idols.

In contrast to religion, the Bible says that the only true way to God was provided by the Lord himself, when in his mercy, *God reached down to man* in the person of Jesus Christ. All the work needed to restore the broken relationship was done by Jesus on the cross.

You can almost see the glimmer of excitement in the disciples' eyes as they listened to God's plan through thousands of years of history being fulfilled in Jesus. For centuries, man had looked forward to the day when he would be delivered from judgment of sin. Now that time had come. But Jesus wasn't finished with his explanation. He continued, no doubt, with the story of Abraham and Isaac.

3 The Emmaus Road Message
— Abraham to the Law —

The disciples must have leaned forward as Jesus launched into his explanation of the story of Abraham and Isaac. They were all direct descendants of these two men.

Remember when God asked Abraham to sacrifice his son? Isaac was under God's order to die and, in reality, he deserved to die for he was a sinner. Isaac was bound and placed on the altar—helpless.

What God was saying is this: Just as Isaac was helpless and could not save himself, so all of us are bound by sin and cannot save ourselves from its consequences.

Remember how Abraham took the knife and prepared to plunge it into Isaac? Abraham was trusting in God's goodness to provide a solution to death. At the last moment, God called from Heaven and stopped him. Because of Abraham's trust, the Lord provided a *substitute* sacrifice for Isaac.

A SUBSTITUTE

Just as the ram died in Isaac's place, so *Jesus died in our place*. We should have died and been punished for our sin, but Jesus died and took our punishment on the cross. He is *our* substitute.

If the ram had not died, then Isaac would have perished. If Jesus had not died, then we would have had to pay our *own* sin-debt.

The Bible says that God honored Abraham's faith.

> *"Abraham believed God, and it was credited to him as righteousness."*   Romans 4:3

Remember that *Certificate of Debt* that every human has as a result of sin? The Bible says that God *credited righteousness* to Abraham's account because of his faith. God did that for Abraham because the Lord was looking ahead to what Jesus would do on the cross. The Bible says that...

> *The words "it was credited to him" were written **not for him** [Abraham] **alone, but also for us**, to whom God will credit righteousness—for us who believe in him who raised Jesus our Lord from the dead.*   Romans 4:23–24

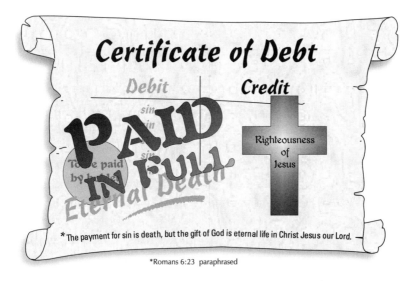

* The payment for sin is death, but the gift of God is eternal life in Christ Jesus our Lord.

*Romans 6:23 paraphrased

DEBTOR

Down through history, every person had carried a *Certificate of Debt*, a massive sin-debt that each one was accountable to pay. The only way that debt could be paid was with one's own eternal death.

CANCELED DEBT

But then Jesus came. His death completely paid man's sin-debt—past, present and future. That is why Jesus cried, "It is finished." *The debt is paid!*

But the payment made by Jesus is only effective if one believes. The Bible says...

*... God will credit righteousness—**for us who believe** in him who raised Jesus our Lord from the dead.*   Romans 4:24

Remember that the word *believe,* as used in the Bible, has a fuller meaning than we sometimes give it.

❖ The terms *faith, belief, trust* and *confidence* all mean essentially the same.

❖ Genuine faith is built on fact (i.e. "Jesus died in our place for our sin"). Faith is not built on *feeling forgiven.*

❖ True biblical belief does not stop with mental assent to the truth. It includes a *heart trust,* a confidence in the facts expressed by a voluntary act of the will. We choose to believe (e.g. "**I** believe that Jesus has paid **my** sin-debt").

All of this would have been good news to the disciples. It should be good news to us as well. The Bible says...

... everything that was written in the past was written to teach us, so that through endurance and the encouragement of the Scriptures we might have hope.   Romans 15:4

The accounts of Abraham and Isaac were stories that the disciples knew well. Although they had heard them since childhood, now they were seeing the whole picture for the first time. As Jesus spoke, one could have heard a pin drop. Every eye was glued on him, THE PROMISED SAVIOR, now in their midst. Jesus continued.

THE PASSOVER

Remember when the children of Israel were slaves in Egypt and God delivered them from Pharaoh with great plagues? The last plague was the death of the first-born child. God had said that if the Israelites followed his Word, they would be safe from this tragedy.

Do you recall how the Israelites were to sacrifice a lamb? Well, the Bible tells us that Jesus is our Lamb.

It seems hardly a coincidence that, from the time of Jesus' birth, he was identified with these harmless creatures. He was born in a stable, a place where little lambs could be sheltered. His first visitors were shepherds, men who cared for lambs and made sure that they came to no harm. We are told that Bethlehem, his birth city, was commissioned by the high priests as a place to raise lamb sacrifices for use in the Temple. John the Baptist said of Jesus:

> "Look, the Lamb of God, who takes away the sin of the world!"
> John 1:29

So when we find Jesus identified as the Passover lamb, we shouldn't be surprised. The parallels are stunning. I will mention only a few.

Remember how the Passover lamb could have *no defect*?
Jesus was *sinless*.

The lamb had to be a *male*.
Jesus was a *man*.

The Passover lamb was killed, dying *in the place of* the first-born.
Jesus died *in our place*.

The blood of the lamb was applied to the door posts and lintel of the house.
> Just as safety was only found by remaining inside, so only by trusting in what Jesus did on the cross brings us safety from eternal death.

When the death angel came, wherever he saw the blood applied, he would *pass over* that house.
> In the same way, God provided a way for his judgment to *pass over* us, and in so doing all the judgment we deserved came to rest upon Jesus.

God had specifically told the Israelites that they must not break any bones when they ate the Passover lamb. This was because the lamb was a *picture*, a foreshadow of Jesus. Jesus' bones were not broken either. When the Roman soldiers...

> ...came to Jesus and found that he was already dead, they did not break his legs.
> John 19:33

As the disciples sat there, hanging onto every word, listening to Jesus explain the real significance of the Passover, they couldn't help but think of what time of year it was. Jesus had been crucified on the very day the Passover lamb died! They had no way of knowing that the priests had hoped to kill him after the feast was over, but they did know that God's plan had triumphed. Jesus not only died on the right day, but he died at the ninth hour (3:00 P.M.), the very hour the temple lamb was offered—the hour of the evening sacrifice. He died right on schedule, just as the Bible said he would.[1] The Scripture says...

> ... Christ, our Passover lamb, has been sacrificed.
>
> 1 Corinthians 5:7

THE LAW

Remember the Ten Commandments? The Israelites thought that it would be easy to obey them. Today, many people believe that you can please God by keeping the ten rules, or some modified version of them. But we saw from our study that God expects nothing less than perfect obedience.

> For whoever keeps the whole law and yet stumbles at just one point is guilty of breaking all of it.
>
> James 2:10

Trying to keep the Ten Commandments does not restore the broken relationship with God.

> Therefore no one will be declared righteous in his sight by observing the law; rather, through the law we become conscious of sin.
>
> Romans 3:20

The law reminds us of our age-old, two-sides-of-the-coin dilemma. *We have something we don't want—sin; and we need something we don't have—righteousness.* The Ten Commandments cannot give us a *righteousness equal to God's righteousness.*

> But now a righteousness from God, apart from law, has been made known, to which the Law and the Prophets testify. This righteousness from God comes through faith in Jesus Christ to all who believe. Romans 3:21–22

Jesus revealed to mankind that there is a type of righteousness totally unrelated to the law, a level of goodness that comes directly from God himself. The Bible says that to obtain this type of righteousness, all we have to do is *believe.* It's just that simple. Simple for us, that is, but for God it involved a lot more.

God's just character could not overlook sin and pretend it had not happened. Sin must be punished—there had to be death. Up to this time, man had been offering animal sacrifices as a death payment, but they were only temporary coverings, because…

> …it is impossible for the blood of bulls and goats to take away sins. Hebrews 10:4 NASB

Was there another solution? Perhaps one man could have died for another, but then he would have had to have been both *sinless* and *willing to be punished.* No such person ever existed. Every man and woman through the ages had been confronted with a personal sin-debt—there was no way they could pay for someone else's. But then God himself left Heaven and became a man—a sinless man. In one remarkable act of selfless love…

> God presented him as a sacrifice of atonement, through faith in his blood. He did this to demonstrate his justice, because in his forbearance he had left the sins committed beforehand unpunished… Romans 3:25

God's just nature was satisfied by the death of Jesus, a death payment for sin. God had left the sins committed beforehand unpunished because he knew that someday Jesus would die for all sin—past, present and future—paying the death penalty in full. Jesus died so God could…

> …demonstrate his justice at the present time, so as to be just and the one who justifies those who have faith in Jesus. Romans 3:26

The word **justified** was a judicial term used in the courtrooms of Jesus' day. Remember the events when man sinned in the garden? At that time God took off the mantle of friendship and donned a magistrate's cloak. As a fair and just judge, God found man GUILTY of a crime, breaking God's perfect law, sinning against a holy God. Man stood before a frowning God, accused and convicted as a perpetual, incurable lawbreaker. The sentence was death—eternal death.

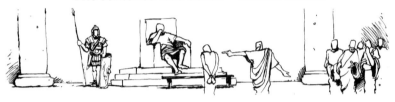

But then God rose from his judgment bench, and taking off the judicial cloak, he put back on the mantle of a friend. God left the lofty heights of Heaven and descended as the God-man, Jesus, to stand with us in front of the bench. He had only one purpose—to take our sentence of death upon himself and pay it for us. Since he had no sin of his own to die for, he was able to die for the sin of others.[2] He died in our place. He was able to pay sin's death penalty for all time, for all mankind.

Sin was gone, but righteousness was still needed. Ah yes, we saw earlier that, just like Abraham, righteousness comes to us by faith. However, to provide *that* purity, something had to happen in God's courtroom. Jesus not only took our putrid rags of sin upon himself, but then—wonder of wonders—he thoroughly wrapped us in the pure, clean robe of *his* righteousness, *a righteousness that is completely <u>equal</u> to HIS holy perfection.*

Now, as God sits as a judge and looks across the faces of humanity, wherever he sees one clothed in Christ's righteousness, he can honestly and justly say, *"In my heavenly courtroom, that man, that woman, stands before me perfect."* The Almighty Judge of Heaven raises his gavel and, with a crash, declares us *"Righteous!"*

That is the meaning of the word JUSTIFIED—*to be declared righteous in God's sight.* But remember: this is only true for those who believe that Jesus died in their place. The Bible says...

> *... that a man is justified by faith ...*   Romans 3:28 NKJV

> *Therefore being justified by faith, we have peace with God through our Lord Jesus Christ…*   Romans 5:1 KJV

No, the Ten Commandments cannot make one righteous.

> *Clearly no one is justified before God by the law…*
> Galatians 3:11

> *…for all have sinned and fall short of the glory of God.*
> Romans 3:23

But the Law had a purpose. The Bible says the ten commands are like a teacher who takes us by the hand, leads us to the cross, and points out to us our need for a Savior.

> *…the law was our schoolmaster to bring us unto Christ, that we might be justified by faith.*   Galatians 3:24 KJV

Everyone needs a Savior. Only when clothed in the righteousness of Christ, can we experience God's welcoming smile.

LOVE AND JUSTICE

On the road to Emmaus, Jesus told the disciples he *had to* die. The idea of Jesus *having to die* makes us uncomfortable—we know we don't deserve such love. Why did he say that? His death was only necessary in this sense:

If God had exclusively allowed the *just* side of his nature to rule, then we would have died for our own sin. That would have been fair, but his *love* would not allow that.

On the other hand, if only *love* had ruled his character, he would have ignored sin for eternity. But that was not an option because of his *just* nature. Sin had to be dealt with.

It was on the cross that we find the complete and perfectly balanced expression of both attributes—boundless *love* shown and infinite *justice* satisfied. From God's point of view, *love* and *justice* made the cross necessary.

> *Greater love has no one than this, that he lay down his life for his friends.*   John 15:13

> *But God demonstrates His own love toward us, in that while we were still sinners, Christ died for us.*
> Romans 5:8 NKJV

4 The Emmaus Road Message
— The Tabernacle to the Brazen Serpent —

You will recall how God instructed Moses to build the Tabernacle. It was an elaborate visual aid to help us understand what the Lord was doing to mend our broken relationship with him. Remember how God showed his presence among the Israelites with a pillar of cloud by day, and a column of fire by night? That *pillar* hovered over the Ark of the Covenant in the Holy of Holies.

One Entrance

As man approached God in the Tabernacle, the first thing he saw was the wall around the courtyard which had only one entrance, a reminder that there is only one way to God. Jesus said...

> *"I am the way and the truth and the life. No one comes to the Father except through me."*   John 14:6

The Brazen Altar

As a person entered the Tabernacle, the first piece of furniture he saw was the Brazen Altar, a reminder that the only way to a right relationship with God was through the blood sacrifice. It's the same with us. The only way to a right relationship with God is through Jesus, who sacrificed his life in our place.

Even a very brief comparison of these two places of death—the Brazen Altar and the Cross—show how Jesus completely fulfilled the graphic picture illustrated in the Tabernacle offerings.

The Brazen Altar	The Cross
The sacrifice was...	Jesus...
...*from either the herd or the flock.*	...is the Lamb of God
...*a male*	...is a male
...*without defect*	...is sinless
...*[to] be accepted on his behalf*	...died in our place
...*to make atonement* [or *covering for sin*] *for him*	...is our way to have forgiveness of sin
...*[a] blood [sacrifice].* Leviticus 1:2–5	...was the blood sacrifice made for us.

THE LAMPSTAND

Remember how God told Moses to make a lampstand of pure gold to light the Holy Place? This is a picture of Jesus who said ...

> *"I am the light of the world. Whoever follows me will never walk in darkness, but will have the light of life."*   John 8:12

Jesus wants to deliver people out of the darkness of sin into the light of eternal life.

THE TABLE WITH THE BREAD

Remember how God told Moses to make a table and place on it twelve loaves of bread, each representing one of the twelve tribes of Israel? Again, this is a picture of Jesus who said ...

> *"I am the bread of life. He who comes to me will never go hungry, and he who believes in me will never be thirsty."*
> John 6:35

Just as the twelve loaves were a picture of sufficient bread for everyone in Israel, so Jesus' death was for the sins of the whole world. As the bread of life, He offers us eternal life.

> *"I tell you the truth, he who believes has everlasting life. I am the bread of life."*   John 6:47–48

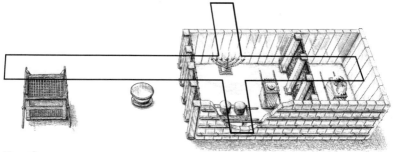

THE CURTAIN

Think again about how God instructed Moses to hang a thick curtain between the Holy Place and the Holy of Holies. Sinful man was barred from entering God's holy presence.

ESTRANGED

The Bible says we are separated from God and cannot come into his presence because of our sin. We are ESTRANGED from God and his love.

But then Jesus came. The Scripture tells us that the Tabernacle curtain was a picture of his physical body. When he died on the cross, the curtain was ripped in two from top to bottom. No man could have torn the veil, but God tore it to illustrate Jesus' body being sacrificed for you and me. When we put our trust in him, our sin is forgiven and we can boldly enter into God's presence. The relationship has been restored.

> *Therefore, brothers, since we have confidence to enter the Most Holy Place by the blood of Jesus, by a new and living way opened for us through the curtain, that is, his body ... let us draw near to God with a sincere heart in full assurance ...* Hebrews 10:19–20, 22

> *But now in Christ Jesus you who once were far away have been brought near through the blood of Christ.* Ephesians 2:13

We are not accepted back simply as a friend. The Scripture tells us that we are placed into God's family as a full member—it says we are *adopted*.

In the Roman world of Jesus' day, adoption was *the legal rite of investing sonship.* In our modern society, a child born into a family is automatically recognized as having all the rights and privileges of that family. But in a world where men had wives, concubines and mistresses, as well as children by their slaves, a child was not a legal heir until invested with that sonship in a separate action. Once adopted as a son, you were a full member of the family.

ADOPTED

So it is with us. We, who once were ESTRANGED from God's love, can now become members of God's family—as SONS.

> *Because you are sons, God sent the Spirit of his Son into our hearts, the Spirit who calls out, "Abba [Daddy], Father." So you are no longer a slave [to sin and Satan], but a son; and since you are a son, God has made you also an heir.*
> Galatians 4:6–7

THE ATONEMENT COVER

The Atonement Cover was that special lid on the Ark of the Covenant, which was located in the Holy of Holies. It was here that the High Priest brought the blood once a year on the Day of Atonement. God gave the Israelites a way to escape judgment of their sin through the shed blood of an innocent lamb. In the same way, Jesus is now our Atonement Cover and, through his shed blood, we find a way to escape eternal death. No longer does man need to offer lambs for a sacrifice. Jesus was the final sacrifice. God says...

> *"**Their sins** and lawless acts **I will remember no more.**" And where these have been forgiven, there is no longer any sacrifice for sin.* Hebrews 10:17–18

With Jesus' death on the cross, the last Lamb had died. Since the beginning of history, it had been God's plan that the way of escape would be provided through Jesus. The sacrifices had only been a picture of what was to come. There was nothing unique about them; they could not take away sin. But now it was no longer necessary to offer any kind of sacrifice, because Jesus' blood paid the sin-debt once for all.

> *...we have been made holy through the sacrifice of the body of Jesus Christ **once for all**.*

> *Day after day every priest stands and performs his religious duties; again and again he offers the same sacrifices, which can never take away sins. But when this priest [Jesus] had offered **for all time** one sacrifice for sins, he sat down at the right hand of God.* Hebrew 10:10–12

God accepted the animals because he was looking forward in history to the time when Jesus would die as the final sacrifice. When Jesus died, he did more than *cover* sin for a year. He blotted it out from God's sight forever. On the cross He cried, "It is finished"—*the final Lamb is found.*

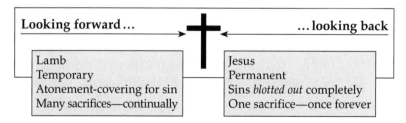

Looking forward...	...looking back
Lamb	Jesus
Temporary	Permanent
Atonement-covering for sin	Sins *blotted out* completely
Many sacrifices—continually	One sacrifice—once forever

Jesus may have told his disciples many more things about himself that are illustrated in the Tabernacle for it is a visual aid of incredible detail, full of comparisons. You can be sure that what Jesus did tell them was unforgettable.

Moses and the Brazen Serpent

Recall how the Israelites sinned and God sent the snakes. They cried out for deliverance, so God instructed Moses to make a bronze serpent and raise it up in the middle of the camp. To be healed, all the people had to do was to LOOK at the serpent. There was nothing else they could do.

"Just as Moses lifted up the snake in the desert, so the Son of Man must be lifted up [on the cross], that everyone who believes in him may have eternal life.

For God so loved the world that he gave his one and only Son, that whoever believes in him shall not perish but have eternal life. For God did not send his Son into the world to condemn the world, but to save the world through him.

*Whoever believes in him is not condemned, but whoever does not believe stands **condemned already** because he has not believed in the name of God's one and only Son."*

John 3:14–18

Man is born into this world *condemned already*. We are like the Israelites who had been bitten by snakes. We are as good as DEAD. We have no relationship with God; our bodies will eventually die and, after death, we will partake of the Second Death, punishment in the Lake of Fire.

But then Jesus enters the picture. He paid the sin-debt with his own death. However Jesus did not remain dead—he came back to life. If we look to him in faith just as the Israelites looked to the bronze snake, then he gives us spiritual life. Just as he came alive, we become spiritually ALIVE, both now and for eternity. The Bible speaks of this as being *born again*.

*When you were **dead** in your sins … God made you **alive** with Christ. He forgave us all our sins.*

Colossians 2:13

*But because of his great love for us, God, who is rich in mercy, made us **alive** with Christ even when we were **dead** in transgressions [sin] …*   Ephesians 2:4–5

Once spiritually DEAD, we are now ALIVE and will dwell forever in Heaven.

5 THE EMMAUS ROAD MESSAGE
— JOHN THE BAPTIST TO THE RESURRECTION —

As Jesus systematically explained to the disciples the significance of the events recorded in the Scripture, it is probable that he elaborated on even more accounts than we have touched on here. No doubt his disciples had keen interest in the subjects with which they had firsthand experience.

THE GOOD SHEPHERD

LOST

The Bible says...

We all, like sheep, have gone astray, each of us has turned to his own way...   Isaiah 53:6

Man chose to go his *own way,* taking a path that led him into a spiritual wilderness. The Bible says that man is LOST.

FOUND

But then Jesus came looking for us. While on earth he told a parable that describes God's concern.

"Suppose one of you has a hundred sheep and loses one of them. Does he not leave the ninety-nine in the open country and go after the lost sheep until he finds it? And when he finds it, he joyfully puts it on his shoulders and goes home. Then he calls his friends and neighbors together and says, 'Rejoice with me; I have found my lost sheep.' I tell you that in the same way there will be more rejoicing in heaven over one sinner who repents than over ninety-nine righteous persons who do not need to repent."   Luke 15:4–7

God could have stayed in Heaven and forever turned his back on mankind, but that isn't what happened. The Bible makes it clear that Jesus took the initiative to seek us out and then, as the good shepherd, went much further.

"I am the good shepherd. The good shepherd lays down his life for the sheep."   John 10:11

That is exactly what Jesus did. He *died for us, in our place, to pay our sin-debt.* That is love in all its perfection. Yes, God is love, but not without tremendous cost. When Jesus was on the cross he cried out,

> *"My God, My God, why have You forsaken Me?"* Mark 15:34

Jesus didn't just die a physical death, there was also a spiritual dimension. *Sin demands separation.* In those desperate hours on the cross, God the Father turned his back on his Son. It must have wrenched his loving heart but, consistent with his holy nature, God could not look upon Jesus as he took our sin upon himself. The Bible says that the sky grew dark although it was midday. It seems as though the Father did not want the world to see the agony that the Son went through, as Jesus willingly took our sin on himself, became our substitute Lamb, and died. God allowed it; indeed, he planned it.

THE GREAT EXCHANGE

The Bible says that...

> *God made him who had no sin to be *sin for us...*
> 2 Corinthians 5:21

This verse is not saying that Jesus became a sinner. The word **sin* has the idea of a sin-offering. *"God made Jesus, who had no sin, to be a sin-offering for us..."* When Jesus took our sin, God poured out on him all the fury of his rightful anger on sin. Then Jesus was able to do something we could not do. He said, *"It is finished."* If we had paid our own sin-debt, we would have gone on and on paying—for eternity. We could never have said, "It is finished." But Jesus paid it all.

The rest of the verse reads:

> *...so that in him we might become the righteousness of God.*
> 2 Corinthians 5:21

It's *in him* we find righteousness! It's not ours. *Jesus took our sin and offers us his righteousness.* It's the greatest of all exchanges. No longer do we need the blood of a lamb to cover our sin; we are clothed in something far better, the righteousness of Christ. When we trust him, God gives us His righteousness! Remember that question from ages past—**"How can man get rid of his sin and gain *a righteousness <u>equal</u> to God's*** *righteousness* **so he can be accepted in God's presence?"** The complete answer is found in this one verse. Read it again.

> *God made him who had no sin to be [a] sin [offering] for us,*
> *so that in him we might become the righteousness of God.*
> *2 Corinthians 5:21*

THE RESURRECTION

Jesus died, yes, but he didn't stay dead like the prophets of the past. Jesus came back to life to prove that death had no power over Him. He said...

> *"The reason my Father loves me is that I lay down my life—only to take it up again. No one takes it from me, but I lay it down of my own accord. I have authority to lay it down and authority to take it up again."* John 10:17–18

The Romans have been blamed for executing Jesus, and the religious leaders for pressuring them to do it. Over the centuries, the Jews have faced immense persecution on the premise that the whole sorry affair was *their* fault. Such a perception is completely false. The Bible states clearly that it was *Jesus* who voluntarily laid down his life. No one forced him to die against his will. It was his choice, motivated by his love for us. The truth of the matter is that the sins of the whole world were responsible for nailing Jesus to the cross.

The resurrection was a powerful display that God's *just* nature was satisfied with Jesus' death on our behalf. The payment had been made and it had been accepted as sufficient! The grave could not hold him in its clutches. He had victory over death! Jesus had broken sin's grip, defeated Satan's power and removed death's terrible finality.

> *Since the children have flesh and blood, he too shared in their humanity so that by his death he might destroy him who holds the power of death—that is, the devil—and free those who all their lives were held in slavery by their fear of death.* Hebrews 2:14–15

An overwhelming feeling of despair must have swept over Satan when Jesus was resurrected. Satan had thought that when he had enticed Judas Iscariot to betray Jesus, *he* was the winner. Now he had been defeated at his own game. His most powerful tool—death—had lost its sting.

Redeemed

For centuries, man had been a SLAVE to Satan's will. Through blatant lies, imitation of the truth, even the denial of his own existence, Satan had manipulated mankind for his own purposes. But even independently of Satan's influence, man could not live a perfect life. Man

SLAVE

was a SLAVE to sin.

 But then Jesus came and REDEEMED us. It is difficult for us to grasp the rich significance connected with this word if we do not understand

SET-FREE
REDEEMED

its association with ancient slavery.

A wealthy man would go to the slave market to buy a slave. There he would see the captives chained, humbled and broken, each being sold for a given sum. The man would pay the asking price and the slave would become his. So far this was nothing unusual, but now the story takes an interesting twist. On rare occasions, the new owner would then take his new slave out of the slave market, break off the chains and set him free. When this happened, it was said that the slave had been REDEEMED.

That is what Jesus did for us. We were bound by the chains of sin and Satan in the slave market of life. We were helpless to deliver ourselves. But then Jesus came and purchased us, paying the price with his own blood. He then took us out of the market, broke off the chains and set us free.

> For you know that it was not with perishable things such as silver or gold that you were **redeemed** from the empty way of life…, but with the precious blood of Christ, a lamb without blemish or defect.　　　　1 Peter 1:18–19

> In him we have **redemption** through his blood, the forgiveness of sins, in accordance with the riches of God's grace.　　　　Ephesians 1:7

THE SHEEP PEN

Now, let's continue with the analogy Jesus used in describing us as sheep. Remember how a good shepherd would sleep in the entrance of the sheep pen to protect the flock? Jesus said...

"I am the gate; whoever enters through me will be saved."
John 10:9

The pen had only one gate. In the same way, Jesus is the only door to eternal life. There is no other way to be saved from the consequences of sin.

> ...Just as there was only one way in which Cain and Abel could approach God;
>
> ...just as there was only one door to safety in Noah's boat;
>
> ...just as there was only one door to the Tabernacle;
>
> ...and just as there is only one door to a sheep pen, so Jesus is the only way to God.

Some people believe you can come to God by another religion, perhaps by some combination of many religions, but the Bible allows no room for other *ways* to God. This may be viewed as discriminatory in our politically-correct age, but repeatedly, the Bible echoes this theme: *Jesus is the only way.*

Salvation is found in no one else, for there is no other name under heaven given to men by which we must be saved.
Acts 4:12

Some may not like this biblical narrow-mindedness, however to be true to the text, I must say that this is what the Bible clearly teaches. It also says that if we don't approve of God's chosen way, we can reject it. God allows us that freedom, but then we must also pay our own debt with our own personal death for eternity. Of course, one can deny the existence of God and ignore the Bible's message entirely, though frankly, a person has to admit, it's a hazardous option.

INTOLERANCE

Though Jesus made it clear that there was no other way to God, he did not advocate violent suppression of other belief systems. His approach was to teach truth. Truth exposes error and people are then free to make their choice.

As the disciples listened to Jesus teach from the Law and the Prophets, they must have had premonitions of the consequences of his message. They lived in the Roman Empire. The Romans were tolerant of other religions up to a point, but they had also come to believe that Caesar was a god. The Romans wouldn't object to Jesus being presented as *another way* to God, but to teach what Jesus taught—that *He* is the *only way*—would jeopardize their lives. According to extra-biblical sources, all but one of the eleven original disciples were put to death for this message. They died for what they knew to be true. The eleventh was exiled.

THE PHARISEES

The Pharisees, of all people, were impeccably religious. They had an extensive list of do's and don'ts.

Today, one of the most common misconceptions about life is that people can earn their way to Heaven by doing enough good to outweigh their bad. Based on *that* kind of thinking, they go to church, pray, burn candles, do penance, give to charity, etc., hoping they will be acceptable to God. That is not what the Bible teaches—anywhere. In fact, it states the opposite.

The Pharisees were very religious, but Jesus condemned both their lives and their teaching as being misleading. Jesus said that the only true way to God was by faith in him.

We put faith into practice every day. You are probably applying a principle of faith right now. If you are sitting in a chair, you are trusting in the chair to hold you up, without collapsing. It's doubtful that you sat down thinking—*"I am going to trust this chair to be sturdy"*—but, nonetheless, you exercised faith in the chair. In a sense, faith in itself is neutral. What is important is this: in what or in whom are you placing your trust? The chair may collapse—but then it's only a chair. However, if you are placing your faith in Jesus having paid your sin-debt, then you can have absolute confidence that he has done just that. He has promised.

> *For it is by grace you have been saved, through faith—and this not from yourselves, it is the gift of God—not by works, so that no one can boast.* Ephesians 2:8–9

The Bible says we are *saved* from the consequences of sin through faith in Jesus Christ. This *salvation* is a *gift* from God. We didn't have to earn it by any religious act or good work.

Gifts are free. If you work for a *gift*, it is no longer a gift.

Gifts in the truest sense are undeserved.

If we feel we deserve it, then it ceases to be a *gift* and becomes an *award*. The eternal life God gives us is truly a gift because we don't deserve it in any way.

The Pharisees were convinced that their good deeds would please God. But God says that if he accepted people based on what they themselves did, then people would *boast* about their goodness. He saves us from judgment, not on the basis of how good we are, but on the basis of his gift to us.

> *For the wages of sin is death, but the gift of God is eternal life in Christ Jesus our Lord.* Romans 6:23

By faith, we believe that Jesus died *in our place* for our sin.

By faith, we believe that Jesus paid *our* sin-debt.

By faith, we believe that God's justice was satisfied by that death. We believe that when He looks at us, He no longer sees our sin, but He sees us clothed in Jesus' righteousness.

By faith, we believe that God gives us the gift of eternal life.

It's all faith, but it's *not* blind faith.

It's *faith* that is built on the *facts* we find in the Bible.

Some people add a spiritual aura to faith. It becomes quantified. You either have a lot of faith or just a little. But that thinking confuses the issue. Putting faith in what Jesus did on the cross for us is similar to a drowning man *nodding* vigorously to his rescuer when the lifesaver says, "Will you trust me to save you?" The size of the *nod* is immaterial. The point is *not* the *nod* at all. The point is that the drowning man is acknowledging and trusting in the lifeguard to rescue him. For the drowning man to later claim that his big *nod* saved his life would be ludicrous. So it is with us. We are to trust in Jesus to save us from our sin, but the size of our trust is not what saves us; it is what Jesus did for us by dying on the cross.

> For in the gospel **a righteousness from God** is revealed, **a righteousness that is by faith from first to last**…
> *Romans 1:17*

In continuing the analogy of a drowning man, let me also add that it is important to *know* that you are drowning. If you think you are floating just fine, you will reject all help. However, even if you *know* you are drowning but are too proud to ask for help, you will drown all the same. Others may see that you are floundering, but they will be unable to help you until you allow them. It's the same spiritually. You must see yourself as a helpless sinner before you can be saved from your sin-debt. That's the starting point.

The Bible is full of illustrations of who Jesus Christ is and what he has done. We can only offer conjecture as to which of those illustrations Jesus used as he taught the disciples. Undoubtedly, he used most or all of the ones we have touched on. He probably used more. When he had finished teaching, the room must have been silent. The question which remained for Jesus' disciples is the same question which remains for us. In whom are you placing your faith? In yourself, your religion, your ideas, your good works, or in the fact that Jesus died in your place to pay your sin-debt?

It should all make sense now. If someone was to ask you, "Why did Jesus die?" you should be able to answer:

Sin demands death. Instead of each of us dying for our sin and paying the eternal consequences, Jesus died in our place, taking those consequences upon Himself. He is our substitute.

If someone was to ask you, "How can I get to Heaven?" you should be able to answer:

To live in Heaven we need to be pure and perfect, just as God is pure and perfect. If we put our faith in God, believing that when Jesus was dying on the cross, he was dying in our place for our sin, then God will clothe us in his righteousness and we will be accepted completely.

Jesus took our sin and offers us his righteousness.

CHAPTER FIFTEEN

1   WHAT DO YOU WANT ME TO DO?

2   A CONVENIENT TIME

1 WHAT DO YOU WANT ME TO DO?

In the days immediately following Jesus' resurrection, he spent time with his disciples and...

> ...showed himself to these men and gave many convincing proofs that he was alive. He appeared to them over a period of forty days and spoke about the kingdom of God.   Acts 1:3

In the end, Jesus took them back to familiar ground, just two miles from Jerusalem.

> When he had led them out to the vicinity of Bethany, he lifted up his hands and blessed them. While he was blessing them, he left them and was taken up into heaven.
>   Luke 24:50–51

> They were looking intently up into the sky as he was going, when suddenly two men dressed in white stood beside them. "Men of Galilee," they said, "why do you stand here looking into the sky? This same Jesus, who has been taken from you into heaven, will come back in the same way you have seen him go into heaven."   Acts 1:10–11

The angels said Jesus would come again. If we were to study the Bible further, we would see that it has a lot to say about that future event.[1] Just as God kept his promise related to prophecies about his first coming, we can be assured that he will keep his Word regarding his second coming. He always does.

The rest of the Bible records the events surrounding the lives of the disciples who became known as apostles. These followers of Jesus told multitudes of people about him.

> So the word of God spread. The number of disciples in Jerusalem increased rapidly, and a large number of [temple] priests became obedient to the faith.   Acts 6:7

Even priests who had been instrumental in Jesus' death believed. But not everyone was convinced and, just as the disciples must have anticipated, there was resistance. One particularly ardent *Jesus-hater* was a young Pharisee named Saul, who murdered and imprisoned followers of Jesus.

Meanwhile, Saul was still breathing out murderous threats against the Lord's disciples. He went to the high priest and asked him for letters to the synagogues in Damascus, so that if he found any there who belonged to the Way, whether men or women, he might take them as prisoners to Jerusalem. As he neared Damascus on his journey, suddenly a light from heaven flashed around him. He fell to the ground and heard a voice say to him, "Saul, Saul, why do you persecute me?"

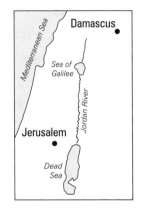

"Who are you, Lord?" Saul asked.

"I am Jesus, whom you are persecuting," he replied.

Acts 9:1–5

This was the beginning of a remarkable life. Saul changed radically. He stopped killing believers and became one himself. The tables turned and the persecutor became the persecuted. On one occasion, he was stoned with rocks and left for dead. Three times he was beaten with rods; five times whipped; three times shipwrecked (during one of which he floated on the sea for twenty-four hours). All of this occurred as Saul tried to tell others about his own belief that Jesus was THE PROMISED SAVIOR. This Saul was none other than the man we know as *Paul the Apostle,* the one who wrote a significant part of the Bible.

Over and over again, we have seen throughout the Scriptures that God asked thought-provoking questions. These queries were designed to expose and clarify a person's innermost thoughts so that the one being addressed would have to grapple with reality. Saul, too, was confronted by God and asked a question:

"Saul, Saul, why do you persecute me?"

In a way, God was saying, "Saul, why are you my enemy when you could be my friend?" Saul's reply revealed that he knew exactly who was quizzing him. He said, *"Lord."*

If we were to be so fortunate as to encounter God in person, I can't help but feel that he would begin the conversation with a question. The likelihood of being confronted the same way as Saul was is very remote; in all of Scripture it happened to only a handful of people. Even though we may not be confronted in person, we are still faced with what God has recorded in the Bible. As I said in the preface, the Bible, by its very nature, demands that we make a choice. God in essence is asking us a question.

As you have read this book, you have heard the facts. You are now accountable for what you know. God now asks, "Will you recognize and believe in Jesus as your own personal SAVIOR—the one who has paid your sin-debt?"

Don't answer without thought. Maybe you have been thinking it through. On the other hand, maybe you need to take some time to ponder the question.

If you answer, "NO, I don't believe Jesus is my DELIVERER," then the rest of this chapter will have little relevance for you. You are welcome to read it, but I would suggest you skip this section and finish with the next section entitled, A CONVENIENT TIME. The Bible says that if we reject the message of the cross, then the rest of the Scripture will not be understood correctly because...

> ... it is veiled to those who are perishing.
>
> The god of this age [Satan] has blinded the minds of unbelievers, so that they cannot see the light of the gospel [the good news] of the glory of Christ, who is the image of God.
>
> 2 Corinthians 4:3–4

On the other hand, if you answer, "YES, I would like to be one who can say that Jesus has paid my sin-debt," or "YES, I believe He has paid my sin-debt," then read on. The rest of the Bible is written for people like you.

If you answered, "YES," then do you understand that God has forgiven you of your sin, and has restored His relationship with you?

If, in all honesty you have answered these questions with a YES, then based on what the Bible says, you can rest assured that your sin is forgiven and that your relationship with God has been restored.

The Facts
Without the Cross

GUILTY

I am accused and found guilty of breaking God's perfect law.

DEBTOR

To break God's law is to sin, and my sin incurs a sin-debt, a consequence I must pay.

ETERNAL JUDGMENT

The debt can only be paid by my death, a payment that is made for eternity in the Lake of Fire.

SLAVE

It is impossible to keep God's law perfectly. Even when I try hard, I still find myself failing. In addition, Satan manipulates me to do his will. I am a slave.

ESTRANGED

My sin has estranged me from God and his love. God seems distant and remote.

ENEMY

When I was born into this world, I joined forces with Satan, who also sinned against God.

LOST

Having chosen my own way, I find myself in a spiritual wilderness, groping for truth. I am like a lost sheep.

Born an Unbeliever ...

I Don't Believe ...

I believe that there may be many ways to be accepted by God— if there is a God. Jesus may be one way. If I live a good life and do my best, then God will not reject me.

THE FACTS
BECAUSE OF THE CROSS

God, as the perfect judge, declares me right with him— justified. He now views me as righteous.

DECLARED RIGHTEOUS

My sin-debt was taken care of on the cross. The debt is gone—paid in full, erased.

CANCELED DEBT

God gives me a new life, both now and for all of eternity in Heaven.

ETERNAL LIFE

... IT'S A CHOICE TO BELIEVE

Once enslaved, I have now been bought with Jesus' blood and set free. I am no longer a slave to Satan's purposes.

SET-FREE REDEEMED

... I DO BELIEVE

I believe that when Jesus died on the cross, he died in my place as my substitute, paying my sin-debt. I trust in him alone to save me from sin's consequences.

Not only have I been born into God's family, but God has given me the full rights of a son.

ADOPTED

Jesus' death and resurrection defeated Satan. I no longer belong to the Devil. I have peace with God.

RECONCILED

Jesus, as the Good Shepherd, has found me and given me new life, eternal life, forgiveness, purpose for living, freedom from guilt, and so much more.

FOUND

If you believe Jesus died in your place for your sin, then you can have complete confidence in the fact that your *Certificate of Debt* has been paid in full.

> *And when you were dead in your transgressions² ... He made you alive together with Him, having forgiven us all our transgressions, having canceled out the certificate of debt consisting of decrees against us and which was hostile to us; and He has taken it out of the way, having nailed it to the cross.* Colossians 2:13–14 NASB

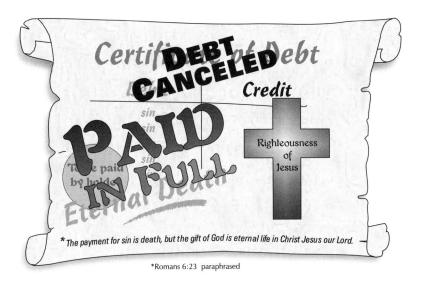

*Romans 6:23 paraphrased

Your sin-debt was nailed to the cross two thousand years ago. Because of your trust in him, God now says that your...

> *"...sins and lawless acts I will remember no more."*
> Hebrews 10:17

God's forgiveness is total.

> *For as high as the heavens are above the earth, so great is his love for those who fear [or respect] him; as far as the east is from the west, so far has he removed our transgressions² from us.* Psalm 103:11–12

> *Therefore, if anyone is in Christ, he is a new creation; old things have passed away; behold, all things have become new.* 2 Corinthians 5:17 NKJV

Now instead of eternal death in the Lake of Fire, Jesus says:

> *"Let not your heart be troubled; you believe in God, believe also in Me. In My Father's house are many mansions; if it were not so, I would have told you. I go to prepare a place for you. And if I go and prepare a place for you, I will come again and receive you to Myself; that where I am, there you may be also. And where I go you know, and the way you know."* John 14:1–4 NKJV

As a believer, life still goes on, but now you are assured of a future destiny in Heaven. Jesus says he is preparing a dwelling place for you. With confidence you can now say that you are a citizen of Heaven. Your **relationship** with God is now restored.

Just as you were once born into an earthly family, the Bible says you have now been born into God's family. And just as your earthly parents will always be your parents regardless of what happens, so it is that once you are born into God's family, you can't be *un-born*. It is important to understand that when it comes to your **relationship** with God, your eternal destiny is settled once for all. You belong to God's family for eternity.[3]

> *I write these things to you who believe in the name of the Son of God so that you may know that you have[4] eternal life.* 1 John 5:13

> *For I am convinced that neither death nor life, neither angels nor demons, neither the present nor the future, nor any powers, neither height nor depth, nor anything else in all creation, will be able to separate us from the love of God that is in Christ Jesus our Lord.* Romans 8:38–39

Even though you are now part of God's family **(relationship)**, the Bible says that you will still sin. When that happens, there is a break in your family **fellowship**.

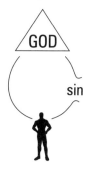

RELATIONSHIP
unbreakable
You have been born into God's family. You are eternally His child.

GOD

sin

FELLOWSHIP
breakable
Your sin breaks the pleasant harmony you have with your Heavenly Father.

Fellowship is different than **relationship**. For instance, if a son is asked by his dad to mow the lawn, but instead he goes fishing, things won't be right when Dad arrives home. There will be a barrier between father and son, and you would probably sense it if you were there. It is true that the son and dad are still related—their **relationship** has not changed—but the family **fellowship** has gone sour. However, the Bible has a solution.

When we sin, we are told to acknowledge that fact to God, and if we have wronged our fellow man, then we must seek to be reconciled to him as well. God has promised that...

> *If we confess our sins, he is faithful and just and will forgive us our sins and purify us from all unrighteousness.* 1 John 1:9

Our **fellowship** with God will be immediately restored when we acknowledge our sin.

Your Responsibility

I remember a time when, after finishing a study of this material with a couple, the husband said to me, "John, I know that I am a helpless sinner." He then gave a brief overview of the Bible to assure me that he knew he couldn't do anything good in himself to please God. He summarized it with a clear explanation of his faith in what Jesus had accomplished on the cross for him. He then said, "John, you have a son. Just as I didn't have to do anything to become a member of God's family, neither did your son do anything to become a member of your family. But now that he is a member, he has responsibilities: he takes out the garbage, he helps with the dishes, and so on." He then asked, *"As part of God's family, what are my responsibilities?"*

That was a very perceptive question, one which the rest of the Bible answers. The Scripture says that the life a person lives is determined by the **focus** he maintains, on *what* he fixes his attention. This is not some sort of mind game. It has to do with your center of attention. If you focus on yourself, you will become very self-centered. If you focus on God, you will find your life bringing him the honor and glory that he deserves. Therefore to be a responsible believer:

1. You need to **focus** on what you *now have* because of Jesus, which includes all the things you see listed on

page 279. What you *now have* is referred to as your *position in Christ*. God wants you to rejoice in the fact that your sin is forgiven and that you now have a new life.

2. You need to **focus** on getting acquainted with Jesus. Paul the Apostle wrote that his life ambition was to…

> …*count all things to be loss in view of the surpassing value of knowing Christ Jesus my Lord, for whom I have suffered the loss of all things, and count them but rubbish so that I may gain Christ, and may be found in Him, not having a righteousness of my own derived from the Law, but that which is through faith in Christ, the righteousness which comes from God on the basis of faith, that I may know Him…*
>
> Philippians 3:8–10 NASB

When you fix your attention on the Lord, you take your eyes off yourself. You become captivated with pleasing him and serving others. It's like a young man with his girlfriend—all taken up with getting to know her.

3. You need to **focus** on trusting Him daily, in all of life's situations, for you can have confidence that he is fully able to handle all your worries and concerns. Jesus said…

> *"Come to me, all you who are weary and burdened, and I will give you rest."*
>
> Matthew 11:28

As you apply these truths, you will find that you will be growing from a spiritual babe into a spiritually mature adult. Should you begin to think that this all happens as a result of some sort of super-discipline you conjure up in yourself, it is important to understand that…

> …*He who has begun a good work in you will complete it until the day of Jesus Christ…*
>
> Philippians 1:6 NKJV

Just as it's not normal or healthy for an infant to remain a baby all its life, it's not right for a person who is a newborn *child of God* to remain a spiritual infant. Unfortunately, this is all too common, but one doesn't need to be that way. Keep your focus in the proper place and you will grow.

Enemies

There are certain things—*enemies*—that can destroy your focus and hinder your spiritual growth.

1. Our human nature:[5] If there ever was a case of being one's own worst enemy, this is it. The Bible says that our sinful human nature is never satisfied. It always desires more money, more attention, a different personality, better looks, nicer this, greater that, ad infinitum it goes. It may be satisfied momentarily, but then it will desire something more to fill the black hole of feelings and wants. Our human nature has one primary focus—our **SELF**. The Scriptures say…

> … *live by the Spirit, and you will not gratify the **desires of the sinful nature.***
> Galatians 5:16

So how do we *live by the Spirit?* It comes back to this matter of focus. As we focus on the things of God, the *desires of the sinful nature* are replaced with a stronger desire to please our Creator-Owner.

We are told to treat our sinful nature as if it were dead. We are to actively and aggressively ignore its demands and desires.

> *Put to death, therefore, whatever belongs to your earthly nature…*
> Colossians 3:5

For example, before I was married I had several girlfriends. They were genuine relationships. But when I got married, those former relationships were over. Dead. Now I am caught up in a new relationship—I desire to please my wife. She has become my focus. It would be wrong for me to allow my thoughts to dwell on a former girlfriend. In the same way, before you believed, you only had your sinful nature to satisfy. But now as a believer, God wants you to put that behind you and be caught up in pleasing Him and in serving others.

> … *let us throw off everything that hinders and the sin that so easily entangles, and let us run with perseverance the race marked out for us. Let us **fix our eyes** [or focus] on Jesus…*
> Hebrews 12:1–2

This biblical counsel runs contrary to much advice we receive today. Nowadays we are told to delve into our past to search for the answers to our problems. Every wrong must be righted and, if we have been hurt, then we are to be pitied as victims.

The end result of all this advice is that we focus on ourselves. We become self-obsessed. By contrast, the Bible tells us to forget about ourselves, including our past. If we have been truly wronged, we are to forgive, as difficult as that may seem.

> *And be kind to one another, tenderhearted, forgiving one another, just as God in Christ forgave you.* Ephesians 4:32 NKJV

It may seem strange, but in the process of forgiving others, we experience healing in our own lives. Jesus, who surely knew what it was to be wronged, said...

> *"I have told you this so that my joy may be in you and that your joy may be complete."* John 15:11

2. The world system: The Bible says that the world system has a negative impact on us spiritually, shifting our focus from Jesus to those things that are fleeting. We are responsible to discern what tends to drag us back into old, sinful patterns and avoid those things that destroy our focus.

> *For the grace of God...teaches us to say "No" to ungodliness and worldly passions, and to live self-controlled, upright and godly lives in this present age, while we wait for the blessed hope—the glorious appearing of our great God and Savior, Jesus Christ...* Titus 2:11–13

3. The Devil: Even though Satan has been defeated, he still actively tries to influence us. God didn't obliterate the Devil when we became believers. Rather, we are responsible to resist his temptations and seek strength from God alone.

> *Submit yourselves, then, to God. Resist the devil, and he will flee from you.* James 4:7

Satan cleverly uses the influence of the world and our self-centered human natures to tempt us, to shift our focus. You can expect him to plant doubt in your mind, even about the choice you have made to trust Jesus. He will say your faith wasn't big enough or question whether you really understood. Remember, he did that with Adam and Eve too. Resist him and do what Jesus did. Go to the Bible for help.

It is interesting that, as we combat the influence of these three enemies, as we maintain our focus, we grow strong spiritual roots.

Friends

The Bible writers also tell us that there are *friends* that will help establish and maintain our focus.

1. God Himself: When you trusted in Jesus, the Bible says the Holy Spirit entered you; he came to live in you. Now he is constantly accessible—to encourage you when you are downhearted, to urge you to earnestly live for him, to rebuke you when you drift into sin. The *Holy Spirit* is such a faithful companion that he is called *the Comforter, the Helper, the Counselor*—all of which are God's names.

> *"But the Helper, the Holy Spirit, whom the Father will send in My name, He will teach you all things, and bring to your remembrance all things that I said to you."*
>
> John 14:26 NKJV

As parents, we are delighted when our children achieve a set goal, or behave themselves in a pleasing manner. As God's children, it is important that we conduct ourselves in a way that will bring honor and not disgrace to our heavenly Father's name. Our obedience shows we are giving to God the proper esteem and respect he deserves.

> *"You are worthy, our Lord and God, to receive glory and honor and power, for you created all things, and by your will they were created and have their being."* Revelation 4:11

2. Faith: The process of growing spiritually is often referred to in Scripture as *walking* with God. It occurs one step at a time. Just as we became members of God's family by *faith*, so we are to walk with God by *faith*.

> *As you have therefore received Christ Jesus the Lord, so walk in Him, rooted and built up in Him and established in the faith, as you have been taught, abounding in it with thanksgiving.* Colossians 2:6–7 NKJV

Remember, *faith* is built on the *facts* that are found in the Bible. It's important not to walk with God based on the way you *feel*. You may get up in the morning feeling congested and running a fever. That does not mean you are no longer part of your parents' family or, for that matter, a part of God's family. Sometimes you may not *feel* very spiritual, but that does not determine how well you are walking with God. Our walk each day is determined by the choices we make. If we make wise choices, we will be learning

God's wisdom. If we make foolish ones, we'll be demonstrating immaturity, and will remain spiritual children. The choices we make are guided by God as we read the Bible.

3. The Bible: It's a source of daily strength, our guide book.

> All Scripture is God-breathed and is useful for teaching, rebuking, correcting and training in righteousness, so that the man of God may be thoroughly equipped for every good work.
> 2 Timothy 3:16–17

The Bible compares itself to spiritual food. The more you study it, the stronger you will become spiritually. God will *speak* to you through the Bible—not audibly, but in your mind. It's one of the keys to developing your *fellowship* with God. Reading the Scripture is how you get to *know* Him. Without its constant nourishment, you will remain a spiritual baby.

If you do not personally own a Bible, purchase one. (See the Appendix for suggestions.) Begin by reading the entire book of the *Gospel of John.* It reads like a story, so it's not difficult. Then re-read this book, THE STRANGER, and look up every reference in your Bible. It will be slow-going at first, but you will be surprised at how quickly you'll catch on. Using a colored pencil, underline the verses. It will help you spot them quickly, and bring back to your memory what you have learned. You may be ready for the books of *Acts* and *Romans* after reading THE STRANGER for the second time. If you don't understand something, mark it down and keep reading. It will slowly come together.

4. Prayer: Prayer is simply talking to God. You don't need to bow your head and close your eyes, although that is appropriate if it helps you avoid distractions. Because God knows your thoughts and is everywhere present, you can silently voice your prayer to him at any time and he will hear it. It is not necessary to pray audibly.

> Do not be anxious about anything, but in everything, by prayer and petition, with thanksgiving, present your requests to God. And the peace of God, which transcends all understanding, will guard your hearts and your minds in Christ Jesus.
> Philippians 4:6–7

Prayer is a way of expressing our concerns, our heartaches, our requests and our thankfulness to God.

5. Other Believers: The Bible tells us that we gain spiritual maturity through friendship with others who believe the Scriptures. This is vital.

> *And let us consider how we may spur one another on toward love and good deeds.*
>
> *Let us not give up meeting together, as some are in the habit of doing, but let us encourage one another—and all the more as you see the Day [of Jesus' return] approaching.*
> Hebrews 10:24–25

Most of your friendships with other believers will be built within the context of a church. However, a few cautions are in order.

Remember, Satan comes as an *angel of light*. He loves religion. Because of that, you need to realize that there are many *false shepherds* and *false sheep* out there. Just because people talk about God does not mean they are true believers. Churches range from good to bad in their understanding and practice of the truth. The Bible says that both true and false teachers will exist until Jesus returns a second time, when he will sort it all out. Until then, be discerning. Ask these questions:

- Does the church believe that the Bible is the true, inspired Word of God, without error in its original writings? Watch out for those who say it only *contains* God's Word.

- Does the church believe the Bible literally, or does it teach that some accounts are just fables or abstract stories? (e.g. The Bible tells us there is a literal Hell, a literal Devil, a literal Heaven, etc.)

- Does the church believe in such events as Jesus' birth by a *virgin* woman? Be alert for those who say it meant only a *young woman*, that Mary wasn't a virgin.

- Does the church believe that Jesus is fully God as well as man? Be on guard for those who say Jesus was just another god, and that we are gods as well. In the same way, avoid those who say Jesus was just a great teacher.

- Does the church believe in the Trinity?

- Does the church understand that Jesus died in our place for our sin-debt? If the church is *fuzzy* on this, or it is felt that you need to do something in addition to be accepted by God, such as baptism or other special rites—beware.

- Does the church have a good reputation? Are the meetings known for bizarre or disorderly behavior? Does it hold high moral standards? Are its business dealings of dubious nature?

If the church is questionable in **one** of these areas, then there is a very great likelihood that it will be off-base in other teachings as well. These questions are targeted to reveal symptoms of deeper problems. You should feel completely free to ask the church leaders to answer specific questions. Any hedging on their part should flash a caution signal. Don't be caught up by how nice the preacher is, or how persuasively he communicates. Remember, many churches are **not** following the Bible. There is no such thing as a perfect church, but these questions will help you find a group of like-minded believers.

The whole notion of *church* may create some derision from your family and friends. It may be a difficult, humbling experience. Your pride may want to come to the rescue, but just remember where pride had its source, and seek out a group of believers anyway. The idea of getting together for mutual strength was God's idea. Let me assure you, it's important for your growth as a Christian. Fellow believers can be a tremendous help in encouraging you in your spiritual journey.

6. Music: King David wrote some of the first songs or *Psalms* for the purpose of encouraging our hearts. Since then, other believers have written excellent lyrics about God. Once again, beware—there is both good and bad music. Use the same discernment you would apply in choosing a church. Based on what you have studied, determine whether the words being sung are *true* or *false*. God will help you.

7. Tell Others: The disciples went everywhere telling others about this *good news*. You can too. It's encouraging to see friends come to the same understanding. But remember, God has given people a free will, so respect it. Be patient in your approach and sensitive in what you say. Don't cram it down their throats. The Bible tells us to be *witnesses*, not *lawyers*. A witness explains something; a lawyer argues and tries to convince. Simply passing this book on to friends may help them understand.

8. Future Hope: The Bible says that one day, Jesus will return to the earth.

> *Brothers, we do not want you to be ignorant about those who fall asleep [or have died], or to grieve like the rest of men, who have no hope. We believe that Jesus died and rose again and so we believe that God will bring with Jesus those who have fallen asleep in him. According to the Lord's own word, we tell you that we who are still alive, who are left till the coming of the Lord, will certainly not precede those who have fallen asleep.*
>
> *For the Lord himself will come down from heaven, with a loud command, with the voice of the archangel and with the trumpet call of God, and the dead in Christ will rise first. After that, we who are still alive and are left will be caught up together with them in the clouds to meet the Lord in the air. And so we will be with the Lord forever. Therefore encourage each other with these words.*
>
> *1 Thessalonians 4:13–18*

Well, there is so much more that could be written. But if you are one of those who has put your trust in Christ, then it is good to know that the Bible says God will lead you, step by step. You have started a spiritual pilgrimage. Keep your eyes on him; let him be your focus. Study your map, the Bible, regularly. The road will not always be smooth, but God will be with you—he has given you his promise. Have a very good journey.

> *May the God of peace, who through the blood of the eternal covenant brought back from the dead our Lord Jesus, that great Shepherd of the sheep, equip you with everything good for doing his will, and may he work in us what is pleasing to him, through Jesus Christ, to whom be glory for ever and ever. Amen.*
>
> *Hebrews 13:20–21*

2 A CONVENIENT TIME

There are those who, after reading the Bible and understanding what it has to say, decide to take a risk. They decide not to believe it. They choose to:

- Ignore its message.
- Reject it outright.
- Get busy with life, and thereby forget it.
- Change its message.
    ...and they hope that the Bible is wrong.

Herod Agrippa took such a risk. As the grandson of Herod the Great and nephew of Herod Antipas, he must have been privy to the gossip about Jesus in the royal household. No doubt, spies had reported every word the prophet from Nazareth spoke. But Herod had status; he was an important man. Rather than humble himself before the King of Kings, he continued to live his life for himself. He even gained an element of popularity by beheading one of Jesus' disciples. But then...

> On the appointed day Herod, wearing his royal robes, sat on his throne and delivered a public address to the people. They shouted, "This is the voice of a god, not of a man." Immediately, because Herod did not give praise to God, an angel of the Lord struck him down, and he was eaten by worms and died.   Acts 12:21–23

God in his grace will tolerate sin for awhile, but then in his justice he will judge it. Judgment may come in this life or it may be withheld until after death, but it will happen. Herod died[6] and faced an eternity in the Lake of Fire. The next verse is noteworthy...

> But the word of God continued to increase and spread.
> Acts 12:24

I would encourage you not to casually ignore the Bible's message or become too busy to properly investigate it. It would be a tragedy not to have taken the time to really discover all you needed to know about life and death.

Another contemporary of Jesus was Herod Agrippa II. As the great grandson of Herod the Great, and son of Herod

Agrippa, he would also have known about Jesus. The Bible says King Agrippa was *well versed* in all the things concerning Jesus. The apostle Paul[7] was arrested and testified before him. In his defense before Agrippa, Paul told him about Jesus. He said...

> *"For the king, before whom I also speak freely, knows these things; for I am convinced that none of these things escapes his attention, since this thing was not done in a corner. King Agrippa, do you believe the prophets? I know that you do believe."*
>
> *Then Agrippa said to Paul, "You almost persuade me to become a Christian."* Acts 26:26–28 NKJV

King Agrippa seemed to understand Paul quite well, so much so that he even admitted that Paul had almost persuaded him to believe. But Agrippa took the risk. He didn't believe. He side-stepped the question in an effort to avoid making a decision. As far as we know, Agrippa never did believe. He went to his grave *understanding* but not believing. It was his choice.

Paul also defended himself before a Roman governor named Felix. Paul always took these opportunities to give a lengthy explanation of who Jesus was and what He had done.

> *Several days later Felix came with his wife Drusilla, who was a Jewess. He sent for Paul and listened to him as he spoke about faith in Christ Jesus. As Paul discoursed on righteousness, self-control and the judgment to come, Felix was afraid and said, "That's enough for now! You may leave. When I find it convenient, I will send for you."* Acts 24:24–25

Felix put off his decision. He was waiting for a more convenient time. It's easy to do that, but the Bible reminds us that *now* is the time to decide...

> *...now is the accepted time; ...now is the day of salvation.* 2 Corinthians 6:2 NKJV

We never know what the future holds, or how quickly our lives can be taken. We need to decide *now*. Of course Felix was afraid, and sometimes we become fearful too. We wonder what others may think. It really doesn't matter. What does matter is what God thinks. Neither biblical nor secular history records what happened to Felix but, to the best of our knowledge, he never did find a convenient time to believe.

Felix also had other hopes...

> ...he was hoping that Paul would offer him a bribe, so he sent for him frequently and talked with him.   Acts 24:26

Felix had ulterior motives. His professed interest in Jesus was distorted by a desire for monetary gain. Nevertheless, he did speak *often* with Paul about Jesus. Many could have interpreted these conversations as Felix having *gotten religion.* Some people are like Felix. They talk a lot about the Bible, but then they use its message for their own profit. Most people recognize the inconsistency, but some are deceived. Because of such hypocrites, some people claim they will never believe the Bible. But hey, wait a minute! Did the Bible's message change? No, not one bit. It still says the same thing no matter how people distort it for their own ends. If you are one who would be tempted to reject the Bible because of guys like Felix, then think again.

If you find yourself vacillating, not understanding, or just outright rejecting what you have read, then might I suggest that you investigate the Bible a little more before you close the case. As we said at the beginning, the Scripture does have a lot to say about life... and death.

Don't stop your investigation now.

Your life—and your life after death—is at stake.

APPENDIX

GLOSSARY

CHOOSING A BIBLE

RESOURCES

END NOTES

Glossary

Abba: (Aramaic) equivalent to the English words *"daddy"* or *"papa"*

Adoption: the rite of investing legal sonship, complete with its obligations and privileges

Altar: a platform made of earth or rocks upon which sacrifices were offered to God or gods

Amen: (Hebrew/Greek) a word of affirmation; a form of agreement, *"That's right!"* or *"I agree!"*

Angel: (Greek) messenger; a created heavenly spirit being

Anoint: to pour oil upon the person's head or on an object for the purpose of setting apart for God's use. The word came to mean or refer to anything chosen for the Lord's service.

Apostle: (Greek) a *sent one;* used most often in reference to the twelve disciples and Paul

Ark: a container; either large (boat) or small (box)

Blessing: the receiving or giving of God's favor

Centurion: (Greek/Latin) a Roman army officer responsible for 100 men

Christ: (Greek) *"the anointed one,"* translated *Messiah* (Hebrew) in the Old Testament

Confess: to *agree with* or *acknowledge*

Covenant: a promise, agreement

Curse: to incur or bestow displeasure

Demon: a created evil spirit being giving allegiance to Satan

Devil: (derived from Greek) false accuser, slanderer; another name for Satan, the most powerful of all evil spirit beings

Disciple: a follower

Faith: to *trust* or *put confidence in* (see pages 104-105)

Genesis: (Greek) *beginnings* or *origins*

Glory: literally *"to have weight,"* as in the sense of worth

Gospel: good news

Grace: God's kindness to undeserving sinners

I AM: a name of God, meaning *"the self-existent one"* or *"the one who exists by His own power."*

Immanuel: (Hebrew/Greek) *"God with us"*

Jesus: (Greek—derived from Hebrew) means *Savior, Deliverer*

Justified: a judicial act whereby God declares a person righteous in His sight

Mercy: God's love demonstrated towards undeserving sinners, pity

Messiah: (Hebrew) *"the anointed one,"* translated *"Christ"* (Greek) in the New Testament

Parable: a short story with a lesson

Pharaoh: the king of Egypt

Pharisee: a Jew who followed God's law meticulously to the point of creating additional laws so as not to break God's laws

Priest: a man who performed assigned duties in the Tabernacle or Temple

Prophet: a messenger who spoke for God

Psalm: (Greek) a song

Rabbi: (Greek) teacher, master

Redeem: *to buy,* as in the sense of purchasing a slave in a market

Repent: to have a *change of mind* (see page 154)

Righteous: to be viewed as right with God. This does not mean that a person is sinless. Can also be used in the sense of how one lives; of having a good or right sort of lifestyle.

Sabbath: the seventh day of the week; Saturday

Sanhedrin: (Greek) a Jewish court comprised of seventy-one men

Satan: (Hebrew/Greek) adversary; the supreme enemy of God

Savior: someone who delivers or rescues another

Scribe: one who made copies of the Scriptures in ancient times

Sin: has the idea of shooting an arrow and missing the mark, in this case aiming for God's holiness, but falling short; to despise God and his Word; refusing to live as God intended

Sin Nature: sometimes referred to as the *human nature* or *Adam's nature*; a condition

Son of God: an idiomatic term, having no physical implications, used to designate the same attributes

Son of man: a phrase used by Jesus in reference to himself to emphasize His humanity, also understood by ancient scholars to be a term referring to Messiah

Synagogue: (Greek) assemblies; commonly used in reference to the building

Transgression: see sin

Worship: to declare God's worth

Choosing a Bible

The Bible was written in the common language of each generation—Hebrew, Aramaic or Greek. God intended it to be accessible to every man, woman and child regardless of their background or social status. Since the age of Greek civilization, translations were made in other languages.

During the period that came to be known as the Dark Ages, the Bible was commonly available only in Latin and only the organized clergy had access to the limited, handwritten copies. It was considered a sin for the man on the street to read or try to understand it for himself. Satan had seemingly succeeded in hiding God's Word behind a clergyman's robe.

Then in the early 1500's, William Tyndale committed himself to putting the Bible into the everyday language of the English-speaking people. It is said that at one time he told a clergyman,

> "If God spare my life, ere many years pass, I will cause a boy that driveth the plough to know more of the Scripture than thou doest."

Tyndale was harshly opposed in his task by both the clergy and the political powers of that day. Suffering shipwreck, loss of manuscripts, pursuit by secret agents and betrayal by friends, he succeeded in translating the Bible into English at the expense of his own life. Captured, imprisoned, sentenced, then strangled and burned—his last words were, "Lord, open the King of England's eyes."

Today, the English language offers a plethora of translations—many with varying degrees of supplementary Bible helps. In choosing a Bible, remember two things:

1. Whatever English Bible you buy, it is a translation of the original languages. Any time you translate a message from one language to another, the accuracy, the readability—the entire production—will have its strengths and weaknesses. Fortunately, the translation of the Bible into English has usually been done with meticulous care, so that what we have today is very accurate. There are, however, both good and not-so-good translations of the Bible. I strongly suggest you aim to get the most precise translation you can, but in so doing, still remember it is a translation. I say this, not depreciating one iota the power of the Bible's message in another tongue.

2. Get a translation that is simple for you to read. Remember, Tyndale gave his life to make the Bible readable to the common man. He wanted people to understand it easily, and not feel like they were reading a foreign language.

In light of the above two points, the following translations are efforts at maintaining accuracy and readability:

Translation	School grade level[1]
New International Version	7.8
New King James Version	9.1
New American Standard Version	11.3
King James Version (old English)	14.0

Although this book uses the New International Version, I have used excerpts from the other translations listed above, when they seemed to give a slightly clearer rendering of the original.

To help explain the Bible in greater detail, many versions come with cross-references, notes on customs, maps, etc.—all listed under the category as Bible helps. These can indeed be helpful, but remember, they are nothing more than man's comments on the Bible text, and are not the Scriptures themselves.

In obtaining a Bible, you may wish to have a small one that can be carried with you, and a larger one that you can leave at home for greater in-depth study.

Resources

Due to the range of issues covered in any list of books, videos, web sites or magazines, by policy, GoodSeed does not issue specific endorsements. Nonetheless, as the time of writting, the following resources contained helpful information on creation/evolution and other Bible/science issues. The following list is representative of many other sources.

Web Sites: www.AnswersInGenesis.org   www.icr.org

Magazines: *Creation ex nihilo*—for adults, with sections for children; also the Technical Journal—for advanced studies. Both are available from www.AnswersInGenesis.org

Books:

An Ice Age Caused by the Genesis Flood—by Michael J. Oard, ICR, El Cajon, CA 243 pp.
Bones of Contention: A Creationist Assessment of Human Fossils—by Marvin L. Lubenow, Baker Bk House, Grand Rapids, MI 295 pp.
Creation and Change: Genesis 1.1-2.4 in the light of changing scientific paradigms— Douglas F. Kelly, Christian Focus Pub., Ross-shire, GB 272 pp.
Creation: Facts of Life—by Gary Parker, Master Bks Green Forest, AR   215 pp.
Darwin's Black Box—by Michael J. Behe, Touchstone, Simon and Schuster, NY, NY 307 pp.
Darwin's Enigma: Ebbing the Tide of Naturalism—by L. Sunderland, MBks, Grn Fst, AR 192 pp.
Evolution: A Theory in Crisis, New Developments in Science are Challenging Orthodox Darwinism—by Michael Denton, Adler & Adler, Pub., Inc., Bethesda, MD 368 pp.
Evolution: The Fossils Still Say NO!—by Duane T. Gish, ICR, El Cajon, CA   391 pp.
Genesis Record—by Dr. Henry M. Morris, Baker Bk House, Grand Rapids, MI 716 pp.
Ice Cores and the Age of the Earth—by Larry Vardiman, Ph.D., ICR, El Cajon, CA 72 pp.
In the Minds of Men: Darwin & the New World Order—by I. Taylor, TFE Pub., Minn., MN 498 pp.
Noah's Ark: A Feasibility Study—by John Woodmorappe, ICR, El Cajon, CA 306 pp.
Refuting Evolution: A Response to the National Acad. of Sciences' Teaching About Evolution & the Nature of Sciences—by J. Sarfati, Ph.D., Master Bks, Green Forest, AR 143 pp.
The Age of the Earth's Atmosphere: A Study of the Helium Flux through the Atmosphere— by Larry Vardiman, Ph.D., ICR, El Cajon, CA 32 pp.
The Controversy: Roots of the Creat.-Evol. Conflict—by D. Chittick, Creation Cps, 280 pp.
The Long War Against God: The History and Impact of the Creation/Evolution Conflict—by Henry M. Morris, Baker Bk House, Grand Rapids, MI   344 pp.
The Modern Creation Trilogy: Scripture & Creation (Three Volume Series)—by Henry M. Morris and John D. Morris, Master Bks, Inc, Green Forest, AR 228 pp.
The Mythology of Modern Dating Methods: Why million/billion-year results are not credible—by John Woodmorappe, M.A. Geology, B.A. Biology, ICR, El Cajon, CA   118 pp.
The Revised & Expanded Answers Book: The 20 Most-Asked Questions about Creation, Evolution, and the Book of Genesis, Answered!—by Ken Ham, Jonathan Sarfati, Carl Wieland, Edited by Don Batten, Ph.D, Master Bks, Green Forest, AR 274 pp.

Videos:

Evidences: The Record and the Flood—Geoscience Rsch. Inst., LL, CA, Rev & Hld Pub. Assoc.
From a Frog to a Prince—Co-prod. by Keiah, Inst. for Creation Research & Answers in Genesis.
Mount St. Helens: Explosive Evidence for Catastrophe—Steve Austin, Ph.D., ICR, El Caj., CA
The Genesis Solution—Ken Ham, Films for Christ, Mesa, AZ
The Grand Canyon Catastrophe: New Evidence of the Genesis Flood—Prod. by Keziah & distrib. by American Portrait Films, Cleveland, OH
The Young Age of the Earth—American Portrait Films, Cleveland, OH
Journeys to the Edge of Creation: (2 Vol.)—Moody Inst. of Science, Chicago IL
The Wonders of God's Creation: (3 Vol.)—Moody Inst. of Science, Chicago, IL

END NOTES

CHAPTER ONE

1. Josh McDowell, compiled by Bill Wilson, *A READY DEFENSE*, Thomas Nelson Publishers, © 1993 pp. 27, 28. Used by permission of Thomas Nelson, Inc.

2. Some English Bibles translate *"God-breathed"* as *"inspired." "God-breathed"* is the more literal translation.

3. *And they came, bringing to Him a paralytic, carried by four men.* Mark 2:3 NASB

4. *ILLUSTRATED BIBLE DICTIONARY*, Pt 3, IVP ©The Universities and Colleges Christian Fellowship 1980, p. 1538

5. Philip W. Comfort, *THE ORIGIN OF THE BIBLE*, Mark R. Norton, Texts & Mscripts of the Old Testament, p. 151ff, ©1992 by Tyndale House Pub., Inc.

6. Translated by William Whiston, *THE WORKS OF JOSEPHUS*, ©1987 by Hendrickson Publishers, Inc., p. 776

7. Norman L. Geisler and William E. Nix, *FROM GOD TO US, HOW WE GOT THE BIBLE*, ©1974 Moody Press, Chicago, p. 7

8. Today, Jewish scholars divide the Hebrew Scriptures into three sections— The Law, The Writings, and The Prophets. Though it may have been established as early as the second century BC, it wasn't until the 5th century that this three-fold division was completed. Ibid., pp. 77–85

9. The American Heritage® Dictionary of the English Language, Third Edition ©1992 by Houghton Mifflin Company.

CHAPTER TWO

1. The Galaxy pictured here is not the Milky Way, as it is impossible to photograph. A similar one, the Andromeda, has been substituted.

2. Statistical data: *THE WORLD BOOK ENCYCLOPEDIA; NIGHTWATCH, A Practical Guide to Viewing the Universe* by Terence Dickinson, pub. Firefly Books, April 1999. The estimated number of galaxies continues to grow.

3. Jude 6

4. Luke 20:36 Death in the physical sense. Angels never cease to exist.

5. Mark 12:25

6. *Lucifer* is Latin for *"light bearer."* It has its source in the Latin name for the planet Venus, which is often referred to as the *"morning star."*

CHAPTER THREE

1. Comparison:

	English	**Hebrew**	**Literal Translation**
Day 1	*light*	*or*	*light*
Day 4	*lights*	*ma-or*	*light-givers*

2. The originally created *kinds* may have given rise to groups, which would subsequently be classified as separate *species* (e.g. dingoes, coyotes and wolves may all have descended from the one *dog kind*). This is not a form of evolution, as no new genetic information has been added that was not in the original ancestral population.

3. "Perfect people" as in the sense of moral perfection.

4 For an example, see Dr. Michael J. Behe, *DARWIN'S BLACK BOX*, Touchstone, Simon and Schuster, NY, NY 307 pp.

5. Geochronology is a vast area of study. A search on the WEB brings up numerous papers on different clock models.

CHAPTER FOUR

1. Revelation 12:3–9; Verses 3 & 4 are generally considered to refer to the fall of Satan. Verses 7–9 are viewed by many scholars as having to do with a yet

future event. I have quoted the entire passage as the latter verses explain the portion we are concerned about—verses 3 & 4—the *who* that is in question.

2. This passage reflects the choices Adam and Eve made.

3. See Romans 5:12–14 for more details. Also see Chapter Ten, end note-1. Adam was the father—the head—of the entire human race. We were *in him* when he sinned.

4. Newsweek, January 11, 1988, pp. 46–52

5. Time, December 4, 1995, USA Edition, p. 29

Chapter Five

1. Some have taught that the reason why God did not accept Cain's sacrifice is because of Cain's attitude. There is no doubt that Cain had an attitude of independence from God, but the Bible clearly states: *"By faith Abel offered God a better* **sacrifice** *than Cain did..."* The Bible does not say: *"a better* **attitude***."* Cain disobeyed God by bringing the wrong sacrifice. See Hebrews 11:4. For a paper giving extensive treatment of this subject, contact the appropriate GoodSeed office as listed in the back of the book.

2. Luke 17:27; Matthew 24:38

3. Romans 1:21–32; Though this passage does not make direct reference to the people of Noah's day, it does reflect the choices they made at the time with the attending ramifications.

4. Probably made from pine-tree resin boiled with charcoal. Bituminous tar would have come into being after the flood.

5. Genesis 6:3

6. 2 Peter 2:5

7. A number of scholars have calculated the "room on the Ark." One helpful resource on this is: *Noah's Ark: A Feasibility Study*—by John Woodmorappe, ICR, El Cajon, CA 306 pp.

8. Dr. John Baumgardner, geophysicist at the Los Alamos National Laboratories in New Mexico, proposes a model known in creationist circles as Catastrophic Plate Tectonics.

9. Job 40:15-24; 41:1-34

10. *"The Lord came down..."* If God is everywhere present at one time, why did he have to *"come down"*? The Bible often uses terms in relationship to God that enhance our understanding of the passage. For example, God is spoken of as "seeing" even though, as a Spirit, he does not have physical eyes.

11. I am indebted to Dr. Carl Wieland for his input on genetics. For a detailed treatment of this subject written for the layman, see: *The Revised & Expanded Answers Book*—by Ken Ham, Jonathan Sarfati, Carl Wieland, Ed. by Don Batten, Ph.D, Master Bks, Green Forest, AR 274 pp.

Chapter Six

1. Notice how life spans decreased dramatically after the flood. Abraham was already considered old at the age of seventy-five.

2. Abram became a great nation: the father of both the Jewish and Arab nations.

3. Abram's name did become great; he is revered by Jew and Arab alike. It is important to note that it was God who made Abram's name great, whereas at Babel the desire was self-motivated.

4. It would seem from history that those who have persecuted the Jews have not prospered over the long run.

5. John 8:56

6. Matthew 17:20

7. *"For the wages of sin is death..."* Romans 6:23. See Chap 4, Death, p. 62.

CHAPTER SEVEN

1. The twelve tribes of Israel are the twelve sons of Jacob. Exceptions: There was no tribe of Levi since they became the nation's religious leaders. There was also no tribe of Joseph—his two sons Ephraim and Manasseh made up the difference.

2. This word can be translated "lice."

CHAPTER EIGHT

1. This paragraph is a loose paraphrase of Exodus 19:5.

2. For the purposes of this book, I have only included the Ten Commandments—often referred to as the Moral Law. In actuality the passages referring to the "whole law" would be including much more—all 613 commands given by Moses.

CHAPTER NINE

1. I am not advocating this approach as an accepted way of saving a drowning man. It is used only as an illustration.

2. ❶ The Bronze Altar: Exodus 27:1,2
   ❷ The Basin: Exodus 30:18
   ❸ The Lampstand: Exodus 25:31
   ❹ The Table with the Bread of the Presence: Exodus 25:23,30
   ❺ The Golden Altar or The Altar of Incense: Exodus 30:1,3
   ❻ The Ark of the Covenant: Exodus 25:10,11
   ❼ The Atonement Cover or Mercy Seat: Exodus 25:17–21

3. The priests could not enter when the pillar of cloud hovered over the Holy of Holies. It signified God's presence. When the cloud moved to lead them on the journey, then they would have been free to pack up the entire Tabernacle and follow.

4. 2 Samuel 7:12–17

5. Scholars differ somewhat on the exact dates associated with Creation, the Noahic Flood and Babel. Taking the Bible at face value does rule out periods of time involving millions or billions of years. All three of these events had to have happened in a period of time of not more than a few thousand years.

CHAPTER TEN

1. This should not be thought of as being some sort of genetic link—that the sin nature can be found in a string of DNA. The association is purely spiritual. God held man responsible for the rebellion in the Garden of Eden, and because of that *"…just as sin entered the world through one man, and death through sin, and in this way death came to all men, because all sinned…"* (Romans 5:12) We all have a human father, therefore we are all sinful. Jesus' father was God, the Holy Spirit, so He had God's nature.

2. Consider what one of the prophets wrote more than 500 years before Jesus' birth. *"I saw in the night visions, and, behold, one like the Son of man came…And there was given him dominion, and glory, and a kingdom, that all people, nations, and languages, should serve him."*
   Daniel 7:13,14 KJV

3. "Lord" is an Old Testament title for Messiah (Ps. 110:1) and emphasizes His authority, His right to rule. J. Dwight Pentecost, *THE WORDS AND WORKS OF JESUS CHRIST*, ©1981 by The Zondervan Corporation, p. 61

4. Ephrathah was a region that distinguished this Bethlehem from another town of the same name near Nazareth.

5. A fragrant perfume

6. This could have been the time of Jesus' bar mitzvah. The Talmud says, *"at the age of puberty."* Some place it a year later.

CHAPTER ELEVEN

1. John was imprisoned by Herod Antipas, son of Herod the Great. John had spoken against Herod's sin, that of living with his half-brother's wife.

CHAPTER TWELVE

1. There is a distinction: *"Then death and Hades [Hell] were thrown into the lake of fire. The lake of fire is the second death."*   Revelation 20:14

CHAPTER THIRTEEN

1. emphatic personal pronoun "I" followed by present indicative active (*". . . at this present time while I am speaking, I Am."*)
2. I have not included all the details of the trial and crucifixion. Of some significance, at this point, is this event: *"As they led him away, they seized Simon from Cyrene, who was on his way in from the country, and put the cross on him and made him carry it behind Jesus."*   Luke 23:26
3. Whiston, *THE WORKS OF JOSEPHUS* p. 720
4. Written in the past tense signifies the certainty of its future happening.
5. What Satan actually thought is not recorded, but because he was the mastermind behind the whole affair, I felt at liberty to conjecture.
6. J. W. Shepard, *THE CHRIST OF THE GOSPELS*, (Eerdmans, Grand Rapids © 1964) p. 604 as quoted by Pentecost, *THE WORDS AND WORKS OF JESUS CHRIST*, p. 487
7. John F. Walvoord, Roy B. Zuck, *THE BIBLE KNOWLEDGE COMMENTARY* ©1983, SP Publications, Inc. p. 340

   Pentecost, *THE WORDS AND WORKS OF JESUS CHRIST*, p. 487

   Warren W. Wiersbe, *THE BIBLE EXPOSITION COMMENTARY*, Vol. 1, ©1989, SP Publications, Inc. p. 384
8. A battalion is an army unit consisting of 300 to 1000 men.
9. The exact sequence of the resurrection morning events is not recorded. I have given one of the more likely scenarios.

CHAPTER FOURTEEN

1. Jesus was nailed to the cross at 9:00 a.m.—the time of the morning sacrifice. He died at 3:00 p.m.—the time of the evening sacrifice.
2. Jesus' perfect life qualified him to be a suitable sacrifice, but it was his death that made the payment for sin. Only by dying could it be said that Jesus had fulfilled the demands of the Law. Matthew 5:17,18

CHAPTER FIFTEEN

1. Approx. 30% of the Bible is prophecy, either completed or yet to be fulfilled.
2. Another word for "sin"
3. This is often referred to as your position in Christ.
4. "have" is present tense, signifying that eternal life is a present possession.
5. Some English Bibles use the term *flesh* in reference to our human nature.
6. Josephus, the first-century historian, also records this man's death.
7. Saul's name was changed to Paul.

APPENDIX

1. Based on computer analysis

Additional copies of this book can be purchased by contacting the appropriate office listed below. A catalogue of current translations of *THE STRANGER* is available upon request.

GOODSEED **Australia**	1800 897 333
	info.au@goodseed.com
GOODSEED **Canada**	800 442 7333
	info.ca@goodseed.com
BONNESEMENCE **Canada**	888 314 3623
Service en français	info.qc@goodseed.com
GOODSEED **UK**	0800 073 6340
	info.uk@goodseed.com
GOODSEED **USA**	888 654 7333
	info.us@goodseed.com

ALSO AVAILABLE

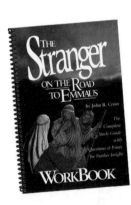

The **WORKBOOK** is a tool to help you determine for yourself whether or not you are understanding the THE STRANGER. It includes additional Bible verses to *look up* that relate to the chapter studied.

The WORKBOOK also teaches Bible navigation skills including the use of a concordance and maps. (Multiple choice, word bank, true/false, fill-in-the-blanks, crossword puzzle)

The **AUDIOBOOK** consists of 10 hours of listening, recorded on nine cds. Recorded professionally using two voices, this product is ideal for the commuter, long-haul driver, the seeing-impaired, or those who would prefer to listen rather than read.

GOODSEED® International is a not-for-profit organization that exists for the purpose of clearly communicating the contents of this book in this language and others. We invite you to contact us if you are interested in ongoing projects or translations.

GOODSEED® International

P. O. Box 3704
Olds, AB T4H 1P5
CANADA
Bus: 403 556-9955
Fax: 403 556-9950
info@goodseed.com

To obtain additional copies of this book, see page 303.

goodseed
see·hear·understand
—— www.goodseed.com ——